AF584667

GALATIANS

THE
TEACHER'S
OUTLINE & STUDY
BIBLE

GALATIANS

THE

TEACHER'S

OUTLINE & STUDY

BIBLE

NEW TESTAMENT

KING JAMES VERSION

Leadership Ministries Worldwide
PO Box 21310
Chattanooga, TN 37424-0310

May our Lord bless us all as we live, preach, teach, and write for Him, fulfilling His great commission to live righteous and godly lives and to make disciples of all nations.

Please address all requests for information or permission to:
Leadership Ministries Worldwide
PO Box 21310
Chattanooga TN 37424-0310
Ph.# (423) 855-2181 FAX (423) 855-8616 E•Mail 74152,616@compuserve.org.
http://www.goshen.net/OutlineBible

HOW TO USE

THE TEACHER'S OUTLINE AND STUDY BIBLE (TOSB)

To gain maximum benefit, here is all you do. Follow these easy steps, using the sample outline below.

1 STUDY TITLE

2 MAJOR POINTS

3 SUB-POINTS

4 COMMENTARY, QUESTIONS, APPLICATION, ILLUSTRATIONS
(Follows Scripture)

	B. The Steps to Peace (Part II): Prayer & Positive Thinking, 4:6-9
1. Peace comes through prayer a. The charge: Do not worry or be anxious b. The remedy: Prayer 1) About everything 2) With requests 3) With thanksgiving	6 Be careful for nothing; but in every thing by prayer and supplication with thanksgiving let your requests be made known unto God.
c. The promise: Peace 1) Peace that passes all understanding 2) Peace that keeps our hearts & minds	7 And the peace of God, which passeth all understanding, shall keep your hearts and minds through Christ Jesus.
2. Peace comes through positive thinking a. The charge: Think & practice things that are... 1) True 2) Honest 3) Just 4) Pure	8 Finally, brethren, whatsoever things are true, whatsoever things are honest, whatsoever things are just, whatsoever things are pure, whatsoever things are lovely, what-

1. First: Read the **Study Title** two or three times so that the subject sinks in.
2. Then: Read the **Study Title** and the **Major Points** (Pts.1,2,3) together quickly. Do this several times and you will quickly grasp the overall subject.
3. Now: Read both the **Major Points** and **Sub-Points**. Do this slower than Step 2. Note how the points are beside the applicable verse, and simply state what the Scripture is saying—in Outline form.
4. Read the **Commentary**. As you read and re-read, pray that the Holy Spirit will bring to your attention exactly what you should study and teach. It's all there, outlined and fully developed, just waiting for you to study and teach.

<u>TEACHERS, PLEASE NOTE</u>:

⇒ Cover the **Scripture** and the **Major Points** with your students. Drive the **Scripture** and **Major Points** into their hearts and minds.

(Please continue on next page)

⇒ Cover *only some of the commentary* with your students, not all (unless of course you have plenty of time). Cover only as much commentary as is needed to get the major points across.

⇒ Do NOT feel that you must…
- cover all the commentary under each point
- share every illustration
- ask all the questions

An abundance of commentary is given so you can find just what you need for…
- your own style of teaching
- your own emphasis
- your own class needs

PLEASE NOTE: It is of utmost importance that you (and your study group) grasp the Scripture, the Study Title, and Major Points. It is this that the Holy Spirit will make alive to your heart and that you will more likely remember and use day by day.

MAJOR POINTS include:

APPLICATIONS:
Use these to show how the Scripture applies to everyday life.

ILLUSTRATIONS:
Simply a window that allows enough light in the lesson so a point can be more clearly seen. A suggestion: Do not just "read" through an illustration if the illustration is a story, but learn it and make it your own. Then give the illustration life by communicating it with *excitement & energy*.

QUESTIONS:
These are designed to stimulate thought and discussion.

A CLOSER LOOK:
In some of the studies, you will see a portion boxed in and entitled: "A Closer Look." This discussion will be a closer study on a particular point. It is generally too detailed for a Sunday School class session, but more adaptable for personal study or an indepth Bible Study class.

PERSONAL JOURNAL:
At the close of every lesson there is space for you to record brief thoughts regarding the impact of the lesson on your life. As you study through the Bible, you will find these comments invaluable as you look back upon them.

Now, may our wonderful Lord bless you mightily as you study and teach His Holy Word. And may our Lord grant you much fruit: many who will become greater servants and witnesses for Him.

REMEMBER!

The Teacher's Outline & Study Bible is the only study material that actually outlines the Bible verse by verse for you right beside the Scripture. As you accumulate the various books of The Teacher's Outline & Study Bible for your study and teaching, you will have the Bible outlined book by book, passage by passage, and verse by verse.

The outlines alone makes saving every book a must! (Also encourage your students, if you are teaching, to keep their student edition. They also have the unique verse by verse outline of Scripture in their version.)

Just think for a moment. Over the course of your life, you will have your very own personalized commentary of the Bible. No other book besides the Bible will mean as much to you because it will contain your insights, your struggles, your victories, and your recorded moments with the Lord.

> **"Study to show thyself approved unto God, a workman that needeth not to be ashamed, rightly dividing the word of truth" (2 Tim.2:15).**
>
> **"All scripture is given by inspiration of God, and is profitable for doctrine, for reproof, for correction, for instruction in righteousness: that the man of God may be perfect, throughly furnished unto all good works" (2 Tim.3:16-17).**

*** All direct quotes are followed by a Superscript Endnote number. The credit information for each Endnote is listed at the end of the individual study session for your reference.

MISCELLANEOUS ABBREVIATIONS

&	=	And
Bckgrd.	=	Background
Bc.	=	Because
Circ.	=	Circumstance
Concl.	=	Conclusion
Cp.	=	Compare
Ct.	=	Contrast
Dif.	=	Different
e.g.	=	For example
Et.	=	Eternal
Govt.	=	Government
Id.	=	Identity or Identification
Illust.	=	Illustration
K.	=	Kingdom, K. of God, K. of Heaven, etc.
No.	=	Number
N.T.	=	New Testament
O.T.	=	Old Testament
Pt.	=	Point
Quest.	=	Question
Rel.	=	Religion
Resp.	=	Responsibility
Rev.	=	Revelation
Rgt.	=	Righteousness
Thru	=	Through
V.	=	Verse
Vs.	=	Verses

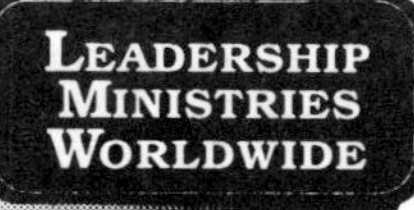

Publisher & Distributor of…

DEDICATED:

To all the men and women of the world who study and teach the Gospel of our Lord Jesus Christ
and
To the Mercy and Grace of God.

- Demonstrated to us in Christ Jesus our Lord.

  "In whom we have redemption through His blood, the forgiveness of sins, according to the riches of His grace." (Eph. 1:7)

- Out of the mercy and grace of God His Word has flowed. Let every person know that God will have mercy upon him, forgiving and using him to fulfill His glorious plan of salvation.

  "For God so loved the world, that he gave his only begotten Son, that whosoever believeth in him should not perish, but have everlasting life. For God sent not his Son into the world to condemn the world; but that the world through him might be saved." (John 3:16-17)

  "For this is good and acceptable in the sight of God our Saviour; who will have all men to be saved, and to come unto the knowledge of the truth." (I Tim. 2:3-4)

&

The Teacher's Outline & Study Bible
is written for God's people to use
in their study and teaching of God's Holy Word.

LEADERSHIP MINISTRIES WORLDWIDE

OUR FIVEFOLD MISSION & PURPOSE:

- To share the Word of God with the world.
- To help the believer, both minister and layman alike, in his understanding, preaching, and teaching of God's Word.
- To do everything we possibly can to lead men, women, boys, and girls to give their hearts and lives to Jesus Christ and to secure the eternal life which He offers.
- To do all we can to minister to the needy of the world.
- To give Jesus Christ His proper place, the place which the Word gives Him. Therefore — No work of Leadership Ministries Worldwide will ever be personalized.

This material, like similar works, has come from imperfect man and is thus susceptible to human error. We are nevertheless grateful to God for both calling us and empowering us through His Holy Spirit to undertake this task. Because of His goodness and grace, *The Preacher's Outline & Sermon Bible™* - New Testament is complete in 14 volumes as well as the single volume of **The Minister's Handbook**.

God has given the strength and stamina to bring us this far. Our confidence is that, as we keep our eyes on Him and grounded in the undeniable truths of the Word, we will continue working through the Old Testament Volumes and on the new, forthcoming series (1995) ***The Teacher's Outline & Study Bible.*** Future materials will include CD-ROM, The Believer's *Outline* Bible, and similar ***Outline*** and **Handbook** materials.

To everyone, everywhere who preaches and teaches the Word, we offer this material firstly to Him in whose name we labor and serve, and for whose glory it has been produced.

Our daily prayer is that each volume will lead thousands, millions, yes even billions, into a better understanding of the Holy Scriptures and a fuller knowledge of Jesus Christ the incarnate Word, of whom the Scriptures so faithfully testify.

As you have purchased this volume, you will be pleased to know that a portion of the price you paid goes to underwrite providing similar volumes at affordable prices in other languages (Russian, Korean, Spanish and others yet to come) to a preacher, pastor, church leader, or Bible student somewhere around the world, who will present God's message with clarity, authority, and understanding beyond their own.
Amen.

For ministry information, prices and shipping details, kindly contact:

LEADERSHIP MINISTRIES WORLDWIDE

P.O. Box 21310, 515 Airport Road, Suite 107
Chattanooga, TN 37424-0310
(615) 855-2181 FAX (615) 855-87616
CompuServe: 74152,616

ACKNOWLEDGMENTS

Every child of God is precious to the Lord and deeply loved. And every child as a servant of the Lord touches the lives of those who come in contact with him or his ministry. The writing ministry of the following servants have touched this work, and we are grateful that God brought their writings our way. We hereby acknowledge their ministry to us, being fully aware that there are so many others down through the years whose writings have touched our lives and who deserve mention, but the weaknesses of our minds have caused them to fade from memory. May our wonderful Lord continue to bless the ministry of these dear servants, and the ministry of us all as we diligently labor to reach the world for Christ and to meet the desperate needs of those who suffer so much.

THE GREEK SOURCES

1 Expositor's Greek Testament, Edited by W. Robertson Nicoll. Grand Rapids, MI: Eerdmans Publishing Co., 1970

2. Robertson, A.T. Word Pictures in the New Testament. Nashville, TN: Broadman Press, 1930.

3. Thayer, Joseph Henry. Greek-English Lexicon of the New Testament. New York: American Book Co.

4. Vincent, Marvin R. Word Studies in the New Testament. Grand Rapids, MI: Eerdmans Publishing Co., 1969.

5. Vine, W.E. Expository Dictionary of New Testament Words. Old Tappan, NJ: Fleming H. Revell Co.

6. Wuest, Kenneth S. Word Studies in the Greek New Testament. Grand Rapids, MI: Eerdmans Publishing Co., 1953.

THE REFERENCE WORKS

7. Cruden's Complete Concordance of the Old & New Testament. Philadelphia, PA: The John C. Winston Co., 1930.

8. Josephus' Complete Works. Grand Rapids, MI: Kregel Publications, 1981.

9. Lockyer, Herbert, Series of Books, including his Books on All the Men, Women, Miracles, and Parables of the Bible. Grand Rapids, MI: Zondervan Publishing House.

10. Nave's Topical Bible. Nashville, TN: The Southewstern Co.

11. The Amplified New Testament. (Scripture Quotations are from the Amplified New Testament, Copyright 1954, 1958, 1987 by the Lockman Foundation. Used by permission.)

12. The Four Translation New Testament (Including King James, New American Standard, Williams - New Testament In the Language of the People, Beck - New Testament In the Language of Today.) Minneapolis, MN: World Wide Publications.

13. The New Compact Bible Dictionary, Edited by T. Alton Bryant. Grand Rapids, MI: Zondervan Publishing House, 1967.

14. The New Thompson Chain Reference Bible. Indianapolis, IN: B.B. Kirkbride Bible Co., 1964,

THE COMMENTARIES

15. Barclay, William. Daily Study Bible Series. Philadelphia, PA: Westminister Press.

16. Bruce, F.F. The Epistle to the Colossians. Westwood, NJ: Fleming H. Revell Co., 1968.

17. Bruce, F.F. Epistle to the Hebrews.Grand Rapids, MI: Eerdmans Publishing Co., 1964.

18. Bruce, F.F. The Epistles of John. Old Tappan, NJ: Fleming H. Revell Co., 1970.

19. Criswell, W.A. Expository Sermons on Revelation. Grand Rapids, MI: Zondervan Publishing House, 1962-66.

20. Green, Oliver. The Epistles of John. Greenville, SC: The Gospel House, Inc., 1966.

21. Green, Oliver. The Epistles of Paul the Apostle to the Hebrews. Greenville, SC: The Gospel House, Inc., 1965.

22. Green, Oliver. The Epistles of Paul the Apostle to Timothy & Titus. Greenville, SC: The Gospel House, Inc., 1964.

23. Green, Oliver. The Revelation Verse by Verse Study. Greenville, SC: The Gospel House, Inc., 1963.

24. Henry, Matthew. Commentary on the Whole Bible. Old Tappan, NJ: Fleming H. Revell Co.

25. Hodge, Charles. Exposition on Romans & on Corinthians. Grand Rapids, MI: Eerdmans Publishing Co., 1972-1973.

26. Ladd, George Eldon. A Commentary On the Revelation of John. Grand Rapids, MI: Eerdmans Publishing Co., 1972-1973.

27. Leupold, H.C. Exposition of Daniel. Grand Rapids, MI: Baker Book House, 1969.

28. Newell, William R. Hebrews, Verse by Verse. Chicago, IL: Moody Press.

29. Strauss, Lehman. Devotional Studies in Philippians. Neptune, NJ: Loizeaux Brothers.

30. Strauss, Lehman. Colossians & Galatians. Neptune, NJ: Loizeaux Brothers.

31. Strauss, Lehman. The Book of the Revelation. Neptune, NJ: Loizeaux Brothers.

32. The New Testament & Wycliffe Bible Commentary, Edited by Charles F. Pfeiffer & Everett F. Harrison. New York: The Iverson Associates, 1971. Produced for Moody Monthly. Chicago Moody Press, 1962.

33. The Pulpit Commentary, Edited by H.D.M. Spence & Joseph S. Exell. Grand Rapids, MI: Eerdmans's Publishing Co., 1950.

34. Thomas, W.H. Griffith. Hebrews, A Devotional Commentary. Grand Rapids, MI: Eerdman's Publishing Co., 1970.

35. Thomas, W.H. Griffith. Studies in Colossians & Philemon. Grand Rapids, MI: Baker Book House, 1973.

36. Tyndale New Testament Commentaries. Grand Rapids, MI: Eerdman's Publishing Co., Began in 1958.

37. Walker, Thomas. Acts of the Apostles. Chicago, IL: Moody Press, 1965.

38. Walvoord, John. The Thessalonian Epistles. Grand Rapids, MI: Zondervan Publishing House, 1973.

OTHER SOURCES

39. Barnhouse, Donald Grey. Let Me Illustrate.Grand Rapids, MI: Fleming H. Revell Co., A Division of Baker Book House,1967.

40. Briscoe, Stuart. Everyday Discipleship for Ordinary People. Wheaton, IL: Harold Shaw Publishers, 1988.

41. Buckingham, Jamie. Into the Glory. Plainfield, NJ: Logos International, 1974.

42. Card, Michael. That's What Faith Must Be. Birdwing Music (a division of The Sparrow Corporation) and BMG Songs, Inc./ Mole End Music [ASCAP], 1988).

43. Christianity Today. Carol Stream, IL: Christianity Today Inc., 1991, 1993.

44. Knight, Walter B. Knight's Master Book of 4,000 Illustrations. Grand Rapids, MI: Eerdmans Publishing Company, 1956.

45. Knight, Walter B. Knight's Treasury of 2000 Illustrations. Grand Rapids, MI: Eerdmans Publishing Company, 1963.

46. Knight, Walter B. Three Thousand Illustrations for Christian Service. Grand Rapids, MI: Eerdmans Publishing Company, 1947.

47. Larson, Craig B., Editor. Illustrations for Preaching and Teaching. Grand Rapids, MI: Baker Books, 1993.

48. Leadership Journal. Carol Stream, IL: Christianity Today Inc., 1994.

49. MacDonald, Gordon. Rebuilding Your Broken World. Nashville, TN: Oliver Nelson Books, 1988.

50. McGee, J. Vernon. Thru The Bible, 5 Vols. Nashville, TN: Thomas Nelson Publishers, 1983.

51. Stanley, Charles. How To Listen to God. Nashville, TN: Oliver-Nelson Books, 1985.

52. Tan, Paul Lee. Encyclopedia of 7,700 Illustrations: Signs of the Times. Rockville, MD: Assurance Publishers, 1985.

Publisher & Distributor of...

"

Go ye therefore, and teach all nations

"

(Mt. 28:19)

OUTLINE OF GALATIANS

<u>**THE TEACHER'S OUTLINE & SERMON BIBLE**</u> is *unique*. It differs from all other Study Bibles & Sermon Resource Materials in that every Passage and Subject is outlined right beside the Scripture. When you choose any *Subject* below and turn to the reference, you have not only the Scripture, but you discover the Scripture and Subject *already outlined for you--verse by verse*.

For a quick example, choose one of the subjects below and turn over to the Scripture, and you will find this marvelous help for faster, easier, and more accurate use.

A suggestion: For the quickest overview of Galatians, first read *all the major titles* (I, II, III, etc.), then come back and read the sub-titles.

OUTLINE OF GALATIANS

THE EPISTLE OF PAUL THE APOSTLE TO THE

GALATIANS

INTRODUCTION

AUTHOR: Paul, the Apostle.
There is little if any question of Paul's authorship.

DATE: Uncertain. Somewhere between A.D. 48-60. Some scholars hold an early date of A.D. 48-50 and some a later date of A.D. 51-60.

TO WHOM WRITTEN: "To the churches of Galatia" (Gal.1:2).
Some believe the letter was written to churches in southern Galatia, others to churches in northern Galatia. Acts 13 and 14 are a record of the southern mission. There is no account in Acts of a northern venture.

PURPOSE: To vindicate Paul's call by God and the gospel of grace.
Paul and the gospel of Christ were both under attack. Some false teachers, who were professing Jewish Christians (called Judaizers), were teaching a double error. They taught (1) that a person was saved partly by faith and partly by works, and (2) that a person grew in Christ partly by faith and partly by his own effort. A person had to believe in Christ, yes, but he also...

- had to undergo the main ritual of religion which was circumcision (compare baptism, church membership, and other requirements today).
- had to observe all the ceremonies and rituals of religion.

(See notes--Gal.1:6-7; 2:3-5; 2:4; 2:11-13 for more discussion.)
Of course, Paul did not teach this. He taught something different--that a man is saved by Christ and by Christ alone. His message was the message of God's grace, of pure grace. A person does not win, earn, or merit salvation. A person is saved by the grace of God through His Son, the Lord Jesus Christ. Because of this, the Judaizers charged Paul with deceit: his apostleship was a false claim of his own making, created in his own imagination. They said that he was not a true minister of God--not a true apostle as he claimed, for he minimized the law of God and no true minister would ever minimize the law of God.
Paul thus sits down and pens Galatians to combat these charges. Writing with great force and stern insistence, he lays down the wonder of God, the wonder of God's glorious grace.

SPECIAL FEATURES:
1. The Area of Galatia. Galatia was a district that stretched across the middle of Asia Minor. The Galatian district sat in the highlands, several thousand feet above sea level. It was formerly settled by the Gauls. The cities visited by Paul stretched across southern Galatia. They were Iconium, Lystra, Derbe, Pisidion, and Antioch of Pisidia. There is no record of Paul ever visiting northern Galatia.
The native Galatians were themselves an emotional, impulsive, and changeable people. They were an impetuous, fickle, arguing, loud, boastful, and immoral people. They had a love for the strange, the curious, the unknown. They were attached to a religion that was mainly the worship of nature. The area was also heavily populated by Jews who clung to their staunch Judaistic religion. Greeks were also numerous and gave the area a strong Hellenistic influence. The nature and strange mixture of people in southern Galatia can be seen in their treatment of Paul. They could both worship and stone him (Acts 14:13-19).
2. The churches in Galatia. Paul visited Galatia on his first and third missionary journeys (Acts 13:14; 18:23f). He was forbidden by the Holy Spirit to preach in Galatia on his second mission (Acts 16:6).
The church was spiritually immature. The very reason for Paul writing the Epistle was to deal with the basic doctrine of Christianity: salvation by grace. As one would expect, there were

Gentile converts in the churches. In Acts 20:4 Paul lists the delegates who were going to Jerusalem with him. There is at least one Gentile delegate, perhaps two, from Galatia. This would point to a large group of Gentiles within the churches. There was also a large number of Jewish converts. The problem of mixing the law with grace is evidence of an influential body of Jewish members.

3. Galatians is "The Heart of the Gospel." Man must receive the gospel by faith. He does not work for it by keeping the law. The law does not produce faith. It only works a curse. Therefore, Christ Himself has to redeem man. But man must go beyond receiving the gospel; he must live it out in his life. This is done by the power of the cross and by the power of the Holy Spirit (Gal.5:1-6:18).

The one point Paul makes is that man cannot earn or win or do anything for salvation. Human effort is nothing more than a fleshly sign, a sign that is born within man himself, of his own thought and energy. It is earthly, and the earthly and corruptible perishes. The works of men and of the law do not last. Human effort is not of a spiritual or eternal nature. It has nothing to do with spirit. Salvation is a free gift of God. It is eternal and lasting. It is spiritual. Therefore, salvation is by the grace of God and by the grace of God alone.

4. Galatians is "The Message of Liberty, yet Subjection; of Unity, yet Diversity; of Oneness, yet Difference."

a. There is a recognition that Gentiles do not have to live as Jews, and Jews do not have to live as Gentiles (Gal.2:11f). Paul never says it is wrong for Jews to be circumcised. He never says it is wrong for them to keep the law or to observe special festivals. What he says is that these have nothing to do with salvation. Customs and practices differ, but salvation never differs. There is only one way to be saved: by the grace of God.

b. There is also a recognition that ministers are not all alike (Gal.2:1f). They are not all called to serve the same kinds of people, nor are ministers themselves called to observe the same customs and life-styles. Paul was called to the Gentiles; Peter to the Jews. The customs and life-styles of Gentiles and Jews differed radically. Yet both Paul and Peter were still ministers of the same Lord.

c. There is also a recognition that all Christians are to fellowship and share with one another, and they are to cooperate. Paul just could not see how two different groups of Christians could be in the same place and refuse to eat with one another because of some theological difference (Gal.2:11f). This was the very point that brought about the crises. And Paul came down hard upon it--fighting tooth and nail for a gospel of grace and a life to match that grace.

5. Galatians has been called "The Magna Charta of the Church." God has used its message to stir world revivals in former generations. The great spiritual awakening of Martin Luther and of the Reformation was stirred as Luther studied its message. John Wesley received peace of heart--peace for which he had so long searched--when he heard a sermon preached from Galatians.

The message of Galatians will pierce the heart of any generation and stir it to action--if that generation will just hear and heed its message.

THE EPISTLE OF PAUL THE APOSTLE TO THE

GALATIANS

CHAPTER 1

I. GREETING, 1:1-9

A. God's Minister & His Authority— Paul, 1:1-5

1. He is commissioned by God alone

2. He is recognized as God's man by Christian believers

Paul, an apostle, (not
of men, neither by
man, but by Jesus
Christ, and God the
Father, who raised
him from the dead;)
2 And all the brethren
which are with me,
unto the churches of
Galatia:
3 Grace be to you
and peace from God
the Father, and from
our Lord Jesus Christ,
4 Who gave him-
self for our sins,
that he might de-
liver us from this pre-
sent evil world, ac-
cording to the will
of God and our Father:
5 To whom be glory
for ever and ever.
Amen.

3. He wishes the very best for other believers

4. He proclaims the work of Christ
- a. The message: Christ gave Himself
- b. Purpose: To deliver us
- c. Reason: God so willed
- d. Result: God is praised

Section I
GREETING, Galatians 1:1-9

Study 1: GOD'S MINISTER AND HIS AUTHORITY

Text: Galatians 1:1-5

Aim: To claim your God-given authority with a life of conviction.

Memory Verse:

"Being confident of this very thing, that he which hath begun a good work in you will perform it until the day of Jesus Christ" (Ph.1:6).

INTRODUCTION:

Have you ever felt intimidated by someone who had more "credentials" to serve than you did? They had all the "right" papers, went to all of the "right" schools, and had been approved by all the "right" agencies? Have you ever felt that you just did not measure up? If you have had these kinds of feelings, you are not alone.

But rest assured, the foundation of Christian service does not rest upon such man-made things as human credentials, schools, and papers of commendation. As helpful as these things may be, they are not the foundation of our service to Christ. The foundation for service is Christ and the great work He has called us to do: that of bearing witness to His death, to the glorious truth that we can be delivered from this present evil world. Men only confirmed the great work and will of God that already works in us.

Now note:

Paul's greeting to the Galatians is different from his greetings to other churches. He was writing under heavy stress and strain. False teachers and critics had arisen in the church who were criticizing and attacking him. They were questioning his call to the ministry and his authority as God's messenger. Some were even questioning the very gospel itself. Therefore, the usual affection expressed toward churches and individuals is missing. From the very first sentence his writing is abrupt. He assails the Galatian churches with words straight to the point: he is a true minister of God, a true apostle and messenger of the Lord Jesus Christ.

GALATIANS 1:1-5

OUTLINE:

1. He is commissioned by God alone (v.1).
2. He is recognized as God's man by Christian believers (v.2).
3. He wishes the very best for other believers (v.3).
4. He proclaims the work of Christ (v.4-5).

1. HE IS COMMISSIONED BY GOD ALONE (v.1).

There were those in the church who questioned Paul's call and ministry, questioned if he had really been called by God to be a minister. They were set on destroying Paul's ministry. Why?

⇒ Because he had lived such a terrible life before his conversion: he had been the savage persecutor of believers (cp. Gal.1:13).

⇒ Because he was not one of the select officials of the church; that is, he had not been taught by the Lord Himself when the Lord was on earth. This was one of the basic qualifications for being recognized as an apostle (cp. Gal.1:17-18).

⇒ Because he had not been appointed by the official or mother church, that is, the home church of the apostles, the church in Jerusalem (cp. Gal.1:17-18).

⇒ Because he by-passed the religious forms and rituals of the official church (cp. Gal.4:9-10; 5:6; 6:12-15).

⇒ Because he preached a different message than the official church: that a person is not saved by ritual and works, but by the love and grace of God demonstrated in the death of Jesus Christ (Gal.1:4-9; 2:16; 3:1f, esp. v.10-11).

Paul answered his critics in no uncertain terms: he was an apostle. The word apostle means a person called and sent forth on a very special commission. The apostle is like...

- an *ambassador* who is sent forth to represent the Person who called and appointed him.
- a very special *messenger* who is called and sent forth to proclaim the message of the Sender.
- a very special *minister* who is called and sent forth to serve as the Leader wills.
- a very special *servant* who is called and sent forth to do the bidding of the Master.

Note that Paul was not arguing with his critics: he was declaring that God had called and appointed him to the ministry. He was making his call a part of his personal testimony (Acts 9:1f; 22:7f; 26:16f; 1 Cor.9:1).

1. His call and ministry were "not of men, neither by man."
   ⇒ "Not of men": men were not the source of his call and ministry. His call had not come *from man*.
   ⇒ "Neither by man": no man had qualified or made him fit for the ministry. He was not made a minister *by man*.
2. His call and ministry were by Jesus Christ and God the Father.
   ⇒ Note that Jesus Christ is placed side by side with God the Father. This is a crucial fact, for it means that Paul's call and ministry came from the highest source possible: from both God the Father and God the Son.

Note also that Jesus Christ is said to be raised from the dead. Therefore, Paul's call and ministry came from the Risen and Living Lord Himself. He was called to *serve* the Living Lord, the very same Lord served by the twelve apostles. If they were true ministers, then he also was a true minister, for he had been called by the same Living Lord who had been raised from the dead by God the Father.

APPLICATION 1:

Critics often arise and cause trouble for the minister of God. At such times the minister must boldly declare his call and ministry, not in a boastful and super-spiritual way but in a humble and clear way.

APPLICATION 2:

Every minister should examine his heart to make sure his call and ministry have been commissioned by God. The ministry is not...

- a profession to be chosen.
- a job to earn a living.
- a position to secure recognition and esteem.
- a service agency founded by men.
- an ordained commission from men.
- a call *of* men nor *by* men.

The ministry is of God; therefore a call to the ministry must come from God. God alone can give a true call and commission to the ministry.

> **"Therefore seeing we have this ministry [from God] as we have received mercy, we faint not; but have renounced the hidden things of dishonesty, not walking in craftiness nor handling the word of God deceitfully; but by manifestation of the truth commending ourselves to every man's conscience in the sight of God" (2 Cor.4:1-2).**

QUESTIONS:

1. How do you think Paul felt as he defended the call of God upon his life? What would you have done if you were the apostle Paul?
2. Do you ever experience feelings of inadequacy in your place of service? What sort of attitude are you to have?
3. How sure are you of God's call upon your life? Why is it important to be sure of His call?
4. What is to be your attitude in serving God?

2. HE IS RECOGNIZED AS GOD'S MAN BY CHRISTIAN BELIEVERS (v.2).

Note: the brothers with Paul were not just sending their greetings to the Galatian churches; they were agreeing with everything that Paul was writing. They were as concerned as Paul over the critics and false teachers in the churches of Galatia, and they clearly recognized Paul's call and commission as being of God. This is the stress of the point. Paul called them *brothers*, not friends. A true brother in Christ is much more than a friend. True brothers have a deeper, richer bond and relationship: they are of one faith, mind, spirit, and purpose. They may have different abilities and be assigned different work, but they believe in and serve the same Lord.

This is what Paul was saying: there were *brothers in the Lord* who knew him and his call. They readily verified his call and ministry. In fact, they *joined him* in writing and declaring the truth.

Note: there was more than one church that was questioning Paul's call and ministry. All the churches in Galatia were attacking him.

> **"And the King shall answer and say unto them, Verily I say unto you, Inasmuch as ye have done it unto one of the least of these my brethren, ye have done it unto me" (Mt.25:40).**

ILLUSTRATION:

Just as you can judge a tree by its fruit, the same is true for any man who claims to represent God. Paul's relationship with the Lord was recognized by other believers because of the fruit he bore. This point is made clear by an example from the life of John Wesley.

> *"In one of his meetings in Spitalfields, John Wesley denounced the sins of the people. Two men, heavily under the influence of liquor, stood on the edge of the crowd. 'He's saying mean things about us,' they said; 'let's do him in.' With large rocks in their hands they crept to a vantage point from which they could hurl them at Wesley's head.*

"As they were about to carry out their murderous plan, Wesley's emphasis suddenly changed from sin to the Saviour, the sinner's Friend. While he lovingly and earnestly spoke of the Saviour, his face shone, and his fervent words burned their way into the hearts of his would-be murderers. The stones were dropped from their hands. They went and knelt at Wesley's feet. He put his hands on their heads and said, 'God bless you, my boys! God bless you!'

"As they walked away one said, 'Was it God Himself?' 'No, Bill, but it was a man like God!' answered the other."[1]

There is no greater way to be recognized as God's man than to proclaim the gospel in power and authority.

APPLICATION:

When critics attack the minister, it is time for *true brothers* in the Lord to step forward and support him in his ministry and in declaring the truth. True brothers always defend and come to the aid of a brother when he is criticized and attacked.

> **"Greater love hath no man than this, that a man lay down his life for his friends" (Jn.15:13).**

QUESTIONS:

1. What person(s) do you trust to confirm God's call in your life? Why do you trust them?
2. As you serve Christ, what difference does it make knowing other Christians believe in your call?
3. What do you think your role is when a fellow believer is being attacked?

3. HE WISHES THE VERY BEST FOR OTHER BELIEVERS (v.3).

The minister, Paul, wanted the believers of Galatia to experience the grace and peace of God and of the Lord Jesus Christ. (Note again how the deity of Jesus Christ is proclaimed: He is placed side by side with God.)

1. Grace means the *undeserved favor and blessings* of God. The word *undeserved* is the key to understanding grace. Man does not deserve God's favor; he cannot earn God's approval and blessings. God is too high and man is too low for man to deserve anything from God. Man is imperfect and God is perfect; therefore, man cannot expect anything from God. Man has reacted against God too much. Man has...

- rejected God
- rebelled against God
- ignored God
- neglected God
- cursed God
- sinned against God
- disobeyed God
- denied God
- questioned God

Man deserves nothing from God except judgment, condemnation, and punishment. But God is love—perfect and absolute love. Therefore, God makes it possible for man to experience His grace, in particular the favor and blessing of salvation which is in His Son, Jesus Christ.

> **"Being justified freely by his grace through the redemption that is in Christ Jesus" (Ro.3:24).**

2. Peace means to be bound, joined, and weaved together with God and with everyone else. It means to be assured, confident, and secure in the love and care of God. It means to have a sense, a consciousness, a knowledge that God will...

- provide
- guide
- strengthen
- sustain
- deliver
- encourage
- save
- give life, real life, both now and forever

GALATIANS 1:1-5

A person can experience true peace only as he comes to know Jesus Christ. Only Christ can bring peace to the human heart, the kind of peace that brings deliverance and assurance to the human soul.

> **"Peace I leave with you, my peace I give unto you: not as the world giveth give I unto you. Let not your heart be troubled, neither let it be afraid" (Jn.14:27).**

The point is this: not everyone in the church was experiencing the grace and peace of God. Some had fallen from the grace of God, no longer trusting Christ to save them; they depended upon their own works and goodness to make them acceptable to God. As a result, they did not have peace of heart. Some had even fallen into all forms of sin and shame (Gal.5:19-21). Others had become extremely critical and divisive, standing against Paul and any who supported Paul. Note: Paul wished the very best for the churches of Galatia—even for the false teachers and critics. He wanted everyone to experience...

- the grace of God by coming to know Jesus Christ as their personal Savior and Lord.
- the peace of God as they walked through life confronting all its struggles and trials.

APPLICATION 1:

Every minister should wish the very best for all believers, even for his critics and enemies. It might be difficult, but his very call to the ministry is to proclaim the grace and peace of God.

ILLUSTRATION:

The Christian believer has been issued a tremendous charge to proclaim the grace and peace of God. As we all journey through life, the footing can become rather treacherous at times. Do you help others as they walk?

> *"A university professor tells of being invited to speak at a military base one December and there meeting an unforgettable soldier named Ralph. Ralph had been sent to meet him at the airport, and after they had introduced themselves, they headed toward the baggage claim.*
>
> *"As they walked down the concourse, Ralph kept disappearing. Once to help an older woman whose suitcase had fallen open. Once to lift two toddlers up to where they could see Santa Claus. And again to give directions to someone who was lost. Each time he came back with a big smile on his face.*
>
> *"'Where did you learn to do that?' the professor asked.*
>
> *"'Do what?' Ralph said.*
>
> *"'Where did you learn to live like that?'*
>
> *"'Oh,' Ralph said, 'during the war, I guess.' Then he told the professor about his tour of duty in Viet Nam, about how it was his job to clear mine fields, and how he watched his friends blow up before his eyes, one after another.*
>
> *"'I've learned to live between the steps,' he said. 'I never knew whether the next one would be my last, so I learned to get everything I could out of the moment between when I picked up my foot and when I put it down again. Every step I took was a whole new world, and I guess I've just been that way ever since.'"*[2]

Do you make the most of every moment? Have you learned to show God's grace and peace every chance you get?

APPLICATION 2:

Believers must guard against falling from grace, guard against trusting their own works and goodness to save them and to make them acceptable to God.

QUESTIONS:
1. How hard is it for you to share God's grace and peace with those who criticize you? What can you do in order to overcome this barrier?
2. Do you think God's peace can be a reality in your life—even when you are walking through "a minefield" of problems? Explain your answer.
3. What things come to your mind when you hear the word grace?
4. Why do more believers not experience God's grace and peace on a consistent basis? Is it possible that God wants you to proclaim His grace and peace to these people? Practically, what can you do?

4. HE PROCLAIMS THE WORK OF CHRIST (v.4-5).

This verse is one of the great summaries of the gospel, that is, of the work of the Lord Jesus Christ. Note four significant points.

1. The message of the gospel is that Christ "gave Himself for our sins." Christ died as our substitute. He took the place of the sinner before God. Two things show this.
   a. The word "for" means instead of, in place of, as our substitute, in behalf of our sins.
   b. The phrase "gave Himself" means that He sacrificed Himself for us. He gave His life for the sinner's life. Jesus Christ...
      - offered Himself to God as the sacrifice for our sin.
      - offered Himself as the sin-offering, the offering that was to stand as the substitute for our sin.
      - accepted the judgment and condemnation of sin for us.
      - bore the punishment of God's justice against sin for us.

Note that "our sins" are not listed or described. This means that Christ died for *all our sins*: big sins as well as little sins, known sins as well as unknown sins, terrible sins as well as mild sins, sins of the flesh as well as sins of the spirit.

> **"Who gave himself for our sins, that he might deliver us from this present evil world, according to the will of God and our Father" (Gal.1:4).**

2. The purpose of Jesus' death was "to deliver us from this present evil world." Note that the present world or age is said to be evil. It is evil in at least two senses:
   ⇒ The present world is sinful: it causes men to ignore, neglect, deny, and curse God. It also stirs and excites ungodliness, unrighteousness, immorality, wickedness, covetousness, maliciousness, envy, murder, strife, deceit, ill will, cruelty, backbiting, gossiping, slander, pride, boasting, inventions of evil things, disobedience to parents, misunderstanding and false undertanding, the breaking of covenants, and the destruction of true love and mercy. (Cp. Ro.1:29-32.)
   ⇒ The present world is corruptible: it keeps both man and his world from being healthy and from living eternally. The present world of corruption causes man and his world to suffer and experience disaster, accident, disease, distress, sorrow, and calamities. It causes everything to age, deteriorate, waste away, decay, and die.
   ⇒ The present world causes man to die and face the judgment of God who is *perfectly holy*. Therefore, the present world dooms man to face the holiness of God as an unholy, sinful, and corruptible creature. The world dooms man to an eternity of death and judgment—dooms him to be separated from God forever.

But note the point: this was the very purpose for Jesus' death. He died to deliver us from this present evil world. The word "deliver" means to rescue and to pluck out. Jesus Christ died to rescue and to pluck us out of this present evil world. How? As stated above, "He gave Himself for our sins." He delivers or rescues us from both *the power and the fate* of the world. The believer experiences both abundant and eternal life now and forever.

"Verily, verily, I say unto you, He that heareth my word, and believeth on him that sent me, hath everlasting life, and shall not come into condemnation; but is passed from death unto life" (Jn.5:24).

3. The reason Christ died for us is because God willed it. This is a most glorious truth: God loves us even as Christ loves us. It was God's will that we be saved and delivered from this evil world. God loves us so much that He wills us to be saved—wills it so much that He sacrificed His own Son for us.

Note that God wills to be our Father. The death of Jesus Christ makes it possible for us to be adopted by God as His sons and daughters (Ro.8:15-16; Gal.4:4-6).

"But God commendeth his love toward us, in that, while we were yet sinners, Christ died for us" (Ro.5:8).

4. The result of Jesus' death is the glory of God. Note: Paul could not mention the death of Christ and the will of God without breaking forth in praise. All men should praise God for His wonderful love and the unspeakable gift of His Son.

"But he was wounded for our transgressions, he was bruised for our iniquities: the chastisement of our peace was upon him; and with his stripes we are healed" (Is.53:5).

ILLUSTRATION:

Have you ever given quality time to meditate on Christ's work on the cross? Take a moment now to fix your attention on Calvary...to a time...to a Savior...to your involvement in His crucifixion.

"Rembrandt, the famous Dutch artist, painted a picture of the crucifixion. Vividly he portrayed Christ writhing in...agony on the cruel cross. Vividly he depicted the various attitudes of those about the cross toward the suffering Saviour by their facial expressions. Apart from the Saviour's death, the most significant thing about the painting is the artist's painting of himself, standing in the shadows on the edge of the onlookers. This was Rembrandt's way of saying, 'I was there, too! I helped to crucify Jesus!' We, too, were there, standing with Rembrandt in the shadows!"[3]

We were there—standing in the shadows of our sin. Christ was there—standing in our sin, dissolving the shadows with His great love for us!

QUESTIONS:

1. What does this section of Scripture tell you about Christ's love for you?
2. Why did Jesus have to die?
3. Could you have done what Jesus did? (Left the glory and perfection of heaven, lived as a pauper, lived with ridicule and mockery, suffered torture and a cruel death for your enemies and then, beyond imagination, bore all the sin and evil of the world for all the sinners of the world?)
4. How should this make you feel when you really think about what Christ did for you?

SUMMARY:

Is God's call upon your life obvious to you and to those who know you? You can sharpen the focus by living a life of conviction for Christ. A life of conviction comes when:

1. You are commissioned by God alone.
2. You are recognized as God's man or woman by Christian believers.
3. You wish the very best for other believers.
4. You proclaim the work of Christ.

GALATIANS 1:1-5

PERSONAL JOURNAL NOTES

(Reflection & Response)

1. The most important thing that I learned from this lesson was:

2. The area that I need to work on the most is:

3. I can apply this lesson to my life by:

4. Closing Statement of Commitment:

---

[1] Walter B. Knight. *Knight's Treasury of 2,000 Illustrations*. (Grand Rapids, MI: Eerdman's Publishing Company, 1992), p.285.

[2] Quoted from Barbara Brown Taylor. *Leadership*. (Carol Stream, IL: Christianity Today, Summer 1993), Vol. XIV, #3, p.61.

[3] Walter B. Knight. *Knight's Treasury of 2,000 Illustrations*, p.96.

Outline	Scripture	Scripture (cont.)	Outline
	B. God's Only Message--the Gospel of Christ, 1:6-9	gospel of Christ.	the gospel
1. God's gospel is the only message (v.4)	6 I marvel that ye are so soon removed from him that called you into the grace of Christ unto another gospel:	8 But though we, or an angel from heaven, preach any other gospel unto you than that which we have preached unto you, let him be accursed.	**3. Preachers of false gospels are accursed** a. The gospel is greater than the apostle b. The gospel is greater than the angels c. The gospel is greater than any man d. The judgment: A double curse
2. Some persons turned to false gospels a. They deserted God b. They turned to another gospel, a false gospel c. They followed those who twisted	7 Which is not another; but there be some that trouble you, and would pervert the	9 As we said before, so say I now again, If any man preach any other gospel unto you than that ye have received, let him be accursed.	

Section I
GREETING
Galatians 1:1-9

Study 2: GOD'S ONLY MESSAGE—THE GOSPEL OF CHRIST

Text: Galatians 1:6-9

Aim: To jealously protect the Gospel of Christ from any falsehood.

Memory Verse:

> **"As we said before, so say I now again, If any man preach any other gospel unto you than that ye have received, let him be accursed" (Gal.1:9).**

INTRODUCTION:

How would your church respond if your young people were approached by an organized cult? One night at a church skating party, a group of teenagers were "befriended" by several men who asked about their spiritual lives. The teenagers were given an invitation to join them for a series of special studies. These strangers also invited themselves to the church of these teens. Like a sinister snake, this cult was moving in for the kill.

Fortunately, the parents of these teenagers knew enough of God's Word to make them cautious and wise. After the next church service, the leaders of this cult were spoken to and in blunt terms told to leave their kids alone and to never return to their church again.

Were these adults being ugly and unloving? No. On the contrary, they were carrying out the Biblical charge: to protect the innocent sheep from the advances of wolves. Paul had the same circumstances to deal with in his time.

The churches of Galatia were being led astray by false teachers, and the very souls of the believers were at stake. Paul had no choice; he had to be strong in what he wrote, for Christ had taught that the value of a single soul was worth more than all the wealth of the world.

> **"For what shall it profit a man, if he shall gain the whole world, and lose his own soul? Or what shall a man give in exchange for his soul?" (Mk.8:36-37).**

Again, the souls of the Galatians were at stake. Forcefully and powerfully, Paul warned both the false teachers and the believers: God has only one message—the gospel of Christ. It is God's gospel and God's gospel alone that must be obeyed, preached, taught, and heeded.

GALATIANS 1:6-9

OUTLINE:

1. God's gospel is the only message (v.6).
2. Some persons turned to false gospels (v.6-7).
3. Preachers of false gospels are accursed (v.8-9).

1. GOD'S GOSPEL IS THE ONLY MESSAGE (v.6).

God's gospel had just been clearly stated by Paul.

> **"[Christ] gave himself for our sins, that he might deliver us from this present evil world, according to the will of God and our Father" (Gal.1:4).**

The message of the gospel is that Christ died to rescue us from this present evil world, that is, from this world's sin:

⇒ lawlessness
⇒ corruption
⇒ deterioration
⇒ judgment
⇒ doom
⇒ unrighteousness
⇒ aging
⇒ death
⇒ condemnation

Christ died that we might be delivered from sin and death to live eternally with God in a new heavens and earth.

Very practically, what happens is this: when a person looks at Jesus Christ and *truly believes* that Christ took his sins upon Himself and died for them, God counts it so. God credits it as a fact. God sees Christ bearing the person's sin, and He looks upon the person as being sinless and perfect, that is, completely free of sin. Therefore, the person becomes acceptable to God. God sees him *in Christ* who is without sin, completely righteous and perfect. But note a critical fact: the person is not sinless; no person is without sin; no person is perfectly righteous. But God counts the person as sinless, as perfectly righteous.

Why does God do such a wonderful and marvelous thing? Because He loves us that much; He loves us with an eternal, unlimited love. This is the message of the glorious gospel. We cannot earn the acceptance of God, for we are unrighteous and imperfect, and only righteousness and perfection can live in the presence of God. But God loves us so much that He has provided the way for us to become righteous and acceptable to him. This is what is meant by justification and the wonderful grace of Christ. This is the glorious message of the gospel.

> **"The next day John seeth Jesus coming unto him, and saith, Behold the Lamb of God, which taketh away the sin of the world!" (Jn.1:29).**

ILLUSTRATION:

Why is it so important to protect the gospel from falsehood? Dave Bass shares this shocking story:

> *"Every day, striking incidents are accumulating in the experience of overseas missionaries and North American Christians alike:*
>
> *"The candidate for elder in an independent suburban church in the Midwest sat with the board for his interview. From all the church's appearances—doctrinal statement, sermons, worship, teaching—he had no reason to doubt that this was a solid, biblical church. In discussing his qualifications, however, he discovered that he was chosen partly because his astrological sign was in harmony with those of the board members. They urged him to pray for a 'spirit guide' who would give him wisdom in his new office. They said he could expect to benefit from 'deep' teachings from the elders themselves. Now the man understood why a friend had earlier declined the position and had been reluctant to discuss it."*[1]

QUESTIONS:
1. How confident are you in your grasp of the essential doctrines of Christianity? What areas need strengthening?
2. What caused Paul to marvel at the Galatians? Are you sometimes guilty of the same thing as the Galatians?
3. What other "gospels" tempt believers? What kinds are a temptation to you?

2. SOME PERSONS TURNED TO FALSE GOSPELS (v.6-7).

This is the subject of The Book of Galatians, the very reason Paul wrote to the churches of Galatia. Some false teachers had joined the church, false teachers who did not believe in the gospel as proclaimed by Paul and the apostles. They were adding to and taking away from the gospel of the Scriptures and attacking the minister. As a result, some believers were following the false teachers and turning to their false gospels. Paul warned the believers of the churches, and his warning was direct and forceful.

1. The believers were deserting God, removing themselves from God. The word "remove" means to turn away, to change places, to transfer elsewhere. The tense of the verb is present which means the Galatians were in the process of turning; they had not yet fully turned. There was still hope for them to repent and return to God. Note three striking facts.

a. A person who turns away from the gospel is not turning away from a set of beliefs or principles nor from a church. The person is turning away from God Himself. It is God who loves us and saves us, not a set of beliefs. It is God who *personally calls* us into the grace of Christ, not a message or a preacher. Therefore, to turn away is to desert God Himself, the Person who has loved us enough to save us and to give us eternal life in His Son, Jesus Christ.

b. The words "so soon" show how quickly people can be led away from God. The false teachers had apparently just joined the church and had impressive ability and charisma, so much so that they were almost immediately accepted as teachers in the church. The result had been devastating: many were immediately swayed by the force of their charisma, ability, ideas, and worldly wisdom.

c. The word "marvel" means astounded, astonished, surprised. Paul could hardly believe the fact, for the Galatians had been grounded in the true gospel and had been growing in Christ. But here they were turning away ever so quickly. The believers needed to be warned: they were walking on thin ice. They were turning away and deserting God Himself.

"And because iniquity shall abound, the love of many shall wax cold" (Mt.24:12).

2. The believers were turning to another gospel, that is, to a false gospel. The word "another" means a different kind of gospel, not just a difference in emphasis or spirit.[2] It means a different kind of gospel that presents…

- a different Jesus
- a different grace
- a different way to be saved
- a different God
- a different picture of God's love

But note what Scripture declares: the gospel to which the Galatians were turning was *not another gospel*. There is no other gospel; there is only one true gospel by which men can become acceptable to God, and that is the gospel of God Himself revealed in the death of His Son, even "the grace of Christ" (v.6).

"Then Simon Peter answered him, Lord, to whom shall we go? thou hast the words of eternal life" (Jn.6:68).

3. The believers were following those who twisted the gospel of Christ. They were following false teachers. Note what it was that made the teachers *false teachers*: a perverting of the gospel. The word "pervert" means to turn about, to change completely, to distort. They were taking the gospel of God's love and grace as demonstrated in His Son, Jesus Christ, and changing it. The false teachers claimed to be Christians, followers of Christ. They even believed with Paul...

- that God did love the world and send His Son into the world.
- that Jesus Christ was the Son of God who did actually come to earth.
- that Jesus Christ did die and arise from the dead.

However, the false teachers were adding to and taking away from the gospel, twisting its meaning and making it say something entirely different from the Scripture Paul preached. They distorted the gospel by saying that...

a. God did show His love for the world by sending His Son, but He sent His Son in particular for the religious person (the Jew and the religionist). They were saying that God loves the world, but He especially loves the people who live religious lives. (Note how this makes God show favoritism and partiality and opens the door for caste systems and prejudice.)
b. Jesus Christ did come to earth; however, it was not to secure a perfect righteousness for men, but to show men how to live a good life that pleases God and merits God's approval.
c. Jesus Christ did die for man; however, He did not die for man's sin, but to show man how he should be so committed to God that he would die for God's cause.
d. The death of Jesus Christ is not sufficient by itself; it cannot stand alone; it is not enough to make man acceptable to God. More is needed than the raw love of God and the pure grace of Christ.
e. A person must undergo the ritual that had been the main ritual of believers down through the centuries: circumcision (church membership, baptism, etc.).
f. A person must work to keep the law of God as well as certain church ceremonies, rituals, rules, and regulations.

Note how devastating the false teaching was: believers were troubled, that is, disturbed, bewildered, perplexed, confused. As pointed out above, they were not only turning away from the gospel but from God Himself and from the glorious grace of Christ (v.6).

APPLICATION:

Note a shocking fact: how close false teaching within the church is to the truth! How a little addition here and a little subtraction there distorts the purity of the gospel! How diligently we must guard against adding our own ideas to the gospel of God.

"Beware of false prophets, which come to you in sheep's clothing, but inwardly they are ravening wolves" (Mt.7:15).

"Be not carried about with divers and strange doctrines" (Heb.13:9).

ILLUSTRATION:

Have you ever thought about the things that pierce God's heart? One of the major things is idolatry, when a person whom He has called turns to a false religion or a false god.

Years ago, a photographer captured on film four men who were struggling to carry a statue of Buddha during the blast of a violent typhoon. As water was rushing up to their knees, their faces grimmaced as they attempted to save their god.

Isaiah the prophet framed this tragic irony—a god who cannot save and has to have the help of people.

"They lift it upon the shoulder and carry it; they set it in its place and it stands there. It does not move from its place. Though one may cry to it, it cannot answer; it cannot deliver him from his distress" (Is.46:7, NASB).

Are you ever tempted to serve this kind of god? Christian believer, let go and let it drown. And then reach out to the one who says...

"When you pass through the waters, I will be with you; and through the rivers, they will not overflow you. When you walk through the fire, you will not be scorched, nor will the flame burn you" (Is.43:2, NASB).

QUESTIONS:

1. What are some of the natural results when a person turns to a false gospel?
2. Do you think it is possible for a Christian believer to turn to a false gospel? How? Why?
3. If you could paint a picture of a false teacher, what would he look like?
4. Can you be too careful about who or what you believe in?

3. PREACHERS OF FALSE GOSPELS ARE ACCURSED (v.8-9).

Accursed means cursed, doomed, damned, cast into hell. This is a strong statement, but it is clearly understandable. The gospel is the means by which men are saved out of the grip of sin, death, and condemnation. Without the gospel no person is saved—no person can become acceptable to God—no person can inherit eternal life. Scripture is clear about the matter and warns all false teachers and all churches.

1. The gospel is greater than the apostle Paul himself. This is a striking statement, for remember who Paul was: probably the most committed servant of God who has ever lived. He had ventured forth as a pioneer into the heathen areas of the world to reach people with the gospel of Christ, the good news that men could be delivered from sin and death and live forever. He loved the Galatians so much that he had risked all he was and had for their sakes. To some Paul must have been a giant, and he must have been held ever so dear to their hearts. But note: Paul says that if he returned to them preaching any other gospel, he was to be accursed. The Galatians were not to receive him no matter how much they esteemed him: they were to reject him. The gospel in all its simplicity and purity was far more important than Paul himself.
2. The gospel is greater than the angels from heaven. Even if an angel came from heaven and began to preach another gospel, he was to be rejected, for he too would be accursed. The glorious message of the gospel is far more important than even the angels in heaven.
3. The gospel is greater than any man (v.9). If any man preached *any other gospel*, he was to be accursed. The gospel is far more important than any man.
4. The preachers of the false gospels shall suffer the judgment of a double curse. The word "anathema" means to be accursed, doomed to destruction, given over to eternal punishment, placed under the wrath of God. The idea is that of eternal death. This is clear from Paul's use of the word elsewhere where he applies it to himself: "I could wish that myself were accursed from Christ for my brethren...." (Ro.9:3). Paul was a Jew; he was saying that he loved his Jewish brothers so much that he would gladly suffer eternal punishment for their salvation (the very same love that Christ had demonstrated for all men).

This is one of the most severe warnings in all of Scripture, and note to whom it is given: it is given to teachers, the *false teachers*. Lehman Strauss points out that every person who does not love the Lord Jesus Christ shall be accursed. How much more, then, shall the false teacher suffer at the hands of God's eternal wrath[3]

"Beware of false prophets, which come to you in sheep's clothing, but inwardly they are ravening wolves. Ye shall know them by their

fruits. Do men gather grapes of thorns, or figs of thistles?...Every tree that bringeth not forth good fruit is hewn down, and cast into the fire" (Mt.7:15-16, 19).

QUESTIONS:

1. What conclusions would you make if a Bible teacher or preacher told you the Bible did not apply to him? What conclusions would you reach if someone said he believed the Bible but refused to live his life according to God's Word?
2. Why is Paul's language so harsh?
3. How can believers recognize false teachers? How does God expect you to deal with false teachers?

SUMMARY:

The Christian believer must become jealous of the gospel of Jesus Christ or else the church will be flooded with a variety of gods that are drowning. If you want to avoid going under with them, remember to apply the major points of this session:

1. God's gospel is the only message.
2. Some persons turned to false gospels.
3. Preachers of false gospels are accursed.

PERSONAL JOURNAL NOTES
(Reflection & Response)

1. The most important thing that I learned from this lesson was:

2. The area that I need to work on the most is:

3. I can apply this lesson to my life by:

4. Closing Statement of Commitment:

---

[1] Selected from Christianity Today. (Carol Stream, IL, April 29, 1991), p.14.

[2] A.T. Robertson. *Word Pictures in the New Testament*, Vol.4. (Nashville, TN: Broadman Press, 1931), p.276.

[3] Lehman Strauss. *Devotional Studies in Galatians and Ephesians*. (Neptune, NJ: Loizeaux Brothers, 1947), p.21

GALATIANS 1:10-16

Outline	Scripture	Scripture	Outline
	II. THE PROOF OF GOD'S MESSENGER & MESSAGE, 1:10-2:21 **A. The Minister's Life Was Completely Changed, 1:10-16**		
1. He sought to please God not men	10 For do I now persuade men, or God? or do I seek to please men? for if I yet pleased men, I should not be the servant of Christ.		
2. He proclaimed the gospel a. Not a man-made gospel b. Not received of man c. A revelation of Christ	11 But I certify you, brethren, that the gospel which was preached of me is not after man. 12 For I neither received it of man, neither was I taught it, but by the revelation	of Jesus Christ.	
		13 For ye have heard of my conversation in time past in the Jews' religion, how that beyond measure I persecuted the church of God, and wasted it: 14 And profited in the Jews' religion above many my equals in mine own nation, being more exceedingly zealous of the traditions of my fathers.	**3. He had a radical change of life** a. His former experience 1) An arch-persecutor 2) A supreme example of self-righteousness
		15 But when it pleased God, who separated me from my mother's womb, and called me by his grace. 16 To reveal his Son in me, that I might preach him among the heathen; immediately I conferred not with flesh and blood:	b. His radical change 1) Set apart & called by God's grace 2) Called as a vessel to reveal Christ 3) Called to preach Christ 4) Called to seek his gospel from God alone

Section II
THE PROOF OF GOD'S MESSENGER AND MESSAGE
Galatians 1:10-2:21

Study 1: THE MINISTER'S LIFE WAS COMPLETELY CHANGED

Text: Galatians 1:10-16

Aim: To pursue a radically changed life through Christ.

Memory Verse:

"For do I now persuade men, or God? or do I seek to please men? for if I yet pleased men, I should not be the servant of Christ" (Galatians 1:10).

INTRODUCTION:

One of the greatest political minds in America in the twentieth century belonged to that of Lee Atwater. He was known for his keen political insight and for his questionable political "techniques" that would help his candidate win the election. Atwater considered politics to be war. Obviously, this kind of life was meant to please only his candidate. His gospel was to win at any cost, and enemies made along the way were considered to be trophies collected during the political war.

One day, his world came to a screeching halt. Atwater discovered that he had a malignant brain tumor. All of a sudden he saw life in a different light. In the remaining months of his life, he gave his heart to Christ. Lee Atwater began to share the gospel of Jesus Christ with whoever would listen (and a lot did). He also made it a point to repent for his political sins and went to each of his self-made enemies to ask for their forgiveness. It was not long after Atwater became a Christian that he left this world for a land where the only politician is the Lord Himself, the Lord Jesus Christ.

What lessons can we draw from this example? It is a very easy thing for us to want to please men instead of God. The gospel we proclaim can become tainted with our own personal agenda. And our life-style can offend unless we...

- set our hearts to please God.
- proclaim the gospel of Christ.
- show that we are different by the example of our lives.

Both critics of Paul and false teachers had arisen in the churches of Galatia. They were saying that Paul's call and the gospel he preached were false, that he was not a true minister of God, that he was a self-made minister who was only using the ministry for a livelihood and other greedy purposes.

Paul's answer was direct and forceful: his message and life were of God. His old life and old message had been radically changed.

OUTLINE:

1. He sought to please God not men (v.10).
2. He proclaimed the gospel (v.11-12).
3. He had a radical change of life (v.13-16).

1. HE SOUGHT TO PLEASE GOD NOT MEN (v.10).

The critics of Paul were saying that he was inconsistent...

- seeking the favor and approval of men instead of God.
- striving to please men instead of God.
- living by the law when he was with the religionists (Jews) and living a looser life when he was with the unsaved and non-religionists (Gentiles).
- saying one thing to one group of people and something else to another group of people.
- living a life of duplicity and deception in order to secure the support of the people.

Paul minced no words; he fired two questions at his critics: "Am I now seeking the favor of men or of God? Do I seek to please men?" As stated, Paul minced no words. He answered his own questions by making a startling statement: he agreed with his critics. **"If I yet [still] pleased men, I should not be the servant of Christ."**

The point is clear: note the word "yet" or *still*. Paul was saying that there was a time when he was a man-pleaser, a time when he sought the favor and approval of men instead of God. But no more: he was not "still pleasing men." He was now seeking to please God and God alone. Pleasing men, courting their favor, securing their acceptance, approval, and recognition, and gaining honor, position, and wealth—none of these things mattered to him anymore. He now wanted one thing and one thing alone: the favor and approval of God. For this reason, he was the slave of Jesus Christ.

> **"If any man serve me, let him follow me; and where I am, there shall also my servant be: if any man serve me, him will my Father honour" (Jn.12:26).**

QUESTIONS:

1. How do believers seek to please men instead of God? What kinds of things do they do?
2. Can you think of a time when you sought to please people and not God? What would you do differently if you had another chance?
3. What should be your motivation to please God?

2. HE PROCLAIMED THE GOSPEL (v.11-12).

Some critics of Paul were saying that he was not a true apostle of the Lord Jesus because he had not been a follower of the Lord when the Lord was upon the earth. Therefore, what he was teaching was a man-made gospel taught by mistaken and misguided men.

Note that the word "certify" is a solemn word, a strong declaration that what follows is of crucial importance and needs to be heard. Paul wants the believers of Galatia to know this fact, know it beyond question.

1. The gospel Paul preached was not a man-made gospel. It was not a gospel created by man's...

- mind
- ideas
- rationalizations
- hopes
- religions
- dreams
- imaginations
- science
- energy

The gospel was not a human thing; it did not originate with man. The gospel was not the good news *of men*.

2. The gospel Paul preached was not received of man. It was *not a taught message*, not a message which he had learned from any man. The gospel he preached was not a message...

- handed down to him like tradition.
- learned by him from an educational institution.
- taught to him by men.

3. The gospel Paul preached was given to him by a *direct revelation* from Jesus Christ. Revelation means a truth that is shared by God to man, a truth that man never knew. It is crucial to note this point, for Paul's call to the ministry and the gospel which he preached rested upon this single fact: did Jesus Christ really reveal Himself and the truth of His death and resurrection to Paul or not? If Paul were lying, then he was not a true minister of the gospel. He would be a fraud, a deceiver, a man who viewed the ministry only as a profession to provide a livelihood and to secure honor and power over people.

However, as Paul plainly declared, he received the gospel by the direct revelation of Jesus Christ. Time and again he declared the fact.

> **"But we speak the wisdom of God in a mystery [revelation], even the hidden wisdom, which God ordained before the world unto our glory" (1 Cor.2:7).**
>
> **"Who will have all men to be saved, and to come unto the knowledge of the truth" (1 Tim.2:4).**
>
> **"But hath in due times manifested his word through preaching, which is committed unto me according to the commandment of God our Saviour" (Tit.1:3).**

ILLUSTRATION:

The apostle Paul's gospel was not a figment of his imagination. His gospel was preached in the power of God; consequently, he got results. The lives of people were changed. No man-made gospel can change the hearts of men.

> *"When George Whitefield was shaking England with the thunders of his revival preaching, a certain baronet said to a friend: 'This man Whitefield is a truly great man. Surely he will be the founder of a new religion.' 'A new religion!' exclaimed the friend. 'Yes,' said the baronet, 'if it is not a new religion, what do you call it?' 'I say of it that it is nothing but the old religion revived and heated with divine energy in a man who really means what he says.'*
>
> *"The old-fashioned Gospel produces old-fashioned conversions when it is preached under the power of the divine Spirit."*[1]

What kind of gospel does your life proclaim? A 'new religion' or the only true gospel of Jesus Christ?

QUESTIONS:
1. What kinds of "man-made" gospels are a part of your culture? Do any of these appeal to you?
2. What distinguishes the gospel of Christ with that of a man-made gospel?
3. If an unbeliever asked you, "What are the basic elements of the gospel of Christ," how would you respond?

3. HE HAD A RADICAL CHANGE OF LIFE (v.13-16).

Paul's radical change of life is clearly seen by comparing his former life with his present life.

1. Paul's former life included two terrible things.
   a. Paul had been the first arch-persecutor of the church. He had been an *inflamed* man who struck out more than anyone else against the early believers.

      "And Saul, yet breathing out threatenings and slaughter against the disciples of the Lord, went unto the high priest....And as he journeyed, he came near Damascus: and suddenly there shined round about him a light from heaven: and he fell to the earth, and heard a voice saying unto him, Saul, Saul, why persecutest thou me?" (Acts 9:1, 3-4).

      Apparently Paul had launched the persecution of the church on the very day of Stephen's death. Saul had wanted to act and act quickly in wiping out the church. The believers were frightened and on the run; therefore, Paul felt that he had to strike immediately in order to catch them before they could escape.

      The point to see is that Paul had been bent on violence; he had sought to utterly stamp out the church; to wipe believers off the face of the earth. The word "wasted" means to make havoc; to utterly rack or lay waste; to devastate, destroy, ruin, or wipe out.

      "As for Saul, he made havoc of the church, entering into every house, and haling men and women committed them to prison" (Acts 8:3).

      "For I am the least of the apostles, that am not meet to be called an apostle, because I persecuted the church of God" (1 Cor.15:9).

   b. Paul had been the supreme example of self-righteousness. Paul declared that he had "profited" in the Jews' religions above and beyond what others had done. The idea is that he had blazed a path and given well beyond what they had achieved. He had been much more *zealous* than they.

      But note where his commitment had laid: in religion and in the traditions of the religious leaders. His focus and fanaticism had been placed upon religion and its traditions, rituals, and ceremonies and not upon God.

      "But he answered and said unto them, Why do ye also transgress the commandment of God by your tradition?" (Mt.15:3).

      "For laying aside the commandment of God, ye hold the tradition of men" (Mk.7:8).

ILLUSTRATION:

Before his conversion, Paul had done all the right things except for one: in spite of all his zeal, he was missing the mark and heading in the wrong direction. Listen to this account:

> *"The space ship Mariner II made big headlines when it completed its thirty-six-million-mile trip towards Venus. Until then, we did not know very much about our closest neighbor.*
>
> *"Most of us have forgotten that Mariner II had a forerunner. Mariner I, which attempted the same journey through space...What happened that time?*
>
> *"Well, there was nothing wrong with Mariner I. It was just as close to perfect as the scientists could make it. But when it was launched, it went off course and missed Venus by tens of thousands of miles. Why?*
>
> *"It seems that in typing out the electronic instructions to the missile, someone left out a hyphen. That meant that the signals were off by one electronic impulse. And, of course, the missile behaved—or misbehaved—in accordance with the faulty instructions.*
>
> *"Damage? The project was held up for two years—and eighteen million tax-payer's dollars were wasted. That's what a hyphen can cost!"*[2]

In Paul's former life, the thing that threw him off course was his misguided sense of self-righteousness. The "hyphen" that put him back on an accurate course for life was the cross. Without the cross, we will be, forever, lost in space.

2. Paul's radical change included four significant points.
   a. God had set Paul apart and called him by His grace. Paul clearly said...
      - that it was *God's grace* that had saved him from a life of self-righteousness and destruction.
      - that God's grace had separated him to serve Christ "from his mother's womb." The idea is that God had Paul in his mind even before Paul's birth. Paul's call and ministry were not due to Paul but to God and His grace. God had His eye on Paul throughout all eternity.

   APPLICATION:

   The believer's call and ministry is of God not of himself.

   > **"For ye see your calling, brethren, how that not many wise men after the flesh, not many mighty, not many noble, are called: but God hath chosen the foolish things of the world to confound the wise; and God hath chosen the weak things of the world to confound the things which are mighty" (1 Cor.1:26-27).**
   >
   > **"For by grace are ye saved through faith; and that not of yourselves: it is the gift of God: Not of works, lest any man should boast" (Eph.2:8-9).**
   >
   > **"Not by works of righteousness which we have done, but according to his mercy he saved us, by the washing of regeneration, and renewing of the Holy Ghost; Which he shed on us abundantly through Jesus Christ our Saviour" (Tit.3:5-6).**

   b. God called Paul as a vessel to reveal Christ. Note the words "in me." God's primary call to Paul was the same as it is for every believer: to reveal His Son Jesus Christ both *to him* and *through him*. God wants the believer both to know Christ and to make Christ known. We are chosen to fellowship and commune with the Lord more and more and to let Him be seen in us more and more. The believer is a mere vessel in and through whom Jesus Christ lives.

"But as it is written, Eye hath not seen, nor ear heard, neither have entered into the heart of man, the things which God hath prepared for them that love him. But God hath revealed them unto us by his Spirit: for the Spirit searcheth all things, yea, the deep things of God" (1 Cor.2:9-10).

c. God called Paul to preach Christ. Believers are not only called to know Christ but also to make Christ known. We must preach and bear witness to Christ.

"And he said unto them, Go ye into all the world, and preach the gospel to every creature" (Mk.16:15).

d. God called Paul to seek his gospel from God alone. Paul was not to seek his gospel from men but from God. He alone is the source of the gospel.

APPLICATION:

This does not mean, of course, that ministers (all believers) are not to learn from other people; it means that ministers (all believers) are not to proclaim the gospel of men. God has given us the gospel to study and preach. It is His message, not man's message, that the world needs.

"For I determined not to know any thing among you, save Jesus Christ, and him crucified" (1 Cor.2:2).

QUESTIONS:

1. Do you believe that your past life keeps you from changing your life now? Why? How?
2. Have you done anything so bad that God cannot forgive you? What does this section of Scripture tell you about God's promise to you?
3. What is the secret to having a radical change of life? What action can you take to bring this change about?

SUMMARY:

Have you heard the challenge to the Christian believer: "If you were on trial for being a Christian, would there be enough evidence to convict you?" There will be if you follow Paul's example!

1. He sought to please God not men.
2. He proclaimed the gospel.
3. He had a radical change of life.

PERSONAL JOURNAL NOTES
(Reflection & Response)

1. The most important thing that I learned from this lesson was:

2. The area that I need to work on the most is:

3. I can apply this lesson to my life by:

4. Closing Statement of Commitment:

---

[1] *Pentecostal Herald.* Walter B. Knight. *Knight's Master Book of 4,000 Illustrations* (Grand Rapids, MI: Eerdmans Publishing Company, 1994), p.252-253.

[2] Robert G. Lee. *Sourcebook of 500 Illustrations.* (Grand Rapids, MI:Zondervan Publishing House, 1970), p.157-158.

GALATIANS 1:17-24

	B. The Minister Followed God First in His Life, 1:17-24	brother. 20 Now the things which I write unto you, behold, before God, I lie not.	b. Gave a solemn protest, cp.11-12
1. First, he went to Arabia: He got alone with God **2. Second, he returned to Damascus: He corrected the wrong he had previously done** **3. Third, he went to Jerusalem: He faced his past, v.13-14** a. Faced Peter & James: Faced them as an equal—did not consult them about the gospel	17 Neither went I up to Jerusalem to them which were apostles before me; but I went into Arabia, and returned again unto Damascus. 18 Then after three years I went up to Jerusalem to see Peter, and abode with him fifteen days. 19 But other of the apostles saw I none, save James the Lord's	21 Afterwards I came into the regions of Syria and Cilicia; 22 And was unknown by face unto the churches of Judaea which were in Christ: 23 But they had heard only, That he which persecuted us in times past now preacheth the faith which once he destroyed. 24 And they glorified God in me.	**4. Fourth, he went to Syria & Cilicia, that is, Tarsus: He faced his hometown** **5. Fifth, the results of a God-centered life were powerful** a. His testimony spread b. His life honored God

Section II
THE PROOF OF GOD'S MESSENGER AND MESSAGE
Galatians 1:10-2:21

Study 2: **THE MINISTER FOLLOWED GOD FIRST IN HIS LIFE**

Text: **Galatians 1:17-24**

Aim: To bear a captivating testimony for Christ.

Memory Verse:

"According to my earnest expectation and my hope, that in nothing I shall be ashamed, but that with all boldness, as always, so now also Christ shall be magnified in my body, whether it be by life, or by death" (Philippians 1:20).

INTRODUCTION:

Think for a moment: What is the most exciting testimony you have ever heard? What struck you the most?

If you were put on the spot today and asked to share your Christian testimony, what would it include? One of the most powerful tools of witnessing is your personal testimony. Unfortunately, many Christians have not lived the kind of life that bears a strong testimony for Christ.

The life of the believer should be so strong that it becomes a *trophy* of what God can do in the heart of a person. Note how stong a life and testimony Paul lived.

Paul was under attack by some critics in the churches of Galatia. They were saying that he was not a God-called minister and that he preached a false gospel. They sowed the poison of gossip: that he was in the ministry only as a profession and for what he could get out of it.

The present passage is a continuation of the former verses. Paul was proving that his call and message did come from God, that he was a God-called minister and his message was the true gospel of the Lord Jesus Christ. In fact, he had never received the gospel from anyone other than Christ Himself. To prove his point, he recounted his journeys right after his conversion.

GALATIANS 1:17-24

The point is this: he sought to learn the truth from God and from God alone. In the first few years after his conversion, he followed God first in his life, not men.

OUTLINE:

1. First, he went to Arabia: he got alone with God (v.17).
2. Second, he returned to Damascus: he corrected the wrong he had previously done (v.17).
3. Third, he went to Jerusalem: he faced his past (v.18-20).
4. Fourth, he went to Syria and Cilicia, that is Tarsus: he faced his hometown (v.21).
5. The result of a God-centered life (v.22-24).

A CLOSER LOOK:

Paul said "immediately...I went into Arabia." The time-table of his ministry would seem to be as follows.

1. His conversion (Gal.1:15-16; Acts 9:1f).
2. His "immediate" preaching and ministry in Damascus (Acts 9:19-22).
3. His time alone with God in Arabia (Gal.1:17). The three years could be three full years or parts of three calendar years. In comparing this passage with Acts, Paul's Arabian experience would seem to fit in best at the close of Acts 9:22. There seems to be a natural break there. Acts 9:23 begins by saying, "And after that many days were fulfilled," which seems to be saying there was a long period of time between his conversion visit to Damascus (Acts 9:3, 10-22) and the ministry which he launched after his Arabian seclusion. He launched the ministry in the most natural place, Damascus, among the believers whom he knew (Acts 9:23).
4. His second ministry in Damascus after returning from Arabia (Acts 9:23-25).
5. His first trip to Jerusalem for fifteen days to see Peter (Gal.1:18-19; Acts 9:23-30). The apostles in Acts 9:27 would be Peter and James, the Lord's brother.
6. His ministry in and around Tarsus which apparently lasted for about eleven years (Gal.1:21-2:1).
7. His call by Barnabas to help him minister in Antioch (Acts 11:25-26).
8. His second trip to Jerusalem to carry relief goods during a famine (Gal.2:1f; Acts 11:30; 12:25). Some say that this return trip to Jerusalem is the trip to the Jerusalem Council described in Acts 15. However, two significant problems exist with this position. First, Paul emphasizes a private interview in Gal.2:2, whereas the Acts account is a public meeting. Second, where does the famine visit fit in? If the account given in the second chapter of Galatians is not the famine visit, then Paul omitted the famine visit altogether from the account in Galatians. This is difficult to explain in light of the fact that Paul goes to extra pains in giving his contacts with the Jerusalem church. In listing his visits, he declares that he speaks the plain truth, **"I lie not" (Gal.1:20).**
9. His call and commissioning as a missionary (Acts 13:2-3).
10. His first great mission to the Gentiles: to Cyprus and Galatia (Acts 13:1-14:28).
11. His return to Antioch after completing his first missionary journey (Acts 14:26-28).
12. His third trip to Jerusalem to defend the gospel of grace before the Jerusalem Council (Acts 15:1-30).
13. His return to Antioch with the message from the Jerusalem Council (Acts 15:30-35).
14. His second great mission to the Gentiles: to Europe (Acts 15:36-18:22).
15. His return to Antioch after completing his second missionary journey (Acts 18:22).
16. His third great mission to the Gentiles: Asia Minor and Europe (Acts 18:23-21:16).
17. His fourth and final trip to Jerusalem when he was arrested (Acts 21:17-26:32).
18. His journey to Rome as a prisoner (Acts 27:1-28:15).
19. His ministry in Rome while a prisoner (Acts 28:16-31).

GALATIANS 1:17-24

QUESTIONS:
1. What lessons can you learn from the time-table of Paul's ministry?
2. What should be our order of priority in serving God?
3. In looking at Paul's life, what special points are challenging to your faith? Why?

1. FIRST, HE WENT TO ARABIA: HE GOT ALONE WITH GOD (v.17).

Paul had just been converted, and his conversion was a most dramatic experience (cp. Acts 9:1f). Paul's former life had taken two terrible turns.

1. Paul had been very self-righteous. He had been steeped in religion and its traditions, form, and ritual. He had felt that he was acceptable to God because he was religious and did as much good as he could. He felt that his own goodness and religion made him righteous before God. He failed to see the absolute perfection and love of God and the absolute imperfection and unlovableness of man. He was utterly deceived about the true nature of man and God, of unrighteousness and righteousness, of sin and forgiveness, of life and death.

2. Paul had become so self-deceived that he had launched a campaign of hatred and murder against the followers of Christ. He had used everything at his disposal to stamp out the name of Christ from the face of the earth.

The point is that Paul was saved from a terrible life of sin and shame, a life steeped in as much sin and shame as a man could be. He was self-righteous and arrogant, full of bitterness, hatred, and murder; and he went about misusing his position and power just like a tyrant—to the point of imprisoning and murdering those who differed with him.

When Paul was converted, he had a dire need to be alone with God. He did not need the counsel and help of men; he needed the presence and help of God and His Spirit. He already knew the Scriptures. He had studied them at the feet of the greatest religious teachers of his day, but he had not known God nor Christ, not in a personal way. Paul had no knowledge of God, not a personal knowledge. What he had known about God had been twisted and corrupted, misapplied and misused. He desperately needed...

- time to learn how to live with Christ day by day, drawing confidence and strength from Him.
- time to learn the real meaning of the Scriptures: how they applied to Christ.
- time to accurately handle the Word of Truth (the Scriptures).
- time to learn how to fellowship with Christ in daily worship (devotions, quiet times).
- time to learn how to walk in the presence and communion and fellowship of Christ all day.
- time to learn the commandments and will of Christ.
- time to think through how to go about making Christ known to a world in dire need and steeped in sin and darkness.

How much time did Paul need? Apparently, he spent about three years in Arabia. Imagine spending three years seeking the Lord and learning how to live and serve Him!

APPLICATION:

What a lesson for all believers, ministers and laymen alike! What power would be in our lives and ministries if we sought to know Christ as Paul did!

> **"Wait on the LORD: be of good courage, and he shall strengthen thine heart: wait, I say, on the LORD" (Ps.27:14).**
>
> **"But they that wait upon the LORD shall renew their strength; they shall mount up with wings as eagles; they shall run, and not be weary; and they shall walk, and not faint" (Is.40:31).**

GALATIANS 1:17-24

"Study to show thyself approved unto God, a workman that needeth not to be ashamed, rightly dividing the word of truth" (2 Tim.2:15).

ILLUSTRATION:

It is during some of the loneliest times of our lives that we find ourselves with God. This seems to be a paradox, but it is true. For when we are truly alone, we can clearly listen to Him. And as Brother Lawrence, a humble Frenchman of the 17th century, stated so well, we can "practice the presence of God." How is that done in a practical sense?

"Jeremiah Denton was a prisoner of war in North Vietnam for seven horrendous years. As one of the highest ranking American captives, he was subjected to particularly grueling torture, spending almost his entire incarceration in solitary confinement. In such a barren, brutal situation, it would be hard not to focus on the pain and [monotony]. Yet, Denton not only survived but also came back and was elected a United States senator from Alabama.

"How did he survive? He stated on many occasions that an essential survival skill was quoting passages from the Bible. Internalized Scripture became the unseen sword that enabled him to fend off the cruelest weapons of the enemy. By inwardly focusing on the power of God to sustain and strengthen him, he was able to rise above the squalor of his lonely existence."[1]

QUESTIONS:

1. When you feel alone, does God seem to be more accessible to you? Why or why not?
2. What barriers stand in the way of your spending quality time alone with God? Which one can you work on now?
3. What tragedy would it take to get you to totally depend upon God?

2. SECOND, HE RETURNED TO DAMASCUS: HE CORRECTED THE WRONG HE HAD PREVIOUSLY DONE (v.17).

When Paul was converted, he was on his way to Damascus to arrest and stamp out the followers of Christ. It was his intent and purpose to literally cleanse Damascus of all Christians. The bitter persecution had, of course, greatly disrupted the lives of believers. It had forced many to flee for their lives, leaving their families, homes, jobs, and all means of livelihood.

The point is this: Paul had returned to Damascus to do what he could to right the terrible wrong he had done to the believers of Damascus. He wanted to ask their forgiveness and assure them that he had been saved; and, no doubt, he wanted to share Christ among the very people he had been so bent on destroying.

"Therefore if thou bring thy gift to the altar, and there rememberest that thy brother hath ought against thee; leave there thy gift before the altar, and go thy way; first be reconciled to thy brother, and then come and offer thy gift" (Mt.5:23-24).

ILLUSTRATION:

Paul did one of the hardest things for a person to do: he went back and made things right with those he had hurt. He wanted a fresh start. Do you? In the book Is it Real When it Doesn't Work?, Doug Murren and Barb Shurin recount:

"Toward the end of the nineteenth century, Swedish chemist Alfred Nobel awoke one morning to read his own obituary in the local newspaper: 'Alfred No-

bel, the inventor of dynamite, who died yesterday, devised a way for more people to be killed in a war than ever before, and he died a very rich man.'

"Actually, it was Alfred's older brother who had died; a newspaper reporter had bungled the epitaph.

"But the account had a profound effect on Nobel. He decided he wanted to be known for something other than developing the means to kill people efficiently and for amassing a fortune in the process. So he initiated the Nobel Prize, the award for scientists and writers who foster peace.

"Nobel said, 'Every man ought to have the chance to correct his epitaph in midstream and write a new one.'

"Few things will change us as much as looking at our life as though it is finished"[2]

Nobel was fortunate--he had a warning that jolted him out of his 'comfort zone.' If you are reading this or listening to this, it is not too late for you to go back and make things right with someone you have hurt--or even to seek peace with someone who has hurt you!

QUESTIONS:

1. What things do you need to make right with others?
2. Has another person done something to hurt you? If he came to you seeking your forgiveness, what would be your reaction?
   ____Total, unconditional forgiveness?
   ____Great caution, watching your back for a knife?
   ____Very sceptical, questioning his true motive?
   ____Unforgiving, the pain is too deep?

3. THIRD, HE WENT TO JERUSALEM: HE FACED HIS PAST (v.18-20).

Before his conversion, Paul had lived in Jerusalem and had been one of the officials of the ruling body (the Sanhedrin) or else had been close to the leaders of the Sanhedrin. We know this because the Sanhedrin had been the official body which stood behind Paul's attack against the Christians. Whatever the case, Paul was well known in Jerusalem, and he knew that some of his former friends would consider him a betrayer to their religion and cause. Nevertheless, Paul wanted to share his testimony with as many of them as could be trusted.

However, Paul's primary reason for going to Jerusalem was to see Peter, the leader of the early Christians. By sharing with Peter, Paul felt that many of the believers would know that he had been truly converted. They would thereby be more ready to accept him and his ministry.

But note: the other apostles were apparently away on evangelistic and mission tours. Paul saw no other Christian leader except James, the Lord's brother, who was pastor of the great Jerusalem church. Imagine the sharing that must have taken place between Paul and Peter...

- as Paul shared his past, his conversion, and his experiences with the Lord in Arabia.
- as Peter shared the life of Christ while on earth.

Remember that Paul was relating his journeys to the Galatians for a very specific purpose: to show that he had not learned the gospel from men; he had received it from the Lord Himself. He was a true apostle and minister of the Lord, and his gospel was the true gospel, the gospel revealed to him by Christ Himself. Paul asserted the truth of his claim with the solemn declaration:

> **"Now the things which I write unto you, behold, before God, I lie not" (v.20).**

APPLICATION:
As much as possible...

- believers should seek to share Christ with former friends and associates. Unbelievers need to see the change Christ can make in lives.
- believers should seek counsel and help as they launch their ministries, in particular the counsel and help of leaders.

"But sanctify the Lord God in your hearts: and be ready always to give an answer to every man that asketh you a reason of the hope that is in you with meekness and fear" (1 Pt.3:15).

QUESTIONS:
1. Have you ever shared Christ with fellow workers? If so, what were their responses? Do they usually see the love of Christ in your life?
2. What was the purpose for Paul's facing his past? What areas of your past do you need to face?
3. Are you comfortable visiting people who knew you before you made a commitment to Christ? Do they see a difference in you now? Do you tell them about what changed your life?

4. FOURTH, HE WENT TO SYRIA AND CILICIA, THAT IS, TARSUS: HE FACED HIS HOMETOWN (v.21).

Tarsus was where Paul's family lived and where his childhood friends were, the place where he had gone to school and played as a child. It was, of course, Paul's desire to share Christ with as many of his family and friends as he could.

"Let your light so shine before men, that they may see your good works, and glorify your Father which is in heaven" (Mt.5:16).

QUESTIONS:
1. Sometimes, one of the hardest mission fields is at home. What difficulties do you face in sharing Christ with unsaved loved ones?
2. What would it take for every member of your family to make a commitment to Christ? What can you do to lead your family to make that commitment?

5. FIFTH, THE RESULTS OF A GOD-CENTERED LIFE WERE POWERFUL (v.22-24).

The results of a God-centered life are twofold, and they are powerful results.

1. The testimony of a God-centered life was spread throughout the whole area. Paul had not yet visited the churches in Judaea, that is, the area surrounding Jerusalem. Nevertheless, the believers of the area had heard about Paul's conversion, that he who had formerly persecuted the church was now preaching Christ.
2. The testimony of a God-centered life stirred believers to honor God. The churches of Judaea had never seen Paul, but they glorified God because of his strong testimony about which they had heard.

"Come and hear, all ye that fear God, and I will declare what He hath done for my soul" (Ps.66:16).

GALATIANS 1:17-24

ILLUSTRATION:

There is a bottom-line when a Christian believer has placed God in the center of his life. Word does get out when God blesses and people want to see living examples of faith. In the book, Everyday Discipleship for Ordinary People, Stuart Briscoe wrote:

> *"One of my young colleagues was officiating at the funeral of a war veteran. The dead man's military friends wished to have a part in the service at the funeral home, so they requested the pastor to lead them down to the casket, stand with them for a solemn moment of remembrance, and then lead them out through the side door.*
>
> *"This he proceeded to do, but unfortunately the effect was somewhat marred when he picked the wrong door. The result was that they marched with military precision into a broom closet, in full view of the mourners, and had to beat a hasty retreat covered with confusion.*
>
> *"This true story illustrates a cardinal rule or two. First, if you're going to lead, make sure you know where you are going. Second, if you're going to follow, make sure that you are following someone who knows what he is doing!"*[3]

Your testimony is either for God or against God. Will your testimony lead others to Christ and stir believers to honor Christ? Or will it lead some innocent souls down the wrong path of life and doom them for eternity?

QUESTIONS:

1. How well is your testimony known? Has your life and testimony been Christ-centered? Has it reached beyond yourself?
2. What difference have you made for the cause of Christ in your family, your church, your community?
3. If you could change one thing about your testimony, what would it be? Why?

SUMMARY:

If you really desire a life that bears a strong testimony, then Paul's life is a great reminder of what it takes...

1. First, he went to Arabia: he got alone with God.
2. Second, he returned to Damascus: he corrected the wrong he had previously done.
3. Third, he went to Jerusalem: he faced his past
4. Fourth, he went to Syria and Cilicia, that is, Tarsus: he faced his hometown.
5. Fifth, the results of a God-centered life were powerful.

PERSONAL JOURNAL NOTES
(Reflection & Response)

1. The most important thing that I learned from this lesson was:

2. The area that I need to work on the most is:

3. I can apply this lesson to my life by:

4. Closing Statement of Commitment:

[1] Charles Stanley. *How To Listen to God*. (Nashville, TN: Oliver-Nelson Books, 1985), p.97.
[2] Craig B. Larson, Editor. *Illustrations for Preaching & Teaching*. (Grand Rapids, MI: Baker Books, 1993), p.123.
[3] Stuart Briscoe. *Everyday Discipleship for Ordinary People*. (Wheaton, IL: Harold Shaw Publishers, 1988, p.25).

1. He defended the work of the gospel
  a. The fact: He made a second Jerusalem trip--14 years later
  b. The reason: God had led him
  c. The purpose for his defense: To protect the work of the true gospel

2. He defended the gospel before false believers
  a. Titus was made a test-case
  b. The false believers
    1) A hypocritical entrance into the church
    2) A false message of bondage
  c. The purpose for his defense: To preserve the pure gospel

CHAPTER 2

C. The Minister Defended the Gospel, 2:1-10

Then fourteen years after I went up again to Jerusalem with Barnabas, and took Titus with me also.
2 And I went up by revelation, and communicated unto them that gospel which I preach among the Gentiles, but privately to them which were of reputation, lest by any means I should run, or had run, in vain.
3 But neither Titus, who was with me, being a Greek, was compelled to be circumcised:
4 And that because of false brethren unawares brought in, who came in privily to spy out our liberty which we have in Christ Jesus, that they might bring us into bondage:
5 To whom we gave place by subjection, no, not for an hour; that the truth of the gospel might continue with you.
6 But of these who seemed to be somewhat, (whatsoever they were, it maketh no matter to me: God accepteth no man's person:) for they who seemed to be somewhat in conference added nothing to me:
7 But contrariwise when they saw that the gospel of the uncircumcision was committed unto me, as the gospel of the circumcision was unto Peter;
8 (For he that wrought effectually in Peter to the apostleship of the circumcision, the same was mighty in me toward the Gentiles:)
9 And when James, Cephas, and John, who seemed to be pillars, perceived the grace that was given unto me, they gave to me and Barnabas the right hands of fellowship; that we should go unto the heathen, and they unto the circumcision.
10 Only they would that we should remember the poor; the same which I also was forward to do.

3. He defended the gospel before any & all persons
  a. Because God shows no partiality
  b. The purpose for his defense: To keep the real gospel from being added to

4. He defended the special call given to each man to proclaim the gospel
  a. A special task is given to each
  b. The purpose for his defense
    1) To assure that each person's task is recognized
    2) To assure that each person has the right to carry out his task: To minister

Section II
THE PROOF OF GOD'S MESSENGER AND MESSAGE
Galatians 1:10-2:21

Study 3: **THE MINISTER DEFENDED THE GOSPEL**

Text: **Galatians 2:1-10**

Aim: To vigorously defend the gospel of Jesus Christ.

Memory Verse:
"Hold fast the form of sound words, which thou hast heard of me, in faith and love which is in Christ Jesus" (2 Tim.1:13).

GALATIANS 2:1-10

INTRODUCTION:

Perry Mason, a fictional but masterful television lawyer, set the standard for every successful trial attorney. In the world of television entertainment, Perry Mason was employed to defend those who had been falsely accused.

In the course of each trial, he would carefully investigate each fiber of evidence. His search for clues enhanced his client's defense. No evidence was overlooked. When the case came to trial, Mason had to present the evidence and defend his client before a prosecutor, jury, and judge. And in the end, after the truth became known, his client would be set free.

The apostle Paul found himself in the postition of being put on trial, of having to defend both himself and the gospel. In the context of the trial, he presented every shred of evidence in defending the gospel and his part in it. In his closing arguments, he challenged each man to proclaim the gospel to men who are guilty of sin.

As you recall, Paul was under attack by some false teachers and critics in the Galatian churches. They were charging him with being a self-proclaimed minister and with preaching a false gospel. He was forced to defend himself and the gospel which he preached. In the present passage, he defended the gospel which he preached in no uncertain terms; and he showed how he defended it before the recognized leaders of the church, the apostles themselves.

OUTLINE:

1. He defended the work of the gospel (v.1-2).
2. He defended the gospel before false believers (v.3-5).
3. He defended the gospel before any and all persons (v.6).
4. He defended the special call given to each man to proclaim the gospel (v.7-10).

1. HE DEFENDED THE WORK OF THE GOSPEL (v.1-2).

It must be remembered that Paul was being very careful and going to extra pains to list his contacts with the Jerusalem church (v.1). He had to show that his call and gospel had come from Christ and not from men, not even from the leaders in Jerusalem. This was absolutely necessary, for the basic qualification for being an apostle was having been called by Christ Himself. Christ had appeared to him on the Damascus road; Christ had saved and called Paul to preach the gospel. Therefore, Paul met the basic qualification of being an apostle: he had seen the Lord Jesus face to face. Christ had confronted him and personally called him to be an apostle.

What Paul was doing in this particular verse was answering his critics: he did not visit Jerusalem to discuss his call and gospel until fourteen years after his first trip to see Peter, whom he had visited for fifteen days (cp. Gal.1:18-20). He had been serving the Lord Jesus as a minister and preaching the gospel for years before he visited the church leaders at Jerusalem. His call and message had been proven by years of service. His ministry for Christ was set; it could not legitimately be questioned and denied--not by an honest person. The critics were terribly wrong to be questioning his call and message.

QUESTIONS:

1. What kinds of things did Paul do to stifle criticisim of his ministry?
2. What can you do to prepare to defend yourself from those who are critical of you, your faith, your beliefs?

Note that God led Paul to go to Jerusalem (v.2). The trip was not a man-planned journey; it was a God-called journey. God wanted Paul to go to Jerusalem to protect the world-wide mission work of the gospel. There were those in the church who were pressing the necessity of ritual and rules for salvation, in particular the necessity of being circumcised and of subjecting oneself to keep the law of Moses.

Paul knew something: if men were allowed to add ritual and rules to the gospel, he and his ministry would have been in vain (fruitless). Every person who had trusted in Jesus Christ and every person who would trust in Jesus Christ for salvation would have to undergo the ritual of circumcision. They would have to focus their lives upon the law instead of upon Jesus Christ.

This was the reason God led Paul to Jerusalem: to save the message and work of the *true gospel.*

⇒ Just imagine the thousands of Gentile believers who had been led to the Lord, and all the churches that had already been established by Paul and others throughout the world.

⇒ Just imagine the catastrophic devastation upon the believers and the churches if they had to return to their conversion experience and add a ritual and other rules to their lives.

Note the method used by Paul to defend his case: private discussions with the leaders, in particular with the apostles.

APPLICATION:

The minister must not run in vain. He must preach only the gospel, and he must build his ministry upon only the gospel. He must not allow ritual or rule, ceremony or law *to be added* to the gospel. People are saved and people grow only by the gospel, only by the good news of God's love for the world--a love that was demonstrated in the supreme gift of His Son to die *for us.*

> **"For God so loved the world, that he gave his only begotten Son, that whosoever believeth in him should not perish, but have everlasting life. For God sent not his Son into the world to condemn the world; but that the world through him might be saved" (Jn.3:16-17).**

ILLUSTRATION:

Does the gospel make a difference? To put it simply, the "proof is in the pudding."

> *"A well-known preacher of the United States was asked to say a few words to a gathering in an open air meeting. At the close of his address an atheist stepped up to him and challenged him to a debate, assuring him that he would bear all the expense of renting the hall and advertising.*
>
> *" 'I accept on one condition: When you bring with you fifty people who have been helped by your philosophy, I am ready. I will bring you hundreds who will testify to the transformation this Gospel has wrought in their lives.'*
>
> *"Needless to say the challenger departed somewhat chagrined"*[1]

Only the true gospel can produce the 'fruit' of changed lives. No false religion or false god can bring about the love, peace, security, and salvation that the gospel can and does produce.

QUESTIONS:

1. What things do some Christians add to the gospel?
2. When there are doctrinal disagreements in a body of believers, what can be learned from Paul's example?
3. If you were asked to defend the gospel, what would you say? Do you feel confident in your answer? What can you do to get a better grasp of the gospel?

2. HE DEFENDED THE GOSPEL BEFORE FALSE BELIEVERS (v.3-5).

A brief look at what lies behind these verses will greatly help the reader. Paul was preaching the gospel of grace alone and this aroused some of the Jewish believers. Remember that most of the believers at Jerusalem were Jews. They had been circumcised when they were eight days old and had been steeped in the law of Moses since childhood. When they accepted Christ, some just refused to forsake their Judaistic religion. They saw Christianity only as an extension of Judaism. In their minds Christ had *only added* new teachings to their existing law and religion. Therefore, if a person wished to accept Christ, he had to become a Jew first...

- to undergo the ritual of circumcision.
- to commit himself to the law of Moses.
- to observe all the ceremonies and rituals of Jewish religion.

Once a person had done these things, that is, become a Jew, then and only then could he receive Christ and be baptized. Only then could he be accepted into the church.

Paul, of course, had gone against these beliefs and practices. He had...

- allowed people to receive Christ by grace through faith alone without undergoing the ritual of circumcision.
- allowed people to follow and focus upon Christ instead of upon the law of Moses.

This shocked those who were still loyal to their Judaistic religion, and they began to form an alliance and oppose Paul vehemently. They felt he was out to destroy their religion and its form and rituals. Therefore, they set out to discredit and destroy him...

- by questioning his salvation and call.
- by denying that his apostleship and ministry were of God.
- by planting their own teachers in the churches where Paul had ministered and by indoctrinating the churches with their own false teaching.
- by sending their own emissaries to follow and hound Paul by stirring up the people against him--stirring them to question his message and call.

These men were called Judaizers, men who mixed ritual and law with the gospel of Christ. Paul's argument was that this teaching was the very opposite of the true gospel. A man is not saved by fleshly signs, by ritual, nor by his own ability to keep the laws, regulations, and rules. A man just cannot earn, win, or do anything to save himself. Salvation is by faith in Jesus Christ alone (Gal.2:16). A man can only accept salvation, and then in thankfulness for God's gift, he must depend upon the power of the Holy Spirit to live for God.

Now to the point of the present verses. When Paul went to Jerusalem, he took Barnabas and Titus, two co-workers, with him. Barnabas was a Jew who had been converted in Jerusalem. He was well known by most believers, for he was one of the very first missionaries, and he had experienced great movements of God wherever he had carried the gospel.

Titus, however, was a different matter. He was a heathen (Gentile) convert. He was not a Jew, which meant he had never undergone the ritual of circumcision, nor had he committed himself to keep the law of Moses and the rituals of religion. Titus was a perfect example of salvation by grace alone, for he had been saved and called by Christ to preach without ever having been circumcised and without submitting to the law of Moses. Apparently, it was Paul's intention to present him as a prime example of God's saving people by grace through faith alone--without any religion, ritual, or rule whatsoever.

However, when the Judaizers heard about Titus, they planted several of their followers in the church who reacted and demanded that Titus undergo the ritual of circumcision and make the law of Moses the focus of his life. Note that they entered the church hypocritically; they were not true believers. Paul calls them *brothers*, but *false brothers*.

Note that Paul refused to be subject to the false teachers. He would not tell Titus he had to undergo a ritual and focus upon the law in order to be saved. Paul fought to preserve the pure gospel in all its truth.

> **"This only would I learn of you, Received ye the Spirit by the works of the law, or by the hearing of faith? Are ye so foolish? having begun in the Spirit, are ye now made perfect by the flesh?" (Gal.3:2-3).**

ILLUSTRATION:

Throughout the ages, men have attempted to *improve* the gospel. Some call it old-fashioned. Others want to repackage it in order to make it *more relevant for today*. And there are some who want to change it by replacing it with something else all-together.

In composing a "new gospel," these people convince themselves that they are right on key. But to a trained ear, the obvious is apparent: this vain rendition is as flat as a pancake!

GALATIANS 2:1-10

"When Lloyd C. Douglas, author of The Robe and other novels, was a university student, he lived in a boarding house, says Maxie Dunnam in Jesus' Claims--Our Promises. Downstairs on the first floor was an elderly, retired music teacher, now infirm and unable to leave the apartment.

"Douglas said that every morning they had a ritual they would go through together. He would come down the steps, open the old man's door, and ask, 'Well, what's the good news?'

"The old man would pick up his tuning fork, tap it on the side of his wheelchair, and say, "That's Middle C! It was middle C yesterday; it will be middle C tomorrow; it will be middle C a thousand years from now. The tenor upstairs sings flat, the piano across the hall is out of tune, but my friend, that is middle C!

"The old man had discovered one thing upon which he could depend, one constant reality in his life, one 'still point in a turning world'"[2]

We live in a world filled with a variety of noises. But, there is still only one 'middle C,' only one gospel of Jesus Christ. Make certain that your song is in tune with Him!

QUESTIONS:

1. What kind of "baggage" (old habits, customs, traditions, etc) do new believers bring into their new lives with Christ?.
2. As you examine your life, do you need to check any of the above baggage at the door? If so, what things have you added to the gospel?
3. What is the end result of a gospel that is not founded upon grace and faith?

A CLOSER LOOK

Judaizers--Legalists: these were Jews who professed Christ but still hung on to their Judaistic religion, in particular to the rite of circumcision and to the law of Moses (cp. Acts 5:1-35, esp. 1, 24-29). They believed a man became a Christian…

- by first becoming a Jew. The man was to embrace Judaism with all its rituals and ceremonies, be circumcised, begin to obey the laws of Moses, and…
- then the man could accept Christ as his Savior.

In the mind of the circumcised, Christianity was a mixture of Judaism and the teachings of Christ. The law was just as important as Christ and Christ was no more important than the law. They failed to grasp…

- that Christ was the fulfillment of the law.
- that Christ had kept the law perfectly, thereby becoming the Ideal Man, the Perfect Pattern of what every man should be.
- that Christ was not only the embodiment of the law, but so much more--the very embodiment of God Himself, the Ideal Man, the Perfect Pattern to whom *all men* were to look for their salvation and standard.
- that Christ, as the Son of God and as the Ideal Man and the Perfect Pattern, was the One to whom *all men* were now to look and obey.

Some Jews were impressed with Christ and professed Him, but they were never able to understand or else were unwilling to accept Christ as the fulfillment of the law and as the Savior of all men. Therefore, they never turned to Christ alone, never broke away from…

- their legalistic religion.
- requiring men (Gentiles) to become Jews before they could become Christians.

This was the great battle the church had to fight in its beginning. It was the great problem that faced God: how to break the church away from its Judaistic roots and away from excluding and shutting out the other people of the world (Gentiles). This had always been the problem of the Jews--the problem of keeping the Gentiles away from God and the glorious salvation He had planned for all men. Now, since Christ had come, God had to lead the early church away from the Judaistic approach, away from making a man become a Jew before he could accept Christ. This just was not the will of God, for God had sent Christ into the world to save all men, not just the Jews. The message had to be carried to all. He had to break the early Jewish believers away from their legalism, away from their...

- making distinctions between themselves and others.
- making others become religionists before accepting Christ.
- discriminating against others.
- building barriers and walls for others to cross (legalistic rules).
- being separatists and being divisive.
- being a people of prejudice and bigotry.

However, note this: all through the history of the church, extending from the early church up to the present time, there have been some who have refused to follow Christ *alone*. They have laid the burden of the law and ritual and ceremony (legalism, becoming a religionist, a Jew) upon people. In the past such people were known as *the circumcision* or the Judaizers; in modern times they are known as religionists or legalists

> **"And certain men which came down from Judaea taught the brethren, and said, Except ye be circumcised [undergo a ritual] after the manner of Moses, ye cannot be saved" (Acts 15:1).**

QUESTIONS:

1. If you saw a modern Judaizer walking down the road, what would he or she look like?
2. What would have happened to the church if the doctrines of the Judaizers had been adopted by Paul?
3. What would happen to your church if the doctrines of the Judaizers were adopted?

3. HE DEFENDED THE GOSPEL BEFORE ANY AND ALL PERSONS (v.6).

The false brothers were saying that Paul should not be followed, for he was not a true minister. His call was not equal to the apostles of Christ: he had never been an associate of Jesus Christ nor of the other leaders of the church. How then could he be a true minister of God? He did not have the right credentials or education, and he was not an associate of the right leaders.

Bluntly, Paul declared the piercing truth:

⇒ God accepts no man's person; God shows no partiality.

⇒ No man, not even a man of reputation, can add anything to another man's call or to the gospel. God is the creator of the gospel and the One who calls men to the ministry. Men have not developed the gospel, not the real gospel, and men do not call other men to the ministry, not to the real ministry.

APPLICATION 1:

All believers, especially ministers, need to search their hearts with such questions as:

⇒ How many of us seek the approval of leaders over the approval of God?

⇒ How many of us seek the call of churches or leaders over the call of God?

⇒ How many of us seek the favor and help of men over the favor and help of God?

⇒ How many of us seek to add to our reputation by associating with leaders instead of seeking God and His place of service?

⇒ And, of extreme danger, how many of us add and teach our own ideas, rituals, and rules instead of the pure gospel?

"Ye have not chosen me, but I have chosen you, and ordained you, that ye should go and bring forth fruit, and that your fruit should remain; that whatsoever ye shall ask of the Father in my name, he may give it you" (Jn.15:16).

APPLICATION 2:

God treats all men alike. He has no favorites and shows no partiality. Every person is saved by the same gospel, and every true minister is called by the same Lord.

"Then Peter opened his mouth, and said, Of a truth I perceive that God is no respecter of persons: but in every nation he that feareth him, and worketh righteousness, is accepted with him" (Acts 10:34-35).

QUESTIONS:

1. Unfortunately, politics creeps into the local church. In a subtle shift, we begin to seek to please men instead of pleasing God. What kinds of things can be done to correct this problem?
2. Why is partiality considered wrong?
3. What dangers result from a man-made gospel?

4. HE DEFENDED THE SPECIAL CALL GIVEN EACH MAN TO PROCLAIM THE GOSPEL (v.7-10).

Note the word "contrariwise" or "to the contrary": the leaders of the church did not agree with the Judaizers as the Judaizers had hoped; on the contrary they stood with and championed the call and gospel of Christ. They saw that God had called Paul to preach to the Gentiles (the uncircumcision) just as he had called Peter to preach to the Jews (the circumcision). They championed the truth that God gives to every man a particular task.

Note who the leaders were in Jerusalem: James, the Lord's brother, who was pastor of the great Jerusalem church, and Peter and John. The point to note is that the great pillars of the church were *now standing together* proclaiming...

- that salvation by grace through faith alone was the true gospel.
- that God was the Person who called Paul and all other ministers to preach the gospel.
- that Paul and all other ministers should remember to minister to the poor, not just to the middle classes and wealthy.

"For though I preach the gospel, I have nothing to glory of: for necessity is laid upon me; yea, woe is unto me, if I preach not the gospel! For if I do this thing willingly, I have a reward: but if against my will, a dispensation [trust, trusteeship, commitment] of the gospel is committed unto me" (1 Cor.9:16-17).

ILLUSTRATION:

As we share the gospel, we need to make sure that every aspect of our community is exposed to the love of God. No one should be left out.

There are many "hidden people" throughout the world--and some even close to home.

"A great life insurance company in New York invited all its agents throughout the country to a conference in New York, and while in attendance one of the agents from the West insured the barber, the elevator man, and a waiter in the restaurant, all of whom had been employed for years by the insurance company in its great building. No one had thought to offer policies to these men in the home office building!

"Exactly so. That is the reason the professional evangelist sweeps in so many; he simply improves the chance that has been there all the time. But why must we wait for him?"[3]

Closer to home, who needs to hear the gospel from you <u>today?</u>

GALATIANS 2:1-10

QUESTIONS:

1. Why are some people in the world overlooked by the witness of the church? What kind of role can you play as a solution?
2. Do you have a burden for the lost? What can you do in order to cultivate this in your life?
3. Who are some of the hidden people--overlooked people--in the world? In what ways does your church reach out to them? What can you do to help your church reach out to them ?

SUMMARY:

God has placed you in the courtroom of the world where your task is to defend the gospel as well as your role in proclaiming the good news. As you face your prosecutors and juries, will you win your case? You will if you faithfully apply these major points to your life as Paul did:

1. Paul defended the work of the gospel.
2. Paul defended the gospel before false believers.
3. Paul defended the gospel before any and all persons.
4. Paul defended the special call given each man to proclaim the gospel.

PERSONAL JOURNAL NOTES
(Reflection & Response)

1. The most important thing that I learned from this lesson was:

2. The area that I need to work on the most is:

3. I can apply this lesson to my life by:

4. Closing Statement of Commitment:

---

[1] *Gospel Herald.* Walter B. Knight. *3,000 Illustrations for Christian Service.* (Grand Rapids, MI: Eerdman's Publishing Company, 1971), p.317.

[2] Craig B. Larson, editor. *Illustrations for Preaching & Teaching*, p.27.

[3] *Sunday School Time.* Paul Lee Tan. *Encyclopedia of 7,700 Illustrations: Signs of the Times.* (Rockville, MD: Assurance Publishers, 1985), p.1327.

GALATIANS 2:11-21

1. A believer who backslides must be confronted
   a. Paul confronted Peter
   b. Peter's failure
      1) A follower of men, of the crowd
      2) A man of prejudice & legalism
   c. The result of Peter's failure: Others were led away—even a leader, Barnabas

2. A believer cannot have double standards
   a. An unrighteous walk: Not true to the gospel
   b. A hypocritical walk: Living one way while telling others to live another way

3. A believer is justified by faith alone
   a. Not by works
   b. By the faith of Christ alone
   c. No one is ever justified by the works of the law

4. A man is not misled by Christ
   a. God forbid such a thought
   b. A man makes himself a sinner

5. A man is justified by living for God
   a. By dying to the law
   b. By being crucified with Christ
   c. By allowing Christ to live His life through his body
   d. By trusting the grace of God: Jesus Christ, who is God's righteousness

D. The Minister Proclaimed the Gospel to Those Who Had Drifted Away, 2:11-21

11 But when Peter was come to Antioch, I withstood him to the face, because he was to be blamed.

12 For before that certain came from James, he did eat with the Gentiles: but when they were come, he withdrew and separated himself, fearing them which were of the circumcision.

13 And the other Jews dissembled likewise with him; insomuch that Barnabas also was carried away with their dissimulation.

14 But when I saw that they walked not uprightly according to the truth of the gospel, I said unto Peter before them all, If thou, being a Jew, livest after the manner of Gentiles, and not as do the Jews, why compellest thou the Gentiles to live as do the Jews?

15 We who are Jews by nature, and not sinners of the Gentiles,

16 Knowing that a man is not justified by the works of the law, but by the faith of Jesus Christ, even we have believed in Jesus Christ, that we might be justified by the faith of Christ, and not by the works of the law: for by the works of the law shall no flesh be justified.

17 But if, while we seek to be justified by Christ, we ourselves also are found sinners, is therefore Christ the minister of sin? God forbid.

18 For if I build again the things which I destroyed, I make myself a transgressor.

19 For I through the law am dead to the law, that I might live unto God.

20 I am crucified with Christ: nevertheless I live; yet not I, but Christ liveth in me: and the life which I now live in the flesh I live by the faith of the Son of God, who loved me, and gave himself for me.

21 I do not frustrate the grace of God: for if righteousness come by the law, then Christ is dead in vain.

Section II
THE PROOF OF GOD'S MESSENGER AND MESSAGE
Galatians 1:10-2:21

(Note: Because of the length of this outline and commentary, you may wish to split this passage into two or three studies.)

Study 4: THE MINISTER PROCLAIMED THE GOSPEL TO THOSE WHO HAD DRIFTED AWAY

Text: Galatians 2:11-21

GALATIANS 2:11-21

Aim: To build strong barriers in order to prevent backsliding.

Memory Verse:

"I am crucified with Christ: nevertheless I live; yet not I, but Christ liveth in me: and the life which I now live in the flesh I live by the faith of the Son of God, who loved me, and gave Himself for me" (Galatians 2:20).

INTRODUCTION:

There is a little bit of the "Prodigal Son" in all of us. Unless we are firmly grasping our Father's hand, we are prone to drift away. Like everyone else, we as believers can become mesmerized by the lures of the world that beckon us. And the longer we listen to the pleas, attractive and appealing as they sound, the less we desire to remain in a place that is safe.

This is a passage packed full of truth and meaning for all men, but especially for the believer. It is a passage that deals with backsliders, with righteousness and self-righteousness, works and faith, the law and God's grace. It is a passage that needs to be proclaimed to the world. It is the message of the gospel proclaimed to those who drift away.

OUTLINE:

1. A believer who backslides must be confronted (v.11-13).
2. A believer cannot have double standards (v.14).
3. A believer is justified by faith alone (v.15-16).
4. A man is not misled by Christ (v.17-18).
5. A man is justified by living for God (v.19-21).

1. A BELIEVER WHO BACKSLIDES MUST BE CONFRONTED (v.11-13).

What happened is simply explained. Paul and Barnabas were ministers of the Antioch church, and they had apparently invited Peter to visit them, or else Peter had taken it upon himself to conduct some services in Antioch (cp. Acts 11:25-26). Antioch was not only a great church, but it was the first great Gentile church and the very first church to send missionaries forth. It was comprised mainly of Gentile believers (cp. Acts 11:20-21; 13:1-3). When Peter began his ministry in Antioch, he joined right in with the Gentiles, fellowshipping, eating, and sharing with them. However, some Judaizers or religionists came to Antioch and began to visit the church. They were astounded to find Peter fellowshipping and eating so freely with Gentiles, even though they were Christians. Remember: the Judaizers believed in the gospel of Jesus Christ, but they thought it was only an addition to the existing religion (Judaism). They said that if people wished to be saved...

- they had to undergo the ritual of circumcision.
- they had to subject themselves to the law of Moses.
- they had to adopt the ritual and ceremonies of the existing religion.
- they had to practice the rules and regulations of religion, for example, observe strict food laws which prohibited the eating of pork and meat bought in the marketplace.
- they had to separate themselves and have no fellowship with Gentiles who had not been circumcised nor subjected themselves to the law of Moses and the rules and regulations of religion.

When the Judaizers saw Peter, the great Jewish apostle, eating with Gentiles who had not done these things, they apparently jumped all over him. They even used James' name to support their position. Of course, James did not support their position or false teaching (cp. Acts 15:24). However, Peter weakened under their attack and withdrew himself from close fellowship with the Gentiles. When Peter withdrew, the inevitable happened: the church split. The church became tragically divided just as any church does when a leader becomes a man-pleaser and begins to follow critics and cliques.

Note how severe the split was: Peter and the other Jews separated themselves from the Gentiles. And note another fact: their argument was so strong that the senior minister, Barnabas, was even led to join their ranks. Paul stood alone among the leaders to fight for the truth of the gospel.

Another way to look at Peter's failure is to look at the three gross sins he committed. (See Gal.2:14 for discussion.)

QUESTIONS:

1. Does anyone love you enough to confront you if you are going astray? Are you able to receive correction from him?
2. Do you love anyone enough to confront him if he is going astray? Is he able to receive correction from you?
3. Everyone has to face peer pressure. In what areas of your life do you feel the pressure to conform to the world and its pressures? What can be done to avoid giving in to these pressuring situations?
4. How does trusting God allow you to accept others who are different?

2. A BELIEVER CANNOT HAVE DOUBLE STANDARDS (v.14).

In common language, Peter was two-faced; he was a man-pleaser. He ate with the Gentile Christians, but when some Judaizers arrived, he separated himself completely from the Gentiles. He feared what the Judaizers would think. His failure was threefold.

⇒ He was hypocritical. He said one thing (Gal.2:9) but lived something else (Gal.2:11-12).

⇒ He followed the crowd simply because they put pressure upon him—even when he knew better.

⇒ He esteemed some persons better than others (Gal.2:12).

1. Peter was walking an unrighteous path, not living according to the truth of the gospel. The gospel declares that God loves and receives *all men*. But Peter was separating himself from those who *followed Christ differently* than he and the mother church at Jerusalem.

2. Peter was walking a hypocritical path, living one way while telling others to live another way. When the Judaizers were not around to see him, he fellowshipped with the Gentiles; but when the strict religionists arrived, he began to be more strict and follow their strict lifestyle. Note: he even began to compel the Gentiles to undergo the ritual of circumcision and submit to the law of Moses in order to be accepted into the true church of Christ.

APPLICATION:

The fact that Peter could be led astray is a strong warning to every believer.

⇒ We must guard against an unrighteous walk, against not being true to the gospel.

> **"That we henceforth be no more children, tossed to and fro, and carried about with every wind of doctrine, by the sleight of men, and cunning craftiness, whereby they lie in wait to deceive" (Eph.4:14).**

⇒ We must guard against a hypocritical walk, against living one way while telling others to live another way.

"And why beholdest thou the mote that is in thy brother's eye, but considerest not the beam that is in thine own eye?" (Mt.7:3).

"And why call ye me, Lord, Lord, and do not the things which I say?" (Lk.6:46).

ILLUSTRATION:

Are you an honest person? If you were given an "honesty test," would you pass or fail? The Lord gave Peter an honesty test in the area of relationships...and he failed, proving to be hypocritical. The Christian believer is charged to be honest in his relationships with others.

"In Moody Monthly...George Sweeting writes about the desperate need for honesty in our culture. He refers to Dr. Madison Sarratt, who taught mathematics at Vanderbilt University for many years. Before giving a test, the professor would admonish his class something like this:

" 'Today I am giving two examinations, one in trigonometry and the other in honesty. I hope you will pass them both. If you must fail one, fail trigonometry. There are many good people in the world who can't pass trig. But there are no good people in the world who cannot pass the examination of honesty' "[1]

QUESTIONS:

1. You have heard it said, "Don't do as I do; do as I say." What expectations do you place on others that you refuse to apply to your own life?
2. Can you identify any reasons why some believers act differently when they get around other people? Do you act differently? Or is your life consistent no matter who you are around?
3. What are some ways you can keep from being hypocritical?

3. A BELIEVER IS JUSTIFIED BY FAITH ALONE (v.15-16).

Note that Paul now identifies himself with the Jews, for he was a Jew by *nature*, that is, by birth. Note also the reference to the Gentiles as "sinners." The meaning is *rank sinners*. The Jews considered themselves to be religionists and considered the Gentiles to be rank sinners. What Paul was saying is this: *all Jews (religionists) who had believed in Christ* had confessed the very same thing the rank sinners had confessed: a person is justified by faith alone and not by the works of the law.

By coming to Christ, the Jewish religionists were confessing that their religion, ritual, works, and law were not able to save them. They needed something more, much more; therefore, they had turned to Christ. Note three crucial points.

1. *A person is not justified and made acceptable to God by works nor by law*. Why? Because man is short of God's glory; he is imperfect, incomplete, and less than what he should be. Yet everything that lives in God's presence must be perfect and complete, full to the ultimate degree, for God is the very embodiment of perfection, completeness, and fulness. Therefore man, who is imperfect and incomplete, cannot stand or live in God's presence.

However, a question needs to be asked: Is there a work that man can do or a law that he can keep that will make him perfect? God says, "No!" For everything that an imperfect being does is imperfect and incomplete. An imperfect being cannot do anything perfectly good, and certainly not good enough to make him perfect. An imperfect man is short of God's perfection; therefore, no matter what man does, he is short of what he should be. He could always be better and do better.

Hence, man is not saved by works nor by law. If our salvation is dependent upon some works that we can do, then we are hopelessly lost. For what work can we do that will make us a perfect and eternal creature? No man can make us perfect and eternal and cause us to live forever in a perfect and righteous world—and we know it. What can any person do to make his loved one live forever—to be perfected and made eternal? There is no work that we can do or law that we can keep to save ourselves from unrighteousness and death. If we are to be justified before God, accepted as perfect and complete, it will not be by the works of the law.

> **"Now we know that what things soever the law saith, it saith to them who are under the law: that every mouth may be stopped, and all the world may become guilty before God. Therefore by the deeds of the law there shall no flesh be justified in his sight: for by the law is the knowledge of sin" (Ro.3:19-20).**

What then is our hope? How can we become justified, made perfect and complete before God? God says there is only one way. Note the middle of the verse: we must believe "in Jesus Christ, that we might be justified by the faith of Christ" (v.16).

2. *A person is justified by the faith of Christ alone* (see **A CLOSER LOOK**, Justification—discussed later in this study).
3. *No person is ever justified by works nor by law* (see **A CLOSER LOOK**, Faith vs. Works—discussed later in this study).

ILLUSTRATION:

Many a man has tried to make it over to the other side (from earth to heaven) without trusting Christ. Every one of them, without exception, has failed.

The Bible says that we are justified by faith in Christ alone. Remember, justification means that God counts our faith in Christ as righteousness, counts us acceptable to Him.

> *"Years ago a strong wire was stretched across Niagara River, just above the roaring falls. It was announced that a tightrope walker would walk on that suspended wire from the American to the Canadian side. The thrilling moment for the death-defying fete arrived. Great crowds watched with wide-eyed wonderment as the man performed, with calm deliberateness, the awesome stunt. The people cheered wildly!*
>
> *"Then the performer did an even more daring thing. He began to push a wheelbarrow with a grooved wheel across the suspended wire. At the conclusion of this breath-taking performance, thunderous applause went up. The performer observed a boy whose wonderment was clearly discernible on his bright face. Asked the man, 'My boy, do you believe that I could put you in this wheelbarrow and push you over the falls?' 'Oh, yes,' said the boy quickly. 'Then, get in the wheelbarrow,' said the man. Instantly the boy dashed away! In reality he did not believe that the tightrope walker could take him safely across the falls."*[2]

Have you come to the place in your life where you trust Christ enough to get into the wheelbarrow?

QUESTIONS:

1. What justifies you in the sight of God?
2. Is perfection in your own strength possible? Why or why not? What does God expect out of you if you cannot perfect yourself?
3. In what practical ways does God challenge you to trust Him even when you do not know the outcome?
4. Why is it sometimes hard to trust God?

A CLOSER LOOK:

Justification: to count someone righteous. It means to reckon, to credit, to account, to judge, to treat, to look upon as righteous. It does not mean to *make* a man righteous. All Greek verbs which end in "oun" mean not to make someone something, but merely to count, to judge, to treat someone as something.

There are three major points to note about justification.

1. Why justification is necessary.
   a. Justification is necessary because of the sin and alienation of man. Man has rebelled against God and taken his life into his own hands. Man lives as he desires...
      - fulfilling the lust of the eyes and of the flesh.
      - clinging to the pride of life and to the things of the world.

      Man has become sinful and ungodly, an enemy of God, pushing God out of his life and wanting little if anything to do with God. Man has separated and alienated himself from God.
   b. Justification is necessary because of the anger and wrath of God. "God is angry with the wicked every day" (Ps.7:11). Sin has aroused God's anger and wrath. God is angry over man's...
      - rebellion
      - ungodliness
      - sin
      - hostility
      - unrighteousness
      - desertion

      Man has turned his back upon God, pushing God away and having little to do with Him. Man has not made God the center of his life; man has broken his relationship with God (discussed later in this study). Therefore, the greatest need in man's life is to discover the answer to the question: How can the relationship between man and God be restored?

2. Why God justifies a man. God justifies a man because of His Son Jesus Christ. When a man believes in Jesus Christ, God takes that man's faith and counts it as righteousness. The man is not righteous, but God considers and credits the man's faith as righteousness. Why is God willing to do this?
   a. God is willing to justify man because He loves man that much. God loves man so much that He sent His Son into the world to sacrifice Him in order to justify man (Jn.3:16; Ro.5:8).
   b. God is willing to justify man because of what His Son Jesus Christ has done for man.
      ⇒ Jesus Christ came into the world to secure (or to become) the *Ideal* righteousness for man. He came to earth to live a sinless and perfect life. As Man He never broke the law of God; He never went contrary to the will of God, not even once. Therefore, He stood before God and before the world as the Ideal Man, the Perfect Man, the Representative Man, the Perfect Righteousness that could stand for the righteousness of every man.
      ⇒ Jesus Christ came into the world to *die* for man. As the *Ideal Man* He could take all the sins of the world upon Himself and die for every man. His death *could stand* for every man. He exchanged places with man by becoming the sinner (2 Cor.5:19). He bore the wrath of God against sin, bearing the condemnation for every man. Again, He was able to do this because He was the Ideal Man, and as the *Ideal Man* His death could stand for the death of every man.
      ⇒ Jesus Christ came into the world to *arise from the dead* and thereby to conquer death for man. As the *Ideal Man* His resurrection and exaltation into the presence of God *could stand* for every man's desperate need to conquer death and to be acceptable to God. His resurrected life could stand for the resurrected life of the believer.

Now, as stated above, when a man believes in Jesus Christ—really believes—God takes that man's belief and...

- counts it as the righteousness (perfection) of Christ. The man is counted as *righteous in Christ*.
- counts it as the death of Christ. The man is counted as having already *died in Christ*, as having already paid the penalty for sin *in the death of Christ*.
- counts it as the resurrection of Christ. The man is counted as already having been *resurrected in Christ*.

Very simply, God loves His Son Jesus Christ so much that He honors any man who honors His Son by *believing on Him*. He honors the man by taking the man's faith and counting (crediting) it as righteousness and by giving him the glorious privilege of living with Christ forever in the presence of God.

3. How God justifies a man. The word justify is a legal word taken from the courts. It pictures man on trial before God. Man is seen as having committed the most heinous of crimes; he has rebelled against God and broken his relationship with God. How can he restore that relationship? Within human courts if a man is acquitted, he is declared innocent, but this is not true within the Divine Court. When a man appears before God, he is anything but innocent; he is utterly guilty and condemned accordingly.

But when a man sincerely trusts Christ, then God takes that man's faith and counts it as righteousness. By such God counts the man—judges him, treats him—as if he were innocent. The man is not made innocent; he is guilty. He knows it and God knows it, but God treats him as innocent. "God justifies the ungodly"—an incredible mercy, a wondrous grace.

How do we know this? How can we know for sure that God is like this? Because Jesus said so. He said that God loves us. We are sinners, yes; but Christ said that we are very, very dear to God.

"And he [Abraham] believed in the LORD; and he counted it to him for righteousness" (Gen.15:6).

"Therefore being justified by faith, we have peace with God through our Lord Jesus Christ" (Ro.5:1).

QUESTIONS:

1. Why is justification necessary?
2. Why is God so willing to justify you?
3. There are a lot of 'good people' in the world. Is that sufficient reason to be called righteous by God? Why or why not?

A CLOSER LOOK:

Faith vs. Works—Self-Righteousness: Why is it that a man can never be justified nor secure righteousness by works and law? Why is it that a man can never approach God by works and law?

1. There are two ways that a man can try to secure righteousness and approach God.
   a. A man can try to work to secure righteousness; he can do all he can to keep the law of God and to please God. But note: a man can do this...
      - only if he can keep the law perfectly, never breaking it once and never violating it a single time...
      - only if he can make sure that every single thing he ever does or thinks is perfectly good and righteous and pure...
      - only if he can please God in every act, word, and thought, never displeasing God in anything.

Only if a man can do this can he secure righteousness by works and law. But what man can be perfect and good and righteous and pure in every single act, word, and thought? It is absolutely impossible to secure righteousness by works and law. A person may try to approach God through works and law, but he can never achieve perfection—not the perfect righteousness and holiness required to see God.

"Follow peace with all men, and holiness, without which no man shall see the Lord" (Heb.12:14).

b. A man can believe that Jesus Christ is God's gift of righteousness to the world--that God so loved the world...
- that He gave His Son to live a perfect life upon earth in order to secure the Perfect and Ideal Righteousness for man.
- that He gave His Son to take the unrighteousness of man upon Himself and to die for man, that is, to bear the judgment of unrighteousness for man.
- that he gave His Son to arise from the dead for man in order to conquer death and to give man a new and perfect life that is eternal.

⇒ A man can believe that God loves him and takes his faith in Christ and counts it as righteousness.
⇒ A man can believe that God loves him and accepts him because he honors His Son Jesus Christ—honors Jesus Christ by believing and following Him.
⇒ A man can believe that God loves His Son so much that He will take any man who honors His Son and do anything for him. If the man believes in Jesus Christ for righteousness, then God will count the man righteous.

"For by grace are ye saved through faith; and that not of yourselves: it is the gift of God: not of works, lest any man should boast" (Eph.2:8-9).

2. Note another point: the two ways that men try to approach God are completely different from each other. Faith and works are incompatible. Faith is always the opposite of works.
⇒ If a man works to keep the law in order to be righteous, then he can offer to God only *self-righteousness*, only the righteousness of the works *he has done*.
⇒ If a man trusts the righteousness of Jesus Christ *for his righteousness*, then he can offer the righteousness of Christ to God. He can come to God in the righteousness of Christ.

God always accepts the righteousness of His Son, Jesus Christ. For any man who truly trusts the righteousness of Christ—who truly gives Christ all he is and has—God accepts that man's trust as righteousness. The man is not righteous, but God takes his trust in Christ and accepts it as righteousness.

3. Note still another fact: a man who *believes God for righteousness* approaches God entirely differently than the man who approaches God in his own self-righteousness.

a. The man who approaches God in his own righteousness...
- presents his self-righteousness to God *by himself*.
- depends upon his own righteousness.
- trust his own righteousness.
- believes in his own righteousness.
- declares that he has the strength and power to make himself righteous and acceptable to God.

b. The man who approaches God in the righteousness of Jesus Christ...
- presents his love and trust in the righteousness of Jesus Christ as his righteousness. (God could never turn down a person who loved and trusted His Son with all his heart.)

- rejects dependence upon himself and depends upon the righteousness of Jesus Christ.
- gives up trusting his own righteousness and trusts the righteousness of Christ.
- no longer believes in his own righteousness, but believes in Christ for righteousness.
- declares that he does not have the power to make himself righteous and acceptable to God; he trusts the power of God to make him righteous and acceptable.

Note what this is saying: a man either believes he has the power to save himself and to keep himself from dying or else he believes that God has the power to save him. A man either trusts his own power for salvation and life or else he trusts God's power. If he believes that he has the power to save himself, then he works to make himself righteous and to live forever. If he believes that God alone has the power to save him, then he trusts God for righteousness and life.

In conclusion, no one is ever justified by works or by law. We may try to secure righteousness by works and law, but it is always self-righteousness, and self-righteousness always ends up with self: in the grave—dead, having passed the way of all flesh—short of God's glory and perfection and disqualified from ever living with God. Self-righteousness is never acceptable to God; works and law can never justify a man and make him perfect.

However, we can secure righteousness by faith. We can trust God as a child trusts his father. We can trust that God loves us enough to count our love and trust for His Son as righteousness.

FAITH IN CHRIST IS GOD'S RIGHTEOUSNESS, THE ONLY RIGHTEOUSNESS THAT MAKES A PERSON ACCEPTABLE TO GOD

"For Christ is the end of the law for righteousness to every one that believeth" (Ro.10:4).

4. Note one other fact: righteousness by works honors and makes man supreme and preeminent, the center and core of life. Righteousness by faith honors God and makes God supreme and preeminent, the center and core of life. God is the One to be obeyed out of a heart of love, adoration, and appreciation for what He has done (Ro.2:29).

QUESTIONS:

1. How many perfect men have lived in this world? How many have tried to be perfect but failed? Would you consider yourself to be in this category? Have you struggled to be righteous enough to please God and earn your salvation by yourself?
2. Why are faith and works incompatible?
3. What would cause a man to believe that he could save himself?

4. A BELIEVER IS NOT MISLED BY CHRIST (v.17-18).

The question is, "Could Christ be making us sinners by our trusting that we are justified by faith in Him alone?" Some argued that Paul was making Christ a *minister of sin*. Their reasoning went like this: when men turned away from the law to trust Christ for righteousness, Christ caused them to sin, for Christ made it easy for them to transgress the law. They said that Christ tore down the law, for He led men away from the law. He removed the restraints and barriers of the law; therefore, men became transgressors by rejecting the law.

Paul simply says two things about this argument. First, God forbid! Second, the man who tries to keep the law makes himself a sinner, for it is the law that condemns him (Gal.3:19).

The believer, of course, rejects the righteousness which comes by law, for the law gives him no righteousness. It only shows him where his failures are. The law condemns his conscience and makes him feel miserable and broken. However, the law has its place in the plan of God just as much as faith does. Very simply, when a man sees what God has done for him, he is driven to please God. The believer sees Christ bearing the guilt and punishment for his crimes (sins) and then bows in love and adoration and arises to work in appreciation for such amazing love. The believer tries to be good, not to earn or to win righteousness but to serve God out of appreciation for salvation. He does not try to put God in debt for salvation, but he thanks God for righteousness. He sees that he owes God whatever service he can perform. The genuine believer has come to know above all others that love is a much stronger force than fear. He follows Christ—does all he can to live like Christ—because he loves Christ. He loves Him because Christ has done so much for Him.

> **"For the love of Christ constraineth us; because we thus judge, that if one died for all, then were all dead: and that he died for all, that they which live should not henceforth live unto themselves, but unto him which died for them, and rose again" (2 Cor.5:14-15).**

QUESTIONS:

1. What is the purpose of the law in the Christian's life?
2. What motivates your love for Christ? Have you ever loved Him for the wrong reasons?
3. Contrast the law with grace. Which one of these has the greatest influence on your life now?

5. A BELIEVER IS JUSTIFIED BY LIVING FOR GOD (v.19-21).

A believer lives for God by doing four things.

1. The believer lives for God by *dying to the law*. The law shows a man that he is a sinner and that he comes ever so short of perfection and righteousness. The law shows man that he is to be punished and separated from the society of God forever. The law shows man that he stands no chance of ever being accepted by God—not if he has to approach God by keeping the law. He just cannot keep the law—not continually, not consistently—for he is always coming short of the law and of God's glory. The law slays man; it kills him and condemns him to death. The only hope man ever has of being acceptable to God is to die to the law—somehow, some way to be delivered out from under the law—to be removed so far away from the law that it has no bearing upon him. How can man do this? By turning away from the law and finding Someone who can stir God to count him righteous and to accept him. The first thing that a man must do in order to live for God is to *die to the law and to self-righteous works*.

2. The believer lives for God by being *crucified with Christ* (v.20). How in the world can a man be crucified with Christ when Christ died so many centuries ago? Scripture tells us how. When a man believes that Jesus Christ died for him—that Jesus Christ bore the punishment of sin for him—God takes that man's faith and...

- counts his faith as his *having died in Christ*.
- counts his faith as his *identification with Christ in death*.
- counts his faith as his having already been punished for sin *in the death of Christ*.

As Scripture says, the man is "crucified with Christ." God counts or credits the believer as having already died—as having died with Christ.

3. The believer lives for God by *allowing Christ to live His life through his body*. Now note: the believer is "crucified with Christ," yet he is still living upon earth. However, he is not to be the one in *charge of his life*. By faith he has died with Christ; therefore, he is to live with Christ. He is to allow Christ to live *in and through his body*, to control and to be in charge of his life.

⇒ The believer is to be so merged into Christ that it is as though Christ is walking upon the earth in his body.

⇒ The believer is to be so much in union and fellowship with Christ that it is as though he be but a branch drawing his very life and nourishment from Christ (cp. the Vine and the branches, Jn.15:1-6).

APPLICATION 1:
Jesus Christ (God's Spirit) lives in the body of the believer.

> **"Abide in me, and I in you. As the branch cannot bear fruit of itself, except it abide in the vine; no more can ye, except ye abide in me. I am the vine, ye are the branches: He that abideth in me, and I in him, the same bringeth forth much fruit: for without me ye can do nothing" (Jn.15:4-5).**

APPLICATION 2:
The believer is to allow Christ to live through his body.

> **"I beseech you therefore, brethren, by the mercies of God, that ye present your bodies a living sacrifice, holy, acceptable unto God, which is your reasonable service. And be not conformed to this world: but be ye transformed by the renewing of your mind, that ye may prove what is that good, and acceptable, and perfect, will of God" (Ro.12:1-2).**

4. The believer lives for God by *trusting the grace of God*, that is, by trusting Jesus Christ who is God's righteousness. The word "frustrate" means to set aside, void, invalidate, make ineffective, and nullify. If a man sets aside the grace of God to seek righteousness by the law, then Christ died in vain. The person who preaches that a man can be good enough—that he can work enough and keep enough law—to become righteous and acceptable to God...

- voids and does away with the love and grace of God.
- makes the death of Christ empty and meaningless.

The only way a man can live for God is by trusting the grace and love of God, that is, by trusting the death of Jesus Christ for His righteousness.

> **"And be found in him, not having mine own righteousness, which is of the law, but that which is through the faith of <u>Christ, the righteousness which is of God</u> by faith" (Ph.3:9).**

ILLUSTRATION:
Have you ever thought about what it means to live a crucified life? Imagine the following happening to a church in your community:

In the middle of a church service, Jesus Christ Himself walked right down the center isle of a large church and positioned Himself behind the pulpit. As you can imagine, there was great excitement. A pulsating electricity ran through the congregation.

On the edge of their seats, the people waited for His profound words. *"Go with Me today to the local shopping mall and witness for Me."* The assembly was a little shocked by His request. After all, their church was trying to do all the right things to bring people in. But, because it was Jesus doing the asking, they decided to do as He said and follow Him to the mall. It would be hard to witness, but they would.

The next week, Jesus came back to the church again. By this time, the congregation was feeling honored that He would take the time to visit their church. Again, they sat in their chairs, wondering what He would say. Truthfully, they expected Him to ease up after the last week's difficult challenge. *"Go with Me and comfort those who are in the prison. And then, reach out to their families by including them in your times of fellowship."* Everyone was shocked! The mall was a safe place to share with people that they would never see again (hopefully). But now, He was asking them to get close to people they had no desire to be around.

But again, because it was Jesus, they did everything that He asked them to do. It was awkward at times, but they all lived through the experience, and those who were visited seemed to really appreciate their efforts.

Jesus came back to the same church for the final time the following week. By this time they had gotten used to His visits. They figured they had passed His test of faithfulness and that He would bless them and go on His way. As was His custom, He walked to the pulpit. One man in the congregation shouted out: *"Jesus, what do you want us to do for you today? We've blocked out the whole afternoon to go with you. What's it going to be today? Nursing homes, soup kitchens, visiting widows? Like I've said; we've scheduled you in for the whole afternoon."* With eyes that pierced through their shallow hearts, He said, *"Today, I want you to take up your cross, deny yourself, and follow Me up that hill and die." "Die?! We don't understand. How can we serve you if we die? We're doing a lot of good things down here and dying on a cross would ruin everything that we've done."*

Like these church people, many of us have missed the purpose of the cross. Crosses were not made for carrying...they were made for dying. There should be no pride in the number and weight of the crosses we carry. Their purpose is for our death to self.

QUESTIONS:

1. What part of you is the hardest to put to death? Your tongue? Your thoughts? Your actions? Why does it have such a powerful grip on your life? What can you do to control it, to squelch it?
2. Do you fully comprehend what it means to have the Holy Spirit living in you? What insights come to your mind as you resist daily temptations?
3. In what practical ways can you nurture and cultivate your trusting God for His grace?

SUMMARY:

If you have wandered away from the Good Shepherd, there is good news for you: He wants you to come back home, and He is coming to meet you with open arms. In the future, instead of backsliding away from Him, run to Him. To review the main points, remember:

1. Paul boldly confronted Peter.
2. A believer cannot have double standards.
3. A believer is justified by faith alone.
4. A man is not misled by Christ.
5. A man is justified by living for God.

PERSONAL JOURNAL NOTES
(Reflection & Response)

1. The most important thing that I learned from this lesson was:

2. The area that I need to work on the most is:

3. I can apply this lesson to my life by:

4. Closing Statement of Commitment:

[1] Paul Lee Tan. *Encyclopedia of 7,700 Illustrations: Signs of the Times*, p.560.
[2] Walter B. Knight. *Knight's Treasury of 2,000 Illustrations*, p.117.

GALATIANS 3:1-5

	CHAPTER 3 **III. THE PROOF THAT A MAN IS JUSTIFIED BY FAITH ALONE & NOT BY WORKS 3:1-4:7** **A. The Proof of a Believer's Experience, 3:1-5**	
1. A believer corrects error (false teaching) a. Because it makes him foolish b. Because it deceives him c. Because it shows that he is disobedient d. Because he has seen Christ so clearly	O foolish Galatians, who hath bewitched you, that ye should not obey the truth, before whose eyes Jesus Christ hath been evidently set forth, crucified among you?	
	2 This only would I learn of you, Received ye the Spirit by the works of the law, or by the hearing of faith?	**2. A believer receives the Spirit by faith, not by works nor by law**
	3 Are ye so foolish? having begun in the Spirit, are ye now made perfect by the flesh?	**3. A believer grows by faith**
	4 Have ye suffered so many things in vain? if it be yet in vain.	**4. A believer suffers by faith**
	5 He therefore that ministereth to you the Spirit, and worketh miracles among you, doeth he it by the works of the law, or by the hearing of faith?	**5. A believer experiences God's miraculous working by faith, not by works nor by law**

Section III
THE PROOF THAT A MAN IS JUSTIFIED BY FAITH ALONE AND NOT BY WORKS
Galatians 3:1-4:7

Study 1: THE PROOF OF A BELIEVER'S EXPERIENCE

Text: Galatians 3:1-5

Aim: To make absolutely sure that your spiritual experience is based on faith alone.

Memory Verse:

"Are ye so foolish? having begun in the Spirit, are ye now made perfect by the flesh?" (Galatians 3:3).

SECTION OVERVIEW:

This passage begins the major teaching of the Book of Galatians, that a man is justified by faith alone and not by good works nor by law. Of course, a man should be as good as he can be and do as much good as he can. A man should live a moral and just life like the law says. But this is not the point; this is not what Scripture is saying. Scripture is saying that a person is *not justified* before God by doing good and keeping the law. No man can do enough good nor keep enough laws to become perfect and acceptable before God. God is perfect, and no matter how much good we do and how much law we keep, we do not become perfect. We still fall short: we still fail, sin, age, and die. Good works and law do not perfect us; they do not make us acceptable to God nor impart to us eternal life. Only God Himself can perfect us, accept us, and give us eternal life. Any thinking and honest person knows that there is nothing on earth--absolutely nothing--that can keep us from coming short and dying. There is absolutely nothing on earth that can give us eternal life in a perfect world where there is nothing but love, joy, and peace. If we are ever to inherit eternal life, then God has to give it to us.

GALATIANS 3:1-5

The point is this: How do we know that God will justify us? How do we know that God will accept us and give us life with Him forever? The answer to this question is the discussion of the present passage. There are six proofs that God will justify us by faith alone, six proofs that God will not justify us by works and law.

SECTION OUTLINE:

1. The proof of a believer's experience (3:1-5).
2. The proof of Scripture (3:6-14).
3. The proof of God's Covenant or promise (3:15-18).
4. The proof of the law's powerlessness (3:19-22).
5. The proof of what faith does for us (3:23-29).
6. The proof of Christ and the fulness of time (4:1-7).

INTRODUCTION:

Christian songwriter Andrae Crouch captured the essence of this session when he wrote, "I didn't think it could be until it happened to me. And you'll never know that it's true until it happens to you." (From *Andrae Crouch and the Disciples: Live at Carnegie Hall*. Light Records, a division of Word).

Until someone has had a spiritual experience with Jesus Christ, their concept of salvation will be built on a foundation of works. The natural mind has no concept of grace and faith. The Christian believer's experience validates the truth of this line from a great hymn: "Just as I am without one plea." You will note that the rendition does not say "Just as I *will be,*" but "just as I am." Hallelujah! We can not add one thing to our salvation. Christ comes to each one of us...just as we are.

Some influential people had joined the churches of Galatia; and the churches took pride in their presence. The new members were so capable and the churches were so glad to have them that they were immediately placed in positions of leadership and teaching. However, these new members had not been truly converted by Christ or else their understanding of the gospel was all confused. They began to teach that faith alone was not enough to save a person, that a person had to undergo the basic ritual of religion (circumcision) and focus his life upon the law in order to become acceptable to God.

Paul's answer is direct: the *experience* of the Galatian believers disproves that a person becomes acceptable to God by law. The *believer's experience* proves that he is justified by faith alone, and all a believer has to do is to rethink his experience and he will see the truth.

OUTLINE:

1. A believer corrects errors (false teaching) (v.1).
2. A believer receives the Spirit by faith, not by works nor by law (v.2).
3. A believer grows by faith (v.3).
4. A believer suffers by faith (v.4).
5. A believer experiences God's miraculous working by faith, not by works nor by law (v.5).

1. A BELIEVER CORRECTS ERRORS [FALSE TEACHING] (v.1).

There are four reasons why a believer must correct the errors that he comes across.

1. Error makes a person "foolish." Note that Paul calls the Galatian believers "foolish Galatians." The word "foolish" means misunderstanding, thoughtless, and unthinking. The Galatians were listening to false teaching and passively drinking it in. They were not thinking through what was being taught. They were lazily sitting and soaking it up, not applying their minds to see if what was being taught was true or not. They were *foolish*, acting like senseless people who were incapable of thinking.

2. Error deceives a person. The word "bewitched" means to fascinate, cast a spell upon, mislead, deceive. The false teachers were, as so many are, very capable, fluent, and persuasive speakers with dynamic personalities and charisma. Their teaching sounded reasonable and logical.

⇒ A man must keep the ritual of religion.
⇒ A man must do good works to be good.
⇒ A man must keep the law in order to be acceptable to God.

It all sounded reasonable and logical, especially to a person who was not thinking and comparing the teaching to the gospel of Christ. The error was *bewitching*, deceiving the believers.

3. Error shows disobedience. The Galatians simply were not obeying the truth. They were trying to become acceptable to God...

- by undergoing the ritual of religion (circumcision, baptism, etc.) instead of trusting the death of Jesus Christ.
- by subjecting themselves and focusing their lives upon the law instead of Christ.

4. Error leads a believer away from Christ. This is tragic, for the true believer is a person who has seen Christ crucified for him. The Galatians had clearly seen the death of Christ through the preaching of Paul. Paul's preaching had plainly pointed out and explained the death of Christ. In fact, the Lord's death had been so clearly explained that it was as though the Lord Jesus had been crucified in their presence, before their very eyes. There was, therefore, no excuse for their following false teachers. They knew what Christ had done for them, that Christ had died for them and had taken their sins upon Himself and borne their punishment for them.

They knew that God loved them, that God so loved the world...

- that He had sent His Son into the world to die *for them*.
- that God expected all men to believe in the death of His Son, Jesus Christ.
- that God took their faith and love in His dear Son and accepted them because they believed and loved His Son.

How then could they be so foolish and bewitched as not to obey the truth--especially when they had clearly seen and understood the death of Jesus Christ?

ILLUSTRATION:

When you were in school, how many papers did you begin to write only to ball them up and throw them into an already over-filled trash can? Did you ever give up and quit? Probably not, because you needed to turn in your assignment in order to pass the class.

If you were to spend some time in the shop of a potter, you would be fascinated to watch the potter at work. Working with a lump of unimpressive clay, the potter beings to form a civilized shape on his wheel. When it appears that he is almost finished, he suddenly smashes his work back into a lump of clay again. "What a waste of time," you think to yourself. It looked pretty good from your perspective.

But, to the trained eye of the potter, an error was easily detected. Because he took pride in what he did, he was not willing to overlook the flaw. His product was going to be a cut above the rest--because of his commitment to quality.

In the same sense, the Christian believer must have the same commitment to correcting errors in the Church. Is it any wonder that a lot of non-Christians are searching for answers elsewhere because the "Christian Potters" are not committed to quality? We must be willing to look for and recognize false teachings and then to get rid of the erroneous teachings. Only then will our witness be pure and appealing to non-believers.

QUESTIONS:

1. What distinguishes the truth from error? Why do some believers fall into error?
2. What can you do to protect yourself from being deceived?
3. What are some of the natural results of a believer who falls into error? What encouragement would you offer to someone who has fallen into the trap of some false teaching?

GALATIANS 3:1-5

2. A BELIEVER RECEIVES THE SPIRIT BY FAITH, NOT BY WORKS NOR BY LAW (v.2).

Note that this whole passage is a series of questions. Paul is stirring the Galatians to think. The present question strikes at the very heart of the gospel: How did you begin your Christian life? Did you receive the Holy Spirit by the works of the law or by the hearing of faith?

There is one thing genuine believers know, and the genuine believers in the Galatian churches knew it too: no person earns, wins, or merits the Spirit of God. Man is too polluted and too short of God's glory to deserve the Spirit of God. His thoughts and behavior are too often...

- ugly
- selfish
- greedy
- unjust
- negative
- immoral
- lustful
- undisciplined
- impure
- unrighteous
- imperfect
- unholy

No matter how much good and how much of the law is kept, the believer knows that he did not and cannot eliminate such thoughts and behavior--not fully, not perfectly. Therefore, he did not become a Christian--he did not receive the Holy Spirit--by good works nor by the keeping of laws. He became a Christian and received the Spirit of God by hearing about faith in Christ. He heard the glorious news that Christ had died for him and his sins, and he believed the news. Therefore, God took his faith and counted it for righteousness. The believer knows that he is not righteous, but God *counts him righteous* because he *believes and loves* His Son. The believer knows that the Holy Spirit does not dwell in him because of any goodness or work of his own; he knows that he has the Holy Spirit because God counts his *faith in Christ* as reason enough to put His Spirit into his heart. That is how the believer receives the Spirit of God, and that is how the Galatians received the Spirit of God.

APPLICATION 1:

Every person must hear the glorious message of faith. The *message of faith* is the gospel of salvation--*faith in the Lord Jesus Christ and His death for our sins.*

> **"How then shall they call on him in whom they have not believed? and how shall they believe in him of whom they have not heard? and how shall they hear without a preacher? And how shall they preach, except they be sent? as it is written, How beautiful are the feet of them that preach the gospel of peace, and bring glad tidings of good things! But they have not all obeyed the gospel. For Esaias saith, Lord, who hath believed our report? So then faith cometh by hearing, and hearing by the word of God" (Ro.10:14-17).**

APPLICATION 2:

The Holy Spirit is the gift of God. No man can earn, win, or merit the Spirit of God. God's Holy Spirit is given by God and by God alone.

> **"And I will pray the Father, and he shall give you another Comforter, that he may abide with you for ever; even the Spirit of truth; whom the world cannot receive, because it seeth him not, neither knoweth him: but ye know him; for he dwelleth with you, and shall be in you" (Jn.14:16-17).**

QUESTIONS:

1. Why has God connected salvation with faith instead of works and the law?
2. How would you explain the concept of faith to a person who was seriously examining Christianity?
3. Why do some people think it takes more than faith in order to be saved?

3. A BELIEVER GROWS BY FAITH (v.3).

Again, note the question: **"Having begun your Christian life in the Spirit, are you now maturing and being made perfect by the flesh?"**

A believer does not become spiritually mature by focusing upon his flesh, upon what he can do with...

- his efforts
- his works
- his goodness
- his discipline
- his morality
- his just behavior

No matter how strong and disciplined his flesh is--no matter how many good deeds and laws he is able to do in his own flesh--the believer's flesh does not make him grow spiritually. Focusing upon his flesh and upon the strength and work of the flesh only causes the believer to concentrate upon himself. It emphasizes self, not the Spirit--the human and physical, not the spiritual and heavenly.

Note another fact: no matter how many good works are done and no matter how many laws are kept, they cannot make a man perfect; they cannot impart eternal life to a man. There is no man upon earth that is living eternally because of works. There is no law whatsoever that can keep a man alive forever and ever. No matter how many works of the law a man has done *in his flesh*, he has not achieved perfection--not the holy perfection that makes him acceptable to God. If he is ever to be perfect enough to be acceptable to a Holy God, it will be because God perfects him, not because he has worked and become perfect through his corruptible flesh and human efforts.

As Paul says, "Are you so foolish?" Is God so low that corruptible and dying man can achieve so much? Is man so exalted that he has so little to achieve in order to be perfected? Any thinking and honest heart knows not.

⇒ A man <u>begins</u> his journey to God when he truly believes in Jesus Christ and is "born again"--*a spiritual thing.*

⇒ A man <u>continues</u> his journey as he is daily renewed by the Holy Spirit--also *a spiritual thing.*

The only way a believer can spiritually grow and mature is to focus his life and mind upon Jesus Christ. The believer must focus his mind upon the things of Christ moment by moment, and as he does, the Spirit of God will draw his mind to spiritual things. Remember: the Spirit of God lives *within* the believer. He is there to work within the believer and to help him grow and mature in Christ.

⇒ The believer keeps his mind and thoughts upon Christ, casting down imaginations and making every thought obedient to Christ.

> **"Casting down imagination, and every high thing that exalteth itself against the knowledge of God, and bringing into captivity every thought to the obedience of Christ" (2 Cor.10:5).**

⇒ The believer focuses and keeps his mind and thoughts upon being conformed more and more to the image of Christ. He keeps his mind and thoughts upon Christ all day long--praising, honoring, worshipping, and asking for His help and guidance. He learns to live and move and have his being in Christ.

> **"For whom he did foreknow, he also did predestinate to be <u>conformed</u> to the image of his Son, that he might be the firstborn among many brethren" (Ro.8:29).**

⇒ The believer who focuses his love, attention, and life upon the Lord Jesus Christ is accepted by God. God loves His Son so much that He accepts any person who truly loves and focuses his life upon His Son. And someday--in the glorious day of redemption--God will perfect the believer and conform him perfectly to the image of Christ.

> **"For our conversation [citizenship, behavior] is in heaven; from whence also we look for the Saviour, the Lord Jesus Christ: who shall change our vile body, that it may be fashioned like unto his glorious body, according to the working whereby he is able even to subdue all things unto himself" (Ph.3:20-21).**

QUESTIONS:

1. It is very fashionable in our culture to be a "self-made" person. In what ways do people try to increase their faith?
2. What is the only way that you can grow in Christ? What are some distractions or barriers to growth that you need to overcome?
3. How does this verse help you to refocus upon the Lord?

4. A BELIEVER SUFFERS BY FAITH (v.4).

When the Galatians accepted Christ, they had suffered ridicule, abuse, isolation and persecution from their neighbors; and apparently the persecution had continued for some time (Acts 14:1-7, 19, 22). The point is this: if the Galatians now turned away from Christ to some false teaching, then the suffering they had borne for Christ would be in vain. They would have suffered for nothing. In fact, they would now appear foolish if they turned away from Christ when they had suffered so much in order to embrace Him.

APPLICATION:

Every believer who truly turns to Christ has some suffering to bear. It may be mild, but some suffering is borne. There is the suffering of...

- separating from the world.
- denying self.
- taking up the cross--dying to one's own will and way every day.
- giving everything that one has to Christ and His cause (money, time, energy, effort).

The list could go on and on, but the point is clearly seen. If Christ is worth suffering for, why then forsake Him and turn to some false teaching?

> **"Blessed are ye, when men shall revile you, and persecute you, and shall say all manner of evil against you falsely, for my sake" (Mt.5:11).**

ILLUSTRATION:

Where is it written in the Bible that a Christian believer is exempt from suffering? Unfortunately, many have bought into a false doctrine that says "bad things don't happen to good people." We need to rest in God's ability to provide everything that we need in order to become more like Jesus.

> *"A man found a cocoon of the emperor moth and took it home to watch it emerge. One day a small opening appeared, and for several hours the moth struggled but couldn't seem to force its body past a certain point.*
>
> *"Deciding something was wrong, the man took scissors and snipped the remaining bit of cocoon. The moth emerged easily, its body large and swollen, the wings small and shriveled.*
>
> *"He expected that in a few hours the wings would spread out in their natural beauty, but they did not. Instead of developing into a creature free to fly, the moth spent its life dragging around a swollen body and shriveled wings.*
>
> *"The constricting cocoon and the struggle necessary to pass through the tiny opening are God's way of forcing fluid from the body into the wings. The 'merciful' snip was, in reality, cruel. Sometimes the struggle is exactly what we need."*[1]

GALATIANS 3:1-5

QUESTIONS:
1. Can you recall an experience when you had to suffer because of your faith? What lessons did you learn from this experience?
2. How can God help you grow through suffering?
3. On a scale of 1 (any time) to 5 (never in my wildest dreams), rate yourself on the following statements. Call this your "suffering index." Would you...
   _____Risk embarrassment by sharing Christ?
   _____Take a short-term mission trip to a third-world country?
   _____Skip a meal once a week and use those funds to feed the hungry of the world?
   _____Get up thirty minutes earlier each day in order to have a quiet-time with God?
   _____Stand up for the rights of the abused and oppressed?
4. Have you become satisfied with your faith, doing only what is easy and comfortable?
5. Does God expect you to suffer sometimes? Why?

5. A BELIEVER EXPERIENCES GOD'S MIRACULOUS WORKING BY FAITH AND NOT BY WORKS NOR BY THE LAW (v.5).

What were the miracles experienced by the Galatians? They were miraculous works of healing (cp. Acts 14:8-15). But note: the miracles were not due to the Galatians; they were due to God. The Galatians did not earn, win, or merit the miracles. They simply *heard about* the power of faith, and they believed God, that God would meet their needs. And God did--God worked miracles among them because of the "hearing of faith." They heard the glorious message of faith in Christ, and they believed in the power of faith in Christ; therefore, God honored their faith and met their needs.

APPLICATION:

What a lesson for us! To believe "the hearing of faith"--the glorious message of *faith in Christ and its power--and then to experience that power*!

> **"And all things, whatsoever ye shall ask in prayer, believing, ye shall receive" (Mt.21:22).**
>
> **"And I say unto you, Ask, and it shall be given you; seek, and ye shall find; knock, and it shall be opened unto you" (Lk.11:9).**

ILLUSTRATION:

In the U.S. Navy, the Seabees have a saying: "The difficult, we do immediately. The impossible takes a little time."

Author Jamie Buckingham shares this story from the missionary adventures of JAARS (Jungle Aviation and Radio Service--the flying arm for Wycliffe Bible Translators). We pick up his story about a pilot who was fighting to keep his plane from a fatal crash:

> *"Never for an instant did Ralph believe they could live through the pending crash...He could feel his wife's warm hand on the back of his clammy knuckles where he gripped the stick. "We do our best, God does the rest." It was the motto of JAARS. During all the time of the emergency, he had not called upon God. Why had he waited? Why had he not cried out at ten thousand feet? Now, with death only seconds away, he gulped the words.*
>
> *" 'Father, if You still have work for me and for my passengers, please bring on the engine...'*
>
> *"It was a sensible prayer. He could have prayed for a giant hand to rise up out of the jungle and cushion his fall. He could have asked for ten thousand angels to bear him up on wings of down. But like Moses at the Red Sea, he was content for God to work in natural ways--not by sending a strong east wind to blow back the sea--but by bringing the engine back to life...The carburetor heat!...[It] was used primarily to prevent ice from forming in the carburetor...But there were no known instances of icing at this altitude.*

GALATIANS 3:1-5

"The carburetor heat! Again he tried to dismiss the thought, to spit it out of his mind. But it pounded against the inside of his temples. It rang in his head. And his hand was obedient. He reached down and jerked the carburetor heat handle and at the same time pulled back on the stick. The jungle had arrived. The only thing to do was flatten his glide just at the treetops, lose as much speed as possible, and settle into the foliage. Certainly forever.

"Suddenly there was a mighty roar up front. The big prop, which had been slowly windmilling in the streaming air, roared to life. As if they had never quit, the thousand horses were up and running again, straining at the traces, trying with all of their might to pull the sinking old Duck out of the jaws of death.

"Ralph's Canadian dignity, shaken all the way to the soles of his soggy socks, finally broke. It came forth like the sound of a shipwrecked sailor thrown at last upon a sandy beach. From the very inner part of his soul, there came forth an utterance of thanksgiving.

"'Praise the Lord!' he said with deep reverence. And then repeated it. 'Praise the Lord!'"[2]

QUESTIONS:

1. Have you experienced any miracles in your life? Do you know anyone else who has?
2. Have you reached a point in your Christian journey where you do not expect miracles?
2. Do you feel you can take good care of yourself without any help from God?
4. Do you think God always has to provide a miracle? Does the miracle always have to be big? Why or why not?

SUMMARY:

Your journey with Christ is meant to be a growing one, full of faith and sometimes full of suffering. Your experience is to be a testimony that has been built on Christ's handiwork, not your own efforts. Remember the challenges from this session:

1. A believer corrects error (false teaching).
2. A believer receives the Spirit by faith, not by works nor by law.
3. A believer grows by faith.
4. A believer suffers by faith.
5. A believer experiences God's miraculous working by faith and not by works nor by law.

PERSONAL JOURNAL NOTES
(Reflection & Response)

1. The most important thing that I learned from this lesson was:

2. The area that I need to work on the most is:

3. I can apply this lesson to my life by:

4. Closing Statement of Commitment:

---

[1] Craig B. Larson, editor. *Illustrations for Preaching & Teaching*, p.266.
[2] Jamie Buckingham. *Into the Glory*. (Plainfield, NJ: Logos International, 1974), p.13-14.

GALATIANS 3:6-14

1. Scripture uses Abraham to illustrate the truth
   a. He believed God—thus he was judged righteous
   b. Those who are of faith are the true sons of Abraham

2. Scripture "preached the gospel of faith to Abraham"
   a. Scripture foresaw that God would judge men righteous through faith
   b. Those who are of faith are judged righteous with Abraham

3. Scripture says the law puts a man under the curse
   a. Because a man does not keep the whole law
   b. Because God's way is to live by faith
      1) The law is not of faith
      2) The man of law will be judged by the law

4 Scripture says "Christ has redeemed us from the curse"
   a. He was made a curse for us
   b. His purpose: To open the door of blessing to all men
      1) Blessing of Abraham
      2) Blessing of the Spirit

B. The Proof of Scripture, 3:6-14

6 Even as Abraham believed God, and it was accounted to him for righteousness.
7 Know ye therefore that they which are of faith, the same are the children of Abraham.
8 And the scripture, foreseeing that God would justify the heathen through faith, preached before the gospel unto Abraham, saying, In thee shall all nations be blessed.
9 So then they which be of faith are blessed with faithful Abraham.
10 For as many as are of the works of the law are under the curse: for it is written, Cursed is every one that continueth not in all things which are written in the book of the law to do them.
11 But that no man is justified by the law in the sight of God, it is evident: for, The just shall live by faith.
12 And the law is not of faith: but, the man that doeth them shall live in them.
13 Christ hath redeemed us from the curse of the law, being made a curse for us: for it is written, Cursed is every one that hangeth on a tree:
14 That the blessing of Abraham might come on the Gentiles through Jesus Christ; that we might receive the promise of the Spirit through faith.

Section III
THE PROOF THAT A MAN IS JUSTIFIED BY FAITH ALONE AND NOT BY WORKS, Galatians 3:1-4:7

Study 2: **THE PROOF OF SCRIPTURE**

Text: **Galatians 3:6-14**

Aim: To be totally convinced by Scripture that man is justified by faith in Christ alone.

Memory Verse:

"Christ hath redeemed us from the curse of the law, being made a curse for us: for it is written, Cursed is everyone that hangeth on a tree" (Galatians 3:13).

INTRODUCTION:

Have you ever thought about what the world would be like if there were <u>no</u> Bible?

"A certain man dreamed that he went to consult his Bible and found every page blank. In amazement he rushed to his neighbor's house, aroused him from sleep, and asked to see his Bible; but they found it also blank. In great consternation they sought other Bibles, with the same result. Then they said, 'We will go to the libraries and gather the quotations from books, and remake our Bible.' But when they examined all the books, they found blank spaces where any Scripture quotations had been. When the

man awoke, his brow was cold, yet covered with perspiration, so great had been his agony during the dream. Oh, how dark this world would be without the Bible!"[1]

Thank God for the truth that His Word is not going to vanish—heaven and earth will pass away, but His Word will remain forever. His eternal Word proves that we are justified by faith in Christ and by faith in Christ alone.

Some false teachers had arisen in the churches of Galatia. They were teaching that a man must focus his life upon the rituals and teachings of religion—upon the works of the law—instead of focusing upon Christ. Simply stated, they were saying that a man had to be ritualized (circumcised, have church membership, be baptized) and give his life to keeping the law in order to be acceptable to God. They placed ritual and law—their own works and effort—before Jesus Christ.

⇒ They focused upon what they had to do instead of Christ.
⇒ They concentrated upon themselves—upon what they could do to save themselves and make themselves acceptable to God—not upon Christ and His saving power.
⇒ They stressed the flesh, the physical and the natural, the strength of man instead of God's love given to the world in His Son, Jesus Christ.

The answer of Paul is forceful: Scripture proves that a man is justified by faith and not by works or law.

OUTLINE:

1. Scripture uses Abraham to illustrate the truth (v.6-7).
2. Scripture "preached the gospel of faith to Abraham" (v.8-9).
3. Scripture says "the law puts a man under the curse" (v.10-12).
4. Scripture says "Christ has redeemed us from the curse" (v.13-14).

1. SCRIPTURE USES ABRAHAM TO ILLUSTRATE THE TRUTH (v.6-7).

Abraham held a unique position in the Jewish nation, for he was the founder of the nation. He was the man whom God had challenged to be a witness to the other nations of the world—a witness to the only living and true God. God had appeared to Abraham to challenge him to leave his home, his friends, his employment, and his country. God made two great promises if Abraham would follow God unquestionably: Abraham would become the father of a new nation, and all nations of the earth would be blessed by his seed (Gen.13:14-17; 15:1-7; 17:1-8, 15-19; 22:15-18; 26:2-5, 24; 28:13-15; 35:9-12).

Note two points.

1. Abraham believed God; therefore, he was judged righteous. He went out—left his home and risked all—not knowing where he was going (Heb.11:8). He completely and unquestionably trusted God and took God at His word.

Now note: it was not Abraham's keeping of the law that pleased God. In fact, the law had not yet been given (Gal.3:17). What pleased God and what caused God to justify Abraham was Abraham's doing as God had said. Abraham simply believed the promise of God that God would give him a new life—in a new nation—with a new people.

a. Abraham and his "seed" were the only ones to whom God gave the promises. This is emphatically stated (Ro.4:13-25; Gal.3:6-16, 26, 29).
b. Only a promise was given to Abraham (Ro.4:13-21; Gal.3:14, 18-21, 29). No other information whatsoever was given. God did not identify the country nor tell Abraham where he was to go. Neither did God tell Abraham when his wife Sarah would bear the seed (the male child) from whom the promised nation would be born. God made a simple promise, and all Abraham had to go on was that simple promise, that is, the sheer Word of God.
c. Only one condition was attached to the promise: Abraham had to believe God. No works whatsoever were involved.

d. Abraham did believe God (Gen.12:4-5; Ro.4:3, 11-22; Gal.3:6; Heb.11:8f).
e. Abraham was counted righteous because he believed God (Ro.4:3-5, 9-13, 19-22; Gal.3:6; cp. Gen.15:6). God did not count him righteous because of who he was or what he had done. He simply believed God. Therefore, God took his faith and counted his faith as righteousness.
f. The proof that Abraham really believed God was that he did what God had said. His faith preceded his obedience. He believed God, and then he obeyed God. If he had not believed God, he would not have left his home or his employment. He would not have left his surroundings and friends, his meaningful relationships and personal attachments. The fact that he did as God asked was evidence that he believed the promise of God.

2. Those who are of faith are the true sons of Abraham. The person who believes God is the person who receives the promises of God (Ro.4:5-12, 16-17, 23-25; Gal.3:7-9, 14, 22, 26, 29). Paul argues that neither heritage nor nationality, neither merit nor works, neither the law nor the rules of the law have anything to do with the promises of God (Gal.3:6-7). The true sons of Abraham are those who believe God—any person of any nation. In fact, God's promise that a nation would be born to Abraham and "his seed" was the promise of an eternal nation. This eternal nation is to be of another world, of another dimension of being: the spiritual dimension, a dimension just as real as the physical dimension. But it is to have one distinction: every citizen is to be a believer—one who has believed God and His Word. This is exactly what this passage is saying: "They who believe are the children of Abraham, the children of God's promise. They are to be blessed along with faithful Abraham. They are to be the citizens of God's Kingdom, 'the new heavens and the new earth.'" (Cp. Heb.11:8-18; 2 Pt.3:10-14.)

QUESTIONS:
1. What condition did God attach to the promise to Abraham? Are His promises to you also conditional? In what way?
2. Contrast the principle of faith with the principle of works. Which one is the easiest for you to live by? Why?
3. Abraham chose to believe God. In what areas of your life do you have a difficult time believing God? What things can you do to help yourself trust in the Lord?

2. SCRIPTURE "PREACHED THE GOSPEL OF FAITH TO ABRAHAM" (v.8-9).

To Paul, Scripture was the Word of God, the very voice of God Himself. Therefore, Paul could just as easily have said that Scripture spoke to Abraham as he could that God spoke to Abraham. (Note Paul's high view of Scripture, a strong rebuke to many.)

1. Scripture declared the gospel of faith long before Christ ever came: Scripture declared the gospel to Abraham. As stated in the former note, God told Abraham that He would accept him and bless him if Abraham would believe (love and follow) the promise of God. What was the promise?

"In thee shall all nations be blessed" (v.8)

Abraham believed God; he separated himself from the world, giving his life totally to God; therefore, God accepted and judged Abraham righteous.

2. Those who are of faith are judged righteous with Abraham. Abraham was justified by believing God. What happened was this. Abraham believed God, and God took Abraham's belief and counted his belief as righteousness. It was not Abraham's works, but his faith that God took and counted as righteousness. It was all an act of God; therefore, all glory belonged to God, not to Abraham. Man is saved by faith; in other words, God takes a man's faith and counts that man's faith as righteousness. This has to be the case:

⇒ God is perfect; He is perfectly righteous. No man can achieve perfection; therefore, no man can live in the presence of God.

⇒ However, God is love; therefore, what God does is take a person's faith and counts that faith as righteousness and perfection. Therefore, a man is able to live in God's presence by faith or justification

> **"But after that the kindness and love of God our Saviour toward man appeared, not by works of righteousness which we have done, but according to his mercy he saved us, by the washing of regeneration, and renewing of the Holy Ghost" (Tit.3:4-5).**

ILLUSTRATION:

How close are you to the Word of God? Is it your desire to absorb it and infuse it into your life or do you read it and hope that something sticks?

"There is a story of a missionary in Korea who had a visit from a native convert who lived a hundred miles away, and who walked four days to reach the mission station. The pilgrim recited proudly, without a single mistake, the whole of the Sermon on the Mount. The missionary was delighted, but he felt that he ought to warn the man that memorizing was not enough—that it was necessary to practice the words as well as to memorize them.

"The Korean's face lit up with happy smiles. 'That is the way I learned it,' he said. 'I tried to memorize it, but it wouldn't stick. So I hit upon this plan—I would memorize a verse and then find a heathen neighbor of mine and practice it on him. Then I found it would stick.'"[2]

The Bible is not just a book about people who have changed...it is a book that changes those who read it and live out what they read!

QUESTIONS:

1. How would you explain to a non-Christian how God speaks to you through His Word? How else can God speak to His children?
2. What attitude should you have if someone claims to speak for God but his words contradict the Scriptures?
3. Did Paul see any difference between the spoken Word of God and the written Word of God? Why do some Christians struggle with this issue? What kind of encouragement can you give to them?

A CLOSER LOOK:

Abraham: the Scripture...preached the gospel to Abraham (Gal.3:8). What does this mean? God had promised Abraham an earthly son and a great earthly nation. But behind God's promise lay something more than just an earthly, human fulfillment. Abraham's son, Isaac, was a type of the real seed that was to come, and the Jewish nation was a type of the real nation that was to be born. (See Ro.4:1-25; 9:7-13; Heb.11:9-19.)

Paul gives at least two proofs for this typology.

1. The word "seed" is singular, not plural (Gal.3:16). God's promise does not point to a great crowd of people but to one single person. That person is Jesus Christ. Jesus Christ is the fulfillment of the promise to Abraham. And the nation promised is the new nation of believers that God is creating to inherit the new heavens and earth (see Gal.3:16; Eph.1:9-10; 2:11-18; 3:6; 4:17-19).
2. The major events of Isaac's life parallel the life of Christ.
   ⇒ First, Isaac was miraculously born (Gen.15:2-3; 18:11; cp. Ro.4:18-22; Heb.11:11).
   ⇒ Second, Isaac was to be offered up as a sacrifice (Gen.22). Abraham was willing to offer up Isaac, and God accepted his willingness and motive as an actual fact. The

word of Heb.11:17 tells us this: "by faith Abraham...[who] received the promise offered up his only begotten son."

⇒ Third, Isaac was delivered from death by a miracle of God (Gen.22:10-13). Abraham knew that God was able to raise up Isaac from the dead in order to fulfil His promise, if need be (Heb.11:19).

QUESTIONS:

1. What does the promise that God made to Abraham mean to your Christian walk?
2. What particular character traits do you find in Abraham's life that you would like to have as your own? What do you need to do in order to achieve this for your life?

3. SCRIPTURE SAYS "THE LAW PUTS A MAN UNDER THE CURSE" (v.10-12).

Note a critical point: in this verse the word "curse" means to be condemned and doomed to punishment by the righteous judgment of God. How do we know this? By verse 13 where it is said that Christ bore the curse of the law for us (the condemnation, doom, death, and punishment due us for having broken the law). The law carries with it a curse. A person either keeps the law or else he is cursed; that is, he is to stand before the Judge and bear the punishment of a lawbreaker. The curse (penalty or punishment) for violating the law is...

- the mark of death (2 Cor.3:7).

> **"For the wages of sin is death; but the gift of God is eternal life through Jesus Christ our Lord" (Ro.6:23).**

- the mark of condemnation (2 Cor.3:9).

> **"And the commandment, which was ordained to life, I found to be unto death. For sin, taking occasion by the commandment, deceived me, and by it slew me" (Ro.7:10-11).**

Why does the law put a curse upon men? There are two clear reasons.

1. The man who approaches God by law is cursed because he does not keep the whole law. Note a crucial fact: there is a righteousness that is of the law (Ro.10:5; Gal.3:12). That righteousness promises life to any man who can obey the law perfectly. If a man can meet every requirement of the law during his lifetime and never once fall below God's holy standard, then that man can escape the penalty for sin, which is death. However, every thinking and honest man knows that he cannot keep the law of God in every single detail—not all the time. He knows that he sometimes comes short in...

- behavior
- motive
- service
- emotions
- worship

Every thinking and honest person knows that he is nowhere close to being perfect nor to attaining perfection. He knows that he fails and comes short too often. He knows that what this verse says is exactly true: no man can continue in and do <u>all things</u> which are written in the law of God.

> **"For Moses describeth the righteousness which is of the law, That the man which doeth those things shall live by them" (Ro.10:5).**

2. God's chosen way for approaching Him is to "live by faith." Scripture declares as clearly as it can: no man is justified by the law in the sight of God. As stated above, God is perfect; He is perfectly righteous. No man can achieve perfection; therefore, no man can live in the presence of God. No matter how good he is or how much good he does, he cannot achieve per-

fection. The fact is evident; for if a man had achieved perfection, he would be perfect—living forever in a perfect state of being, even on this earth.

But note this: God is love. So what God does is take a person's faith and count that faith as righteousness, as perfection. Therefore, a man is able to live in God's presence by faith or justification. The point is this: God's way for a man to approach Him is the way of faith: "The just shall live by faith."

Note also that the law is not of faith, but any man who attempts to live by the law will be allowed to so live. But the man must realize: he shall be judged by the law.

> **"Therefore by the deeds of the law there shall no flesh be justified in his sight: for by the law is the knowledge of sin" (Ro.3:20).**

QUESTIONS:

1. Do you believe that men are under a curse? What is a curse? What steps have you taken to escape this curse?
2. What are some of the logical results of a man who lives under the curse?
3. Why do you think God wants you to approach Him by faith?

A CLOSER LOOK:

Chapter 3 gives an excellent study of the law.

1. The law carries with it a curse (Gal.3:10). The curse is the mark of death and the mark of condemnation or guilt: alienation from God both in this life and throughout all eternity (cp. Dt.27:1f; 28:15; Ro.6:23; 2 Cor.3:7, 9).
2. There is a righteousness which is of the law (Ro.10:5-10; Gal.3:12). That righteousness promises life to any man who can obey the law perfectly. If a man can meet every requirement of the law during his lifetime and never once fall below God's holy standard, then that man can escape the penalty of sin which is death.
3. Jesus Christ delivers man from the curse of the law (Gal.3:13). What does this mean? Jesus Christ kept the law in every single detail. Therefore, He bore no guilt; and He bore no penalty, no mark of death. He had the right to stand before God and claim eternal life, the right to never experience death. He was perfect; He had secured incorruptible righteousness. The glorious gospel is that instead of claiming this right for Himself, He offered to give His perfection and righteousness to the people of the earth and to take their sins upon Himself. He offered to swap His righteousness for man's unrighteousness, to swap His life for man's life. This glorious expression of substitutionary love was the very purpose for which God had created the earth. God willed to show His great and unsearchable love that gave itself so perfectly (Eph.1:5f). The great tragedy is that man has so much difficulty accepting so great a love (1 Cor.1:18).

   It also means another thing. Jesus Christ accomplishes the same purpose that God intended for the law, except much more. He not only sets the same ideals and standards before us, but He also relates Himself to us. Whereas the law is a set of cold letters with no power to give life (Gal.3:21), Jesus Christ is a living person possessing the power to raise the dead to life again. He sets the standards and gives the power to keep the standards. He has replaced the law in showing men the awfulness of their sin (through His death), and He adds the extra dimension of strength to live as He lived (Gal.5:22f; Eph.1:19f; 3:20).
4. The law was only meant to be a temporary arrangement between God and man (Gal.3:16). It was to extend only from Moses to Jesus Christ, for Jesus Christ is "the seed" to whom the promise of righteousness was given (see Mt.5:17). God never intended the law to be the way of salvation. It was for the temporary purpose of showing men their sin and its awfulness. Since Jesus Christ has come, He (His perfect life and righteousness) is to be the standard for men.
5. The law was given to show men their sin and to instill within them a personal guilt for disobeying God and His law (Ro.3:19-20; 7:7; Gal.3:19). This guilt was to lead men to seek and

trust God for salvation. Thus, the law stops every mouth from claiming self-righteousness and makes all the world guilty before God.

6. The law is inferior to God's promise of grace (Gal.3:19c-20). Three arguments show this.

⇒ First, the law was not given directly by God. The law was given by angels to men through Moses. Moses was a mediator. But God and God alone gave the promise of grace and righteousness to Abraham.

⇒ Second, the law was between two parties—man and God. If man kept the law, he would receive the reward of righteousness. The gift of righteousness was conditional under the law. But the promise of grace is given by God alone. No one can break that promise. If man simply believes, he receives the promise of righteousness.

⇒ Third, the giving of the law came after the promise to Abraham—four hundred and thirty years after. The promise of grace was given first before the law. Therefore, the law cannot void the promise. The promise of God stands.

7. The law has no power to give life (Gal.3:21). The law demands that each commandment be kept and obeyed. But it is mere words, cold and lifeless. It is entirely external to man; it sets outside the being of man. It has no energy whatever to help in keeping the law.

8. The Scripture is conclusive: all men are lawbreakers and under sin (Gal.3:22).

9. The believer is no longer under the law but under grace (Ro.6:14; 7:4; Gal.3:22). Man is unable to participate in the righteousness of the law, for he is totally incapable of fulfilling the law. But he can experience the grace of God by trusting the righteousness which Jesus Christ has secured. When a man believes in Jesus Christ, Jesus Christ judges that man righteous. That man becomes a "partaker of the divine nature of God" (2 Pt.1:4).

10. The law shuts man up under sin (Gal.3:23). Man is a permanent prisoner under the law. Under the law he is put in bondage and held captive all the days of his life. The only avenue of escape is Jesus Christ, that is, faith in Him. If Christ fails to deliver, then there is no escape, for the law does not free man; it enslaves.

11. The law was man's guardian to lead him to see his need for Christ (Gal.3:24). The schoolmaster was usually a trusted slave who was in charge of a child's moral welfare, but he had one particular duty to which Paul was referring. Every day the guardian took the child to school and delivered him to the teacher. And then at the end of the day, he returned for the child and brought him safely back home. This was what the law was to do. The law was to lead man to Christ, the true Teacher. The law does this by showing man that he cannot secure righteousness by himself. He must look to Christ, the real Teacher, for righteousness and acceptance by God. And once faith in Christ has come, there is no need for the law nor for any other guardian, for Jesus Christ brings us face to face with God.

12. The law is still in force for the unbeliever (1 Tim.1:8-14). It remains in force to condemn and to lead the unbeliever to see his need for God.

13. Men were not always transgressors (Ro.4:15; 5:20). There is no transgression where there is no law, for there is no law to transgress. But men were still sinners before the law was given to Moses. They were just not as aware of their sin nor did they sense as much guilt as was necessary to show their need for God. For that reason the law was given, that men might be more and more aware that they were sinners before God.

QUESTIONS:

1. Why did not Christ abolish the law when He came to earth?
2. Contrast the law with God's grace. How have you learned to balance the two in your life?

A CLOSER LOOK:

Justification—Faith: this verse is used three times in the new Testament. A different point is emphasized each time it is used. It tells how a man can be just with God (cp. Hab.2:3-4).

1. **"<u>The just</u> shall live by faith"** (Ro.1:17). Who can live by faith? Only the just. People make two claims to justification. The man who says "I am justified by doing the best I can" is simply saying that he expects God to excuse his sin. But God does not excuse sin; God forgives sin. Excusing sin is nothing more than license—allowing man to go on living as he wishes and always coming up short. Therefore, a man is not justified by doing the best he can—by living after the law. He is justified by faith, by trusting God to forgive him. Once a man has really trusted God, he is just. And the just then begins to live by faith. The former man, whether a legalist or a man of fleshly indulgence, has no opportunity to live by faith. Why? Simply because he never started the life of faith. It is the just, not the legalist or the man of sinful indulgence, who lives by faith.

2. **"The just <u>shall live</u> by faith"** (Gal.3:11). By what rule does a person live? By the principle of faith, not by the principle of works. The person declared just by faith shall live apart from works. The believer is saved by faith, and the believer lives by faith (Gal.3:11).

3. **"The just shall live <u>by faith</u>"** (Heb.10:38). By what power does a person live? By the power that is given him by God because of faith. The Christian believes God, believes in the promises God has made. Therefore, the believer does what God says. The power of faith energizes him to live a just life. Works have nothing to do with making him just nor with keeping him just.

<u>QUESTIONS:</u>
1. What do you think of when you hear the word justification?
2. What effect should justification have upon you day by day?

4. SCRIPTURE SAYS "CHRIST HAS REDEEMED US FROM THE CURSE" (v. 13-14).

The word "redeemed" means to buy back or to buy from or to ransom. Christ has bought man back and ransomed him from the curse of the law. That man has broken the law of God is unquestionable; every honest man knows this. Therefore, every man stands guilty before God and must be judged and condemned to bear the curse and punishment of the law. But this is the glorious news: Jesus Christ has redeemed us from the curse of the law. How?

1. Jesus Christ was made a curse for us. Simply stated, Jesus Christ took our condemnation, doom, death, and punishment upon Himself, bearing them all for us. Jesus Christ took our place as the lawbreaker and guilty party before God, and He bore the punishment of the lawbreaker for us. How was this possible?

   ⇒ Because Jesus Christ had obeyed and kept the law of God perfectly. He had never broken the law, not even once. He was sinless and perfect. He had secured the Ideal Righteousness and Perfection before God. Therefore, He bore no guilt and no penalty and no mark of death. He had the right to stand before God to claim eternal life, the right to be accepted by God so as never to experience death. He was perfect; He had secured incorruptible righteousness.

   ⇒ Because God is love. The glorious gospel is that instead of claiming the right to live in God's presence, Christ determined to give His perfection and righteousness to the people of the earth and to take their sin upon Himself. He was determined to swap His ideal righteousness for man's unrighteousness, to swap His ideal life for man's sinful life.

Stated as simply as possible, Jesus Christ substituted Himself, His perfect life, for man's sinful life. He substituted His obedience to God for man's disobedience. He bore man's sin and punishment so that man might stand righteous and perfect before God. Jesus Christ bore the curse of the law for us.

Note the Old Testament quotation: "Cursed is everyone that hangs on a tree" (Dt.21:23). This does not mean that a man is cursed because he is executed upon a tree, but rather that a man who is executed upon a tree is there because he is cursed, having been judged as a lawbreaker. Jesus Christ was the lawbreaker, taking the place of the transgressor; therefore, He was cursed (condemned) to die as the unlawful and disobedient sinner.

2. The purpose for Jesus Christ's bearing the curse of the law was to open the door of blessing to all men. Christ's bearing the curse of the law was the way God fulfilled His promise to Abraham: that all nations would be blessed in him. Christ's bearing the curse of the law is also the way that God gives the promises made to Abraham to the world. Any man who believes in Jesus Christ—that Christ bore the curse of the law for him—is accepted by God and given the blessings of the promised land eternally.

In summary, the man who believes in Christ receives the promise of God's Holy Spirit, that is, the promise...

- of the divine nature.

> **"Whereby are given unto us exceeding great and precious promises: that by these ye might be partakers of the divine nature, having escaped the corruption that is in the world through lust" (2 Pt.1:4).**

- of the new birth.

> **"Jesus answered and said unto him, Verily, verily, I say unto thee, Except a man be born again, he cannot see the kingdom of God. Nicodemus saith unto him, How can a man be born when he is old? can he enter the second time into his mother's womb, and be born? Jesus answered, Verily, verily, I say unto thee, Except a man be born of water and of the Spirit, he cannot enter into the kingdom of God. That which is born of the flesh is flesh; and that which is born of the Spirit is spirit" (Jn.3:3-6).**

- of being made a new creature.

> **"Therefore if any man be in Christ, he is a new creature: old things are passed away; behold, all things are become new" (2 Cor.5:17).**

- of being made into a new man.

> **"And that ye put on the new man, which after God is created in righteousness and true holiness" (Eph.4:24).**

ILLUSTRATION:

It took a "curse-breaker" to set us free from the guilt of sin. Jesus Christ took our place and took the curse upon Himself when He shed His blood for our sins.

> *"In his book Written in Blood, Robert Coleman tells the story of a little boy whose sister needed a blood transfusion. The doctor had explained that she had the same disease the boy had recovered from two years earlier. Her only chance for recovery was a transfusion from someone who had previously conquered the disease. Since the two children had the same rare blood type, the boy was the ideal donor.*
>
> *"'Would you give your blood to Mary?' the doctor asked.*
>
> *"Johnny hesitated. His lower lip started to tremble. Then he smiled and said, 'Sure, for my sister.'*
>
> *"Soon the two children were wheeled into the hospital room—Mary, pale and thin; Johnny, robust and healthy. Neither spoke, but when their eyes met, Johnny grinned.*

GALATIANS 3:6-14

"As the nurse inserted the needle into his arm, Johnny's smile faded. He watched the blood flow through the tube. With the ordeal almost over, his voice, slightly shaky, broke the silence. 'Doctor, when do I die?'

"Only then did the doctor realize why Johnny had hesitated, why his lip had trembled when he'd agreed to donate his blood. He'd thought giving his blood to his sister meant giving up his life. In that brief moment, he'd made his great decision.

"Johnny, fortunately, didn't have to die to save his sister. Each of us, however, has a condition more serious than Mary's, and it required Jesus to give not just His blood, but His life."[3]

QUESTIONS:

1. What are some ways you can thank Jesus for breaking the curse upon your life?
2. Why did Jesus go to the cross for you?
3. How would you explain His willingness to become a curse for you? Is this kind of love a part of your character—to lay your life down for others?

SUMMARY:

Throughout the ages, men have hammered away at the Word of God. But as men have come and gone, the Scriptures, like an anvil, remain unmarred. This *anvil* proves that a man is justified by faith:

1. Scripture uses Abraham to illustrate the truth.
2. Scripture "preached the gospel of faith to Abraham."
3. Scripture says "the law puts a man under the curse."
4. Scripture says "Christ has redeemed us from the curse."

PERSONAL JOURNAL NOTES
(Reflection & Response)

1. The most important thing that I learned from this lesson was:

2. The area that I need to work on the most is:

3. I can apply this lesson to my life by:

4. Closing Statement of Commitment:

---

[1] From the King's Business. Walter B. Knight. *3,000 Illustrations for Christian Service*, p.40-41.
[2] From Earnest Worker. Walter B. Knight. *Knight's Master Book of 4,000 Illustrations*, p.26-27.
[3] Craig B. Larson, Editor. *Illustrations for Preaching & Teaching*, p.25.

	C. The Proof of God's Covenant & Promise, 3:15-18		
1. God expects any covenant to be honored a. A man's covenant stands b. The point: God's covenant stands even more **2. God made His covenant with Abraham & his seed** a. Stated emphatically	15 Brethren, I speak after the manner of men; Though it be but a man's covenant, yet if it be confirmed, no man disannulleth, or addeth thereto. 16 Now to Abraham and his seed were the promises made. He saith not, And to seeds, as of many; but	as of one, And to thy seed, which is Christ. 17 And this I say, that the covenant, that was confirmed before of God in Christ, the law, which was four hundred and thirty years after, cannot disannul, that it should make the promise of none effect. 18 For if the inheritance be of the law, it is no more of promise: but God gave it to Abraham by promise.	b. The seed is Christ **3. God gave His covenant of faith before He gave the law** **4. God gave His covenant or inheritance (righteousness) by promise not by law**

Section III
THE PROOF THAT A MAN IS JUSTIFIED BY FAITH ALONE AND NOT BY WORKS, Galatians 3:1-4:7

Study 3: **THE PROOF OF GOD'S COVENANT & PROMISE**

Text: **Galatians 3:15-18**

Aim: To cling to the assurance of God's promises.

Memory Verse:

"For if the inheritance be of the law, it is no more of promise: but God gave it to Abraham by promise" (Galatians 3:18).

INTRODUCTION:

Do you *really* believe that God will keep His promises to you? Have you ever felt that God has forgotten you?

When God made a covenant with Abraham, it was more than just a few legal terms pasted on a piece of paper. God chose to take full responsibility for Abraham's destiny. God guaranteed His commitment to him, unconditionally.

As Christian believers, we also benefit from the Abrahamic Covenant. How? It guarantees our justification. What justification? That we are made righteous and acceptable to God through Jesus Christ. With that guarantee set in place, we need to do something: *live* our lives like we belong to God. Living a justified life affects the total person. Myron Augsburger speaks toward this gripping truth:

> *"The words holiness and sanctification are not prominent in much of Protestant theology. We have tended to speak of justification without [an] emphasis on sanctification...Holiness means that one belongs wholly to God. This is also the meaning of sanctification, being set apart as God's own possession. When this begins internally, with the heart, the transformation becomes something that affects the total person."*[1]

Some teachers in the Galatian churches were teaching a false doctrine, a very dangerous doctrine. They were saying that a person was not saved by the grace of God through faith alone; a man had to keep the rituals of the church and focus his life upon the law and upon doing all the good works he could possibly do. Very simply stated, if a man wanted to be acceptable to God, he had to be the very best person he could, be as religious as he could, and keep all the laws of God that he could.

This, of course, is totally wrong. A person is justified by faith alone; he is not justified by being religious and doing good and keeping the law. Religion, good works, and the law all have their place in the plan of God and in the life of man. But man is not saved and made acceptable to God by his own effort. Man cannot earn, win, or merit God's acceptance; for no matter how good and disciplined man may become, he is still short of God's glory which is perfection. Despite all of man's goodness and achievements, man is still too often polluted with...

- selfishness
- injustice
- transgressions
- pride
- lack of love
- envy
- anger
- bitterness
- unkindness
- favoritism
- lust
- evil thoughts
- immorality
- prejudice
- impatience
- being puffed up
- anger
- hatred
- failure to hope
- greed
- trespasses
- aloofness
- failure to honor God
- failure to worship
- unbecoming behavior
- being easily provoked
- failure to endure
- failure to pray

The list could go on and on. The point is that no matter how good we are, we are still guilty of sin and failure—we are short of God's glory, ever so short of perfection. Our goodness just cannot earn or merit acceptance with God. If God is going to accept us, it will be because we *believe Him*, truly <u>believe that He will accept us</u> and that He loves us enough to honor that belief. If God does not love us enough to accept our faith in Him, then we are hopelessly lost forever. Faith in Him—in His love and in His promise—is our only hope for salvation and acceptance by God.

This is the point of the present passage. God's covenant and promise to Abraham proves that justification is by faith and not by works of the law.

OUTLINE:

1. God expects any covenant to be honored (v.15).
2. God made His covenant with Abraham and his seed (v.16).
3. God gave His covenant of faith before He gave the law (v.17).
4. God gave His covenant or inheritance (righteousness) by promise—not by law (v.18).

1. GOD EXPECTS ANY COVENANT TO BE HONORED (v.15).

There is the illustration of a covenant between men. A covenant is an agreement made between two parties, a special relationship set up and established by two or more persons. The point is that once a covenant has been made and executed, it stands: it cannot be annulled or added to. By law, the promises of the covenant are sealed; both parties are bound to keep their word, their promise.

<u>ILLUSTRATION:</u>

We live in a society where promises are expected to be broken. Are you a man or woman of your word? Or are your commitments made or broken as a matter of "convenience"?

Years ago a department manager, Harry, in a retail store seemed to be bound for a steady rise up the corporate ladder in the company. As he worked faithfully and kept his witness for Christ before all of the employees, he was offered a position as a youth leader in a local church. With great excitement, he accepted the offer and turned in his notice to his manager. After he turned in his resignation, he asked for permission to select and train his replacement.

Tim was a non-Christian friend who had been an end-of-Christmas-layoff casualty. Harry had befriended Tim and had shared Christ with him. Sensing an opportunity to reach out in a practical way, Harry chose Tim to be his replacement. Harry had it all figured out: Train Tim for a month and then start at the church the next day.

Along the way, something went wrong. Either Harry was a good trainer or Tim was a fast learner, but Tim learned the job in two weeks and not four. Observing this, the store manager called Harry in his office and said, "Harry, I can't afford to pay two men to do the same job. Are you sure this church job is a guaranteed position? If not, I'll keep you and release Tim."

There was no struggle for an answer in Harry's heart. He had given both his job and his word to Tim. He quickly remembered the words of King David, **"He swears to his own hurt, and does not change" (Ps.15:4[b], NASB).** It turned out that the church position fell through. But did God honor Harry's integrity? Of course, God always takes care of those who are promise keepers. Did it make a difference in Tim? You bet! Years later, he became one of the key employees in his company. And to this day, he still remembers what Harry did for him.

QUESTIONS:

1. Are you in the habit of keeping promises that you make to others? What are the hardest promises for you to keep? Why?
2. For you, what is a stronger commitment: your *word* or your *name* written on a contract?
3. Do you think that God would ever break His covenant with you? What factors brought you to your conclusion?

2. GOD MADE HIS COVENANT WITH ABRAHAM AND HIS SEED (v.16).

How do we know that a person is justified by faith alone? Because God made His covenant with Abraham and *his seed*. Note that the promise was not given to Abraham alone, but it was also given to the *seed*, the descendants and offspring of Abraham. The promise or covenant with Abraham is covered in the Book of Genesis:

> **"And I will establish my covenant between me and thee and thy seed after thee in their generations for an everlasting covenant, to be a God unto thee, and to thy seed after thee. And I will give unto thee, and to thy seed after thee, the land wherein thou art a stranger, all the land of Canaan, for an everlasting possession; and I will be their God" (Gen.17:7-8).**

The important question is: Who is meant by the seed of Abraham? Scripture declares that it is Jesus Christ. The word "seed" is singular, not plural. Therefore, God's promise points to one single person, and that person is Jesus Christ. Jesus Christ is...

- the *seed* promised to Abraham.
- the *seed* who is to receive the promises made to Abraham. This is a phenomenal truth, and it means three significant things.

1. It means that the promises made to Abraham have passed down to Jesus Christ. Jesus Christ is the descendent who is to inherit the *promised land*, the land of Canaan for an *everlasting possession*. Canaan, of course, is a type of heaven and of the new heavens and earth which God has promised to recreate. The point is that Jesus Christ is to inherit the world and be exalted as the Sovereign Majesty of the universe, ruling and reigning forever and ever.
2. It means that believers, too, shall inherit the world and reign with Christ through all eternity. Abraham was promised that he would be the father of many nations or of many children, and believers are those children.

> **"Blessed are the meek [the humble, trusting, believing]: for they shall inherit the earth" (Mt.5:5)**

3. It means that faith is the way men become justified and acceptable to God.

> **"For the promise, that he should be the heir of the world, was not to Abraham, or to his seed, through the law, but through the righteousness of faith" (Ro.4:13).**

In summary Abraham believed God, and because he believed, God kept His covenant and promise.

⇒ Abraham has been given a *seed*, a descendent who has blessed the whole world, that is, Jesus Christ.

⇒ Abraham has also been given nations of people who are heirs of his and of Christ. And there is only one condition to receiving the inheritance: believing God, that is, following in the "steps of that faith of our father Abraham" (Ro.4:12).

"For what saith the scripture? Abraham believed God, and it was counted unto him for righteousness" (Ro.4:3).

⇒ He, Christ, and his descendents are to receive the promised land—a new heavens and earth that will be perfected eternally.

"For the promise, that he should be the heir of the world, was not to Abraham, or to his seed, through the law, but through the righteousness of faith. For if they which are of the law be heirs, faith is made void, and the promise made of none effect" (Ro.4:13-14).

QUESTIONS:
1. Who is Abraham's seed? Why is this important to know?
2. Do you think any of the promises made to Abraham have lost their power over the course of thousands of years? What is the secret behind the enduring quality of God's promises?
3. What part, if any, does the believer have in God's promises to Abraham?

3. GOD GAVE HIS COVENANT OF FAITH BEFORE HE GAVE THE LAW (v.17).

How do we know that a person is justified by faith alone? Because God gave His covenant of faith to Abraham before He gave the law to Moses. The covenant of faith preceded the covenant of law. The law of God did not even appear upon the scene until four hundred and thirty years after Abraham. Note two significant things.

1. When the law was given, the promise to Abraham had not yet been fulfilled; therefore, the law could not void or change the covenant of faith with Abraham. The promises of God to Abraham and his descendent, Jesus Christ, still stood. As Lehman Strauss points out:

⇒ The covenant of faith finds its roots in eternity past.

"For the law was given by Moses, but grace and truth came by Jesus Christ" (Jn.1:17).

⇒ Since Jesus Christ, who is eternal, existed before Abraham, the covenant of faith was given to Christ even before it was given to Abraham.[2]

2. The covenant made with Abraham told man how he was to follow God and receive the promises of God, that is, by faith. Therefore, when the law was given, it must have been given for a different purpose entirely. It could not have been given to show men how to follow God, for that truth was already established in the covenant of faith given to Abraham.

The point is clear: no man is justified by the law, that is, by self-effort and works, trying to become good and righteous through obeying the law. That was not the purpose of the law. A person is justified by faith and by faith alone.

APPLICATION:

God's covenant of faith or of grace is sure. It cannot be revoked or changed. *Believers* shall inherit the promises made to Abraham and Christ.

"Heaven and earth shall pass away: but my words shall not pass away" (Lk.21:33).

QUESTIONS:
1. Which is older: the law or God's covenant? That is, the law given to Moses or God's covenant given to Abraham? Why is this significant?
2. Why did God not "change the rules" when He gave the law regarding how to follow Him?
3. What difference does it make how God wants you to follow Him?

4. GOD GAVE HIS COVENANT OR INHERITANCE (RIGHTEOUSNESS) BY PROMISE—NOT BY LAW (v.18).

How do we know that a person is justified by faith alone? Because God gave His covenant or inheritance by promise, not by law.

William Barclay sums up this passage in a most descriptive way.

> *"Again and again Paul comes back to the same point. The whole problem of human life is to get into a right relationship with God. So long as we are afraid of God, so long as God is a grim stranger, there can be no peace in life. How can we achieve this right relationship? Shall we try to achieve it by a meticulous and even self-torturing obedience to the law, by performing endless deeds, by observing every smallest regulation the law lays down? If we take that way we are forever in default, for man's imperfection can never fully satisfy the perfection of God; we are forever frustrated, forever climbing up a hill in which the peak never comes in sight, forever under condemnation; but if we simply abandon this hopeless struggle and bring ourselves and our sin to God, then the grace of God opens its arms to us and we are at peace with a God who is no longer judge but father. Paul's whole argument is that that is what happened to Abraham; it was on that basis that God's covenant with Abraham was made. And nothing that came in later can change that covenant any more than anything can alter a will that has already been ratified and signed."*[3]

The inheritance given to Abraham is that of righteousness, of being accepted by God and given the privilege of living forever with Him in the new heavens and earth. The inheritance was not given to Abraham by law, that is, Abraham could not earn, win, or merit it; but as Scripture declares: "God gave it [the inheritance] to Abraham by promise."

APPLICATION:

The same promise is given to believers, that is, to all those who walk in the faith of Abraham: the promise of being counted righteous and acceptable to God, and of being given the privilege of living forever in the new heavens and earth.

"Let not your heart be troubled: ye believe in God, believe also in me. In my Father's house are many mansions: if it were not so, I would have told you. I go to prepare a place for you" (Jn.14:1-2).

ILLUSTRATION:

We should be thankful that God kept His promise after the law came to Moses. Can you imagine what life would be like if our justification came because of our ability to keep all of the rules—perfectly?

Booker T. Washington describes meeting an ex-slave from Virginia in his book Up from Slavery:

GALATIANS 3:15-18

"I found that this man had made a contract with his master, two or three years previous to the Emancipation Proclamation, to the effect that the slave was to be permitted to buy himself, by paying so much per year for his body; and while he was paying for himself, he was to be permitted to labor where and for whom he pleased.

"Finding that he could secure better wages in Ohio, he went there. When freedom came, he was still in debt to his master some 300 hundred dollars. Notwithstanding that the Emancipation Proclamation freed him from any obligation to his master, this black man walked the greater portion of the distance back to where his old master lived in Virginia, and placed the last dollar, with interest, in his hands.

"In talking to me about this, the man told me that he knew that he did not have to pay his debt, but that he had given his word to his master, and his word he had never broken. He felt that he could not enjoy his freedom till he had fulfilled his promise."[4]

The law did not change this man's commitment to keep his promise. Even more so, the law did not change God's plan for man. As Malachi 3:6 says: **"I am the LORD, I change not."**

QUESTIONS:

1. Can you really trust God to give you an inheritance--even through you sin and fall short?
2. How can you back up what you believe about God's promises?
3. Do man-made laws have any bearing or effect on God's promises?

SUMMARY:

The Christian believer has no reason to doubt God's promises. In particular, His promise to justify us has been guaranteed by His covenant to Abraham. The major points of our lesson reinforce this great truth:

1. God expects any covenant to be honored.
2. God made His covenant with Abraham and his seed.
3. God gave His covenant of faith before He gave the law.
4. God gave His covenant or inheritance (righteousness) by promise—not by law.

PERSONAL JOURNAL NOTES
(Reflection & Response)

1. The most important thing that I learned from this lesson was:

2. The area that I need to work on the most is:

3. I can apply this lesson to my life by:

4. Closing Statement of Commitment:

---

[1] From *The Christ-Shaped Conscience*. Selected from Christianity Today, (March 8, 1993), p.45.
[2] Lehman Strauss. *Devotional Studies in Galatians and Ephesians*, p.45.
[3] William Barclay. *The Letters to the Galatians and Ephesians*. "The Daily Study Bible." (Philadelphia, PA: Westminister Press, 1954), p.30.
[4] Craig B. Larson, editor. *Illustrations for Preaching & Teaching*, p.190.

	D. The Proof of the Law's Powerlessness, 3:19-22	but God is one. 21 Is the law then against the promises of God? God forbid: for if there had been a law given which could have given life, verily righteousness should have been by the law.	4. The law has no power to give life
1. The law was given to reveal sin—to make men more aware of their sins 2. The law was temporary 3. The law was not given by God but through a mediator; therefore, it is inferior	19 Wherefore then serveth the law? It was added because of transgressions, till the seed should come to whom the promise was made; and it was ordained by angels in the hand of a mediator. 20 Now a mediator is not a mediator of one,	22 But the Scripture hath concluded all under sin, that the promise by faith of Jesus Christ might be given to them that believe.	5. The law imprisons all men under sin

Section III
THE PROOF THAT A MAN IS JUSTIFIED BY FAITH ALONE AND NOT BY WORKS, Galatians 3:1-4:7

Study 4: THE PROOF OF THE LAW'S POWERLESSNESS

Text: **Galatians 3:19-22**

Aim: To expose the law's powerlessness to justify us.

Memory Verse:

"But the Scripture hath concluded all under sin, that the promise by faith of Jesus Christ might be given to them that believe" (Galatians 3:22).

INTRODUCTION:

One of the corny gags from the days of Vaudeville theater was someone pointing a gun at someone else, pulling the trigger and...BANG! said the flag as it hung from the barrel. The gun looked real and sounded real, but it proved to be harmless.

The law has the same affect on the Christian believer. It looks intimidating and it sounds intimidating, but it is powerless. The law cannot justify us. Those who claim that the law does justify are just shouting BANG!

There were some teachers in the Galatian churches who were teaching a false doctrine: that a person is justified (acceptable to God) because...

- he does the very best he can: he honestly tries to obey the law of God and to do as much good as he can.
- he practices religion: he keeps the rituals, ceremonies, and rules of the church.
- he has submitted to the basic ritual of the church (circumcision, church membership, baptism, or whatever).

All of these are important: everyone should be faithful in obeying the law and in practicing religion and in being baptized. However, Scripture is abundantly clear: these are not the things that *actually justify* a person. Jesus Christ alone justifies a person. Man can do nothing whatsoever—exert no energy, no effort, no work—to make himself acceptable to God. A person is acceptable and justified before God only when he truly believes in God's Son, Jesus Christ. There are many people who...

- exert all kinds of energy and effort in keeping the law and doing the best they can, but they *do not believe in Jesus Christ*.

- practice religion, but they *do not believe in Jesus Christ.*
- have been circumcised and baptized, but they *do not believe in Jesus Christ.*

The raw energy—the fundamental act—that saves a person is *faith in Jesus Christ, true faith* in God's very own Son. When a person truly believes in God's Son, God takes that person's belief and counts his belief as righteousness. God accepts that person because he honors God's Son—honors Jesus Christ by entrusting and giving all he is and has into His keeping.

Since this is so, why then did God give the law to man? If we are not saved and justified by obeying the law of God and doing the best we can, what is the purpose of the law? This is the discussion of this passage: to show that the law is powerless in saving a man. And the powerlessness of the law actually proves that a person is justified or made acceptable to God by faith.

OUTLINE:

1. The law was given to reveal sin—to make men more aware of their sins (v.19).
2. The law was temporary (v.19).
3. The law was not given by God, but through a mediator; therefore, it is inferior (v.19-20).
4. The law has no power to give life (v.21).
5. The law imprisons all men under sin (v.22).

1. THE LAW WAS GIVEN TO REVEAL SIN—TO MAKE MEN MORE AWARE OF THEIR SINS (v.19).

How do we know that the law does not justify or make a person acceptable to God? Because the law was given to reveal sin—to make people more aware of their sins. Note the crucial fact: the law was not given to make men righteous, but...

- to make men aware of their sin and condemnation.
- to show men that they are short of God's glory.
- to stir men to pay attention to the fact that they are sinners.
- to stop every mouth from boasting and claiming self-righteousness.
- to awaken men to their crying need for God's help.
- to plant in man's mind that he desperately needs God to save him from sin and death.
- to arouse every mouth to confess its need for a Savior from sin and its punishment (death).

> **"Therefore by the deeds of the law there shall no flesh be justified in his sight: for by the law is the knowledge of sin" (Ro.3:20).**
>
> **"Wherefore the law was our schoolmaster to bring us unto Christ, that we might be justified by faith" (Gal.3:24).**

ILLUSTRATION:

What does God use to get your attention, to show that you are a long way from perfection? Does He use other people or circumstances?

Long ago a story was told about a proud fishing pond and a fish. Across the land, fishermen would come and exclaim how clear the water was in this pond. Upon hearing yet another positive accolade, the pond's level of pride began to reach flood stage. "I must be the best and clearest pond in the world!" It didn't take long for the old fish at the bottom to grow weary of this overdone pride. He had heard it for years. And he, better than anyone, knew what was really in this pond.

Resting on the bottom of the pond, the old fish began to rapidly flutter his fins. As he did the motion of the water began to stir up the silt on the bottom. It did not take long for the pond to fill up with a murky cloud.

"Stop! What are you doing to me? What have you done? How dare you dirty me up?!" screamed the offended pond. The fish responded in measured and striking words: "I haven't done a thing to you except to show what has been in you all the time.

And that is what the law does to us. It simply shows us the sin that has settled in the bottom of our hearts. Just in case we forget who we really are, the law reminds us how desperately we need the cleansing power of our precious Savior, the Lord Jesus Christ.

QUESTIONS:
1. How can you know that the law is powerless to save you?
2. Since the law is powerless to justify you, why did God give the law?
3. When the "old fish" swims at the bottom of your heart, what kinds of things is he likely to stir up? Which one of these things need your immediate attention?

2. THE LAW WAS TEMPORARY (v.19).

How do we know that the law does not justify or make a person acceptable to God? Because the law was temporary. It had a certain course to run and when it was run, it was to be set aside. To say that the law was temporary frightens some believers, for they fear that such a teaching makes way for loose living. Nothing could be further from the truth. Note what Scripture says:

> **"[The law] was added because of transgressions, till the seed should come" (Gal.3:19).**

When Jesus Christ came, the law was to be set aside. The law was *meant* to have only a temporary purpose and life span. It was to extend only from Moses to Jesus Christ, for Jesus Christ is "the seed" to whom the promise of righteousness was given. God *never intended the law* to be the way of salvation. It was only for the temporary purpose of showing men their sin and its awfulness.

⇒ However, note: since Jesus Christ has come, He (His perfect life and righteousness) is to be the standard for men. Jesus Christ fulfilled the law; that is, in Jesus Christ, God gave man more than just mere words to describe how He wants man to live. He gave man the Life, the Person who perfectly pictures and demonstrates the law before the world's very eyes. Jesus Christ is the Picture, the Living Example, the Pattern, the Demonstration of life as it is to be lived. He is the Perfect Picture of God's will, the Ideal Man, the Representative Man, the Pattern for all men.

> **"And the Word was made flesh, and dwelt among us, (and we beheld his glory, the glory as of the only begotten of the Father,) full of grace and truth" (Jn.1:14).**
>
> **"Who is the image of the invisible God, the firstborn of every creature" (Col.1:15).**

Now note: since the law was meant to be temporary until Christ came, does that mean that the law has no value for men today? Could we just cut the law out of our Bibles and be just as well off? No, a thousand times no! Jesus Christ *fulfilled the law*; therefore, the law and its righteousness is part of His nature. Therefore, when a man looks at Jesus Christ, he sees the perfection of His nature, and that perfection includes the righteousness of the law. To cut the law out of our Bibles would be to erase part of our understanding of Jesus Christ and part of His very nature.

"Think not that I am come to destroy the law, or the prophets: I am not come to destroy, but to fulfil" (Mt.5:17).

"For what the law could not do, in that it was weak through the flesh, God sending his own Son in the likeness of sinful flesh, and for sin, condemned sin in the flesh" (Ro.8:3).

Note another point as well: the law is still in force for the unbelieving world. Why? Because all unbelievers who have not trusted Jesus Christ are trusting their own righteousness to make them acceptable to God. They are still trying to become righteous by the law. Therefore, God shall judge them by the law.

"For they being ignorant of God's righteousness, and going about to establish their own righteousness, have not submitted themselves unto the righteousness of God. For Christ is the end of the law for righteousness to every one that believeth" (Ro.10:3-4).

Matthew Henry points out another fact that should be noted: the law can still be used to convince men of sin and to restrain them from living loose and evil lives.[1]

QUESTIONS:

1. Even though the law was only temporary, it still serves a useful purpose today. What does it do in your life?
2. What does the Bible mean when it says that Christ came to fulfil the law?
3. What kind of harm do you create if you separate Christ from the law?
4. Can an unbeliever achieve perfection through the law? Why or why not?

3. THE LAW WAS NOT GIVEN BY GOD BUT THROUGH A MEDIATOR; THEREFORE, IT IS INFERIOR (v.19-20).

How do we know that the law does not justify or make a person acceptable to God? Because the law was not given directly by God, but through a mediator; therefore, it is inferior. Two arguments show this.

1. The law was not given directly by God. The law came from God, but it was given by angels to Moses and then to man. Moses stood as a mediator between God and man in the giving of the law; therefore, the law came to man as a second-hand thing. But not the promise of God. God Himself gave the promise of grace and righteousness (that is, of His acceptance and eternal life). Abraham received the promise of God directly from God. Therefore, the promise of God is bound to be superior to the law, for it involves a more personal contact (relationship) with God.

2. The law was between two parties—man and God. In the covenant of law, man and God both had responsibilities or work to do. Man had to keep the law, and if he did, God would act and reward him with the gift of righteousness. The gift of righteousness was conditional under the law.

However, the promise of righteousness or grace was given by God alone. No one could break that promise. If man (Abraham) simply believed God's promise, he received the promise of righteousness and grace.

QUESTIONS:

1. To whom was the law first given? Why does this make the law inferior?
2. What was man's responsibility to the law?
3. Exactly what has qualified you to receive God's promise of righteousness and grace?

4. THE LAW HAS NO POWER TO GIVE LIFE (v.21).

How do we know that the law does not justify or make a person acceptable to God? Because the law has no power to give life.

1. The law is only words and rules. It can only inject the idea of behavior into the mind of a person. It can only demand—demand that each precept be kept and obeyed. The law is mere words, cold and lifeless. It is entirely external to man, outside the body of man. It has no spirit, no life, no power to enable a person to do the law. It cannot help man to any degree whatsoever as he tries to keep the law. The law demands obedience, but it leaves man entirely on his own as he struggles to obey.

2. The law cannot give life to man. It is not a living being with the power to give life. If it were, then righteousness would have come by law. But, as stated, the law has no life and it has no power. It is mere writing, mere words and rules. However, this is not true of Jesus Christ. Jesus Christ is both a Person and a life. Therefore, He is able to put spirit and life to the words and rules of the law. He is able to live the life described by the words and rules. As such, He is able to inject both the idea and the power to behave into a person's mind and life. It is now His life that sets the standard and the rule for the believer; it is His spirit and life that give the believer power to obey.

> **"For what the law could not do, in that it was weak through the flesh, God sending his own Son in the likeness of sinful flesh, and for sin, condemned sin in the flesh" (Ro.8:3).**

ILLUSTRATION:

Doing all the right things and having all the right titles are of no benefit to the Christian believer. There is only one thing that will grant us justification. David Seamands ends his book Healing Grace with this story:

"For more than six hundred years the Hapsburgs exercised political power in Europe. When Emperor Franz-Joseph I of Austria died in 1916, his was the last of extravagant imperial funerals.

"A procession of dignitaries and elegantly dressed court personages escorted the coffin, draped in the black and gold imperial colors. To the accompaniment of a military band's somber dirges and by the light of torches, the cortege descended the stairs of the Capauchin Monastery in Vienna. At the bottom was a great iron door leading to the Hapsburg family crypt. Behind the door was the Cardinal-Archbishop of Vienna.

"The officer in charge followed the prescribed ceremony, established centuries before. 'Open!' he cried.

"'Who goes there?' responded the Cardinal.

"'We bear the remains of his Imperial and Apostolic Majesty, Franz-Joseph I, by the grace of God Emperor of Austria, King of Hungary, Defender of the Faith, Prince of Bohemia-Moravia, Grand Duke of Lombardy, Venezia, Styriga…" The officer continued to list the Emperor's thirty-seven titles.

"'We know him not,' replied the Cardinal. 'Who goes there?'

"The officer spoke again, this time using a much abbreviated and less ostentatious title reserved for times of expediency.

"'We know him not,' the Cardinal said again. 'Who goes there?'

"The officer tried a third time, stripping the emperor of all but the humblest of titles: 'We bear the body of Franz-Joseph, our brother, a sinner like us all!'

"At that, the doors swung open, and Franz-Joseph was admitted.

"In death all are reduced to the same level. Neither wealth nor fame can open the way of salvation, but only God's grace, given to those who will humbly acknowledge their need."[2]

The law is powerless. It cannot open heaven's door for you. It cannot give you life. Where have you placed your trust? In the law or in Christ?

QUESTIONS:
1. What can you count on the law to do for you?
2. Why would someone think that the law gives life to men?
3. Why is Jesus Christ superior to the law?
4. In what ways are you tempted to look to the law for direction? What can you do in order to redirect your focus upon the Lord?

5. THE LAW IMPRISONS ALL MEN UNDER SIN (v.22).

How do we know that the law does not justify or make a person acceptable to God? Because the law imprisons all men under sin. Note several significant facts.

1. "The Scripture" refers to the law. The law of God, or the Scripture, is conclusive: all men are lawbreakers—all men are under sin.

2. "Under sin" means to be shut up as a prisoner in the solitary hopeless depths or solitary confinement of a dungeon.

> **"What then? are we better than they? No, in no wise: for we have before proved both Jews and Gentiles, that they are all under sin; as it is written, There is none righteous, no, not one....Therefore by the deeds of the law there shall no flesh be justified in his sight: for by the law is the knowledge of sin" (Ro.3:9-10, 20).**

3. The great purpose of the law is stated again: to drive men to seek the promise of Jesus Christ, that is, righteousness by faith. When men look at the law and see that they are sinners, they are driven to seek a Savior. Man can seek and trust the righteousness which Jesus Christ has secured. When a man believes in Jesus Christ, Jesus Christ judges that man righteous, and that man becomes a **"partaker of the divine nature of God" (2 Pt.1:4).**

> **"Therefore being justified by faith, we have peace with God through our Lord Jesus Christ" (Ro.5:1).**

ILLUSTRATION:

No matter who we are, the law pulls us down. No one can defy the law's lethal gravitational pull. J. Vernon McGee illustrates this point for us:

> *"Picture a building about twenty-four stories high. There are three men on top of the building, and the superintendent goes up to see them and warns, 'Now be very careful, don't step off of this building or you will be killed. It will mean death for you.' One of the fellows says, 'This crazy superintendent is always trying to frighten people. I don't believe that if I step off this building I will die.' So he deliberately steps off into the air. Suppose that when he passes the tenth floor, somebody looks out the window and asked him, 'Well how's it going?' and he says, 'So far, so good.' But, my friend, he hasn't arrived yet. There is death at the bottom...*
>
> *"Now suppose another fellow becomes frightened at what the superintendent said. He runs for the elevator, or the steps, and accidentally slips. He skids right off the edge of the building and falls to the street below....The third fellow...is thrown off the building by some gangsters...Now the man who was thrown off the building is just as dead as the man who deliberately stepped off and the man who accidentally slipped off the building. All of these men broke the law of gravitation, and death was inevitable for all of them. It is in the fact, you see, and not the de-*

gree. It is the fact that they went over the edge—they all broke the law of gravitation."[3]

If you are going to take a leap, leap into the waiting arms of the Lord Jesus Christ. Allow Him to pull you close to His side.

QUESTIONS:

1. The law continually convicts man of sin. What solution has God provided?
2. What feelings would a prisoner experience if he were trapped in a dungeon? Have you ever experienced some of the same feelings? What one thing freed you from a prison of sin, a "life without parole"?
3. What does this verse teach you about the nature of man? Why do some people tend to think that man is basically good? How does Scripture address this misconception?

SUMMARY:

Is the law pointing a gun at you? Are you afraid of what will happen when the trigger is pulled? BANG! It's only a cruel gag. Remember, the law has no power over you because...

1. The law was given to reveal sin—to make men more aware of their sins.
2. The law was temporary.
3. The law was not given by God, but through a mediator; therefore, it is inferior.
4. The law has no power to give life.
5. The law imprisons all men under sin.

PERSONAL JOURNAL NOTES
(Reflection & Response)

1. The most important thing that I learned from this lesson was:

2. The area that I need to work on the most is:

3. I can apply this lesson to my life by:

4. Closing Statement of Commitment:

---

[1] Matthew Henry. *Matthew Henry's Commentary,* Vol.5 (Old Tappan, NJ: Fleming H. Revell Co.), p.661.

[2] *Alan J. White* (Selected from *Leadership*, Fall, 1994), p.42.

[3] J. Vernon McGee. *Thru The Bible, Vol.5* (Nashville, TN: Thomas Nelson Publishers, 1983), p.171.

GALATIANS 3:23-29

	E. The Proof of What Faith Does for Us, 3:23-29	26 For ye are all the children of God by faith in Christ Jesus.	2. Faith makes us children of God a. By causing us to focus upon Christ
		27 For as many of you as have been baptized into Christ have put on Christ.	b. By clothing us with Christ, with His righteousness & Sonship
1. Faith in Christ was before the law: Two pictures of the law a. Before faith: The law was a prison for man	23 But before faith came, we were kept under the law, shut up unto the faith which should afterwards be revealed.	28 There is neither Jew nor Greek, there is neither bond nor free, there is neither male nor female: for ye are all one in Christ Jesus.	3. Faith in Christ makes us one: Eliminates all distinctions & prejudices
b. Before faith: The law was a guardian for man	24 Wherefore the law was our schoolmaster to bring us unto Christ, that we might be justified by faith.		
	25 But after that faith is come, we are no longer under a schoolmaster.	29 And if ye be Christ's, then are ye Abraham's seed, and heirs according to the promise.	4. Faith in Christ makes us heirs of the promise

Section III
THE PROOF THAT A MAN IS JUSTIFIED BY FAITH ALONE AND NOT BY WORKS, Galatians 3:1-4:7

Study 5: THE PROOF OF WHAT FAITH DOES FOR US

Text: Galatians 3:23-29

Aim: To grasp the great benefits of faith.

Memory Verse:
"And if ye be Christ's, then are ye Abraham's seed, and heirs according to the promise" (Galatians 3:29).

INTRODUCTION:

How many times have you begun a journey, only to realize that you made a wrong turn along the way? You wanted to go south, but you were actually heading west. Sincere as you were about wanting to go south, your destination was westward bound.

Many of us have turned down the wrong road in life, trusting in our works and the law to save us. We have been sincere, but we have been sincerely wrong. How can we make a mid-course correction? By faith, we must begin to trust the Lord to show us the way.

Some people in the churches of Galatia were spreading a false teaching. They were saying that a person is justified by works and law; that is, that a person becomes acceptable to God by subjecting himself to Christ, but he must also subject himself to the law and do the very best he can. They were saying that, yes, Christ is important; but a commitment to live by the law—a commitment to do the very best one can—is also essential in order to be saved and acceptable to God.

The false teaching sounds good, for a person not only should, but he must, do the best he can. Actually a person should not only do the best he can in seeking God but in everything he undertakes. However, Scripture is very clear: man is not justified by being good and doing good. Man just cannot be good enough nor do enough good to become perfect. God is perfect; therefore, man must become perfect if he is to live with God.

How then can a person become acceptable to God? By faith in Jesus Christ. When a person believes in Jesus Christ, he honors God's Son, and God honors the person who honors His Son. God honors the person by doing the very thing for which the person trusted Christ. For example, if a person believes that Christ died for his sins, God counts it so. If a person believes that God considers him righteous in Christ, God considers it so. And so on. Note, however: belief does not mean *mental assent*, just believing in one's thoughts and mind that Jesus Christ is the Savior. True belief is *spiritual commitment*, the commitment of one's heart and life--all that one is and all that one has--to Christ.

How do we know that we are justified by faith and not by the law and doing the best we can? Because of what faith does for us.

OUTLINE:

1. Faith in Christ was before the law: Two pictures of the law (v.23-25).
2. Faith makes us children of God (v.26-27).
3. Faith in Christ makes us one: eliminates all distinctions and prejudices (v.28).
4. Faith in Christ makes us heirs of the promise (v.29).

1. FAITH IN CHRIST WAS BEFORE THE LAW: TWO PICTURES OF THE LAW (v.23-25).

There are two pictures which clearly illustrate the purpose of the law.

1. The law was a prison for man. Before faith came, that is, before Christ died, man was "kept under the law." The word for "kept under" means to be guarded, kept in custody, imprisoned, held in bondage. Very simply, the law shuts man up under sin; it imprisons and holds man in bondage to sin. How?

   a. The law shows man exactly where he fails—exactly where he comes short. There is no question about it: the law said to do this, but the man did that. He failed or disobeyed. The failure is clearly spelled out, just as clearly as a speed limit sign spells out the violation of the speeder.

   b. The law accuses and condemns man. As soon as a person violates the law, the law charges him. The law is in black and white, written down, so there is no question about its having been broken. Therefore, it preys upon his mind, cuts and convicts his heart. Guilt and conviction take over, and the man is troubled and vexed to varying degrees, all dependent on the seriousness of the violation.

   c. The law has no life and no power to deliver man from the punishment due him for his violation. This is the whole point: the law reveals the violation and condemns man; it imprisons him. The law does not deliver man; it condemns man to bondage. It continues and continues to point out man's sins and failures. And the case of the law is endless: its finger of accusation points out the man's failure every time he violates it. The bondage to the law is ongoing.

   The only hope for man is for someone to appear on the scene with the power to release him. That someone has appeared: Jesus Christ has come to set us free. But note: as prisoners we have to accept His deliverance. The choice is ours. We can believe and trust His power to deliver us or not.

2. The law was a schoolmaster or guardian for man. The law was man's guardian to lead him to see his need for Christ. He was usually a trusted slave who was in charge of a child's moral welfare, but he had one particular duty to which Paul was referring. Every day the guardian took the child to school and delivered him to the teacher. And then at the end of the day, he returned for the child and brought him safely back home. This was what the law was to do. The law was to lead man to Christ, the true Teacher. The law does this by showing man that he is utterly unable to secure righteousness by himself. He must look to Christ, the real Teacher, for righteousness and acceptance by God, that is, for justification by faith. And once Christ (faith in Him) has come, there is no need for the law nor for any other guardian, for Jesus Christ brings us face to face with God.

QUESTIONS:
1. The law is a prison for man. Can anyone successfully escape from this prison? Why do men think they can escape on their own?
2. Does the law have any power to deliver its prisoners? Where does your hope of deliverance come from? Where does your faith come in?
3. In what practical ways does God use the law to bring us to Christ?

2. FAITH MAKES US CHILDREN OF GOD (v.26-27).

How do we know that we are justified by faith instead of by the law and by doing the best we can? Because faith makes us children of God. As stated in the previous point, Jesus Christ brings us face to face with God. He stirs God to adopt us as children of God. How? By faith. Note two crucial points.

1. Faith causes us to focus upon God's Son, Jesus Christ. Man can rest upon one thing: God will accept anyone who *focuses* upon His Son Jesus Christ, for God loves His Son to the ultimate degree. God is no less than any normal father who loves his son. In fact, God is much more than man; He is perfect. Therefore, God loves His Son, Jesus Christ, with a perfect love. This simply means that God will honor any person who honors His Son by believing and trusting Him. If a person believes in Jesus Christ for righteousness, then God will honor that man by counting him righteous.

The point is this: the person who tries to become acceptable to God by the law and by doing the best he can—the man who focuses upon the law and good works—keeps his mind upon the law and struggles to be good. God is not the center and focus of his thoughts and life; the law and works are.

But the person who has *faith in Jesus Christ* focuses upon Christ. He honors God's Son; therefore, God accepts his faith, the focus of his life, as righteousness. The person becomes acceptable to God. God actually accepts the person as a child of His. How is this possible? The answer is the subject of the following point.

2. Faith clothes us with Christ, with His righteousness and Sonship. This is a most wonderful truth, for it tells us that we can actually "put on" Christ—a glorious revelation! The phrase "put on" is the picture of putting on clothes, of covering oneself. All that Christ is can cover us. Christ is two things that hold great significance for us.

a. Christ is the very embodiment of righteousness. He is the Son of God who came to earth to secure righteousness for us. He lived a sinless and perfect life; He always obeyed God, never violating the law or will of God—not even once. Therefore, He was the Perfect, Ideal Man; He was the Pattern of what every man should be. As the Ideal and Perfect pattern, He could represent all men; and this is exactly what happened. Jesus Christ is our righteousness. When we believe in Him, God clothes us with Christ, with His righteousness. And, because we are clothed with the righteousness of Jesus Christ, God sees us in His Son and accepts us.

ILLUSTRATION:

Picture this illustration. Let your left hand represent Christ, and your right index finger represent you. Now, wrap your left hand around your index finger. What do you see? You see Christ, not yourself, for Christ is covering you. So it is with faith. When you believe in Jesus Christ, your faith covers you with Jesus Christ and His righteousness.

"For he hath made him to be sin for us, who knew no sin; that we might be made the righteousness of God in him" (2 Cor.5:21).

b. Christ is the Son of God; therefore, to be clothed with Christ means that we are covered with His Sonship. When God looks at the believer, He sees His Son Jesus Christ covering him; therefore, He counts the believer as a son of His. This is the way we become children of God: by faith in Jesus Christ, God's Son. When we believe that Jesus Christ is God's Son, God takes our faith and places us in Christ, and to be in Christ is to be in the Sonship of Christ. God actually sees us in Jesus Christ, in His Son. Therefore, he accepts us as children of His—all because our faith has covered us with Christ.

> **"But as many as received him, to them gave he power to become the sons of God, even to them that believe on his name" (Jn.1:12).**

ILLUSTRATION:

How much do you value your relationship as a child of God? Sometimes, we might be tempted to doubt God's love. We fail time and again and come up so short. Some of us even commit terrible sin. We wonder, "How could God forgive me? How could He love me after I've failed so much and so terribly? Jim Adams shares this eye-opening story with us:

> *"Perhaps no composer has captured the musical heart and soul of America as did Irving Berlin. In addition to familiar favorites such as 'God Bless America' and 'Easter Parade,' he wrote, 'I'm Dreaming of a White Christmas,' which still ranks as the all-time best-selling musical score.*
>
> *"In an interview for the San Diego Union, Don Freeman asked Berlin, 'Is there any question you've never been asked that you would like someone to ask you?'*
>
> *"'Well, yes, there is one,' he replied. 'What do you think of the many songs you've written that didn't become hits?' My reply would be that I still think they are wonderful.'*
>
> *"God, too, has an unshakable delight in what—and whom—He has made. He thinks each of His children is wonderful, and whether they're a 'hit' in the eyes of others or not, He will always think they're wonderful."*[1]

QUESTIONS:

1. What is a person's relationship to God before he is saved?
2. Can you be a child of God without having faith in Christ? Why or why not?
3. Why does God accept only our faith when He adopts us?
4. What good works have you done that convinced God to adopt you into His family?

A CLOSER LOOK:

Baptism: note the reference to *baptism* instead of *belief*:

> **"For as many of you as have been baptized into Christ have put on Christ" (v.27).**

Why did Paul switch from using the word *believe* to the word *baptism*? Why did he not say:

"For as many of you as have believed in Christ have put on Christ"?

Is Paul saying that a person is *saved by* baptism? Any thinking and honest person knows that there are thousands and thousands of people who have been baptized, and yet they live like the devil himself. Therefore, Paul could not mean that it is baptism that causes God to clothe a person with Christ.

Similarly, any honest and thinking person knows that there are thousands and thousands of people who *profess faith* and yet live like the devil himself. Therefore, Paul could not mean what the general public means by faith.

What Paul is saying is what Scripture declares: a true believer fulfills all the righteousness of Christ which includes baptism. The believer lives for Christ, and living for Christ includes the ordinance of being baptized, for baptism pictures his faith. Baptism (and repentance) is the *first and immediate* evidence of faith; therefore, faith and baptism are closely linked, so closely that Paul can speak of baptism as faith.

QUESTIONS:

1. Why is baptism important?
2. Why do some people think that baptism saves them? What does the Scripture say?
3. What is the relationship between faith and baptism? Do you think that it is possible to have a meaningful relationship with God with only one of these? Explain your answer.

3. FAITH IN CHRIST MAKES US ONE: ELIMINATES ALL DISTINCTIONS AND PREJUDICES (v.28).

How do we know that we are justified by faith rather than by the law and by doing the best we can? Because faith in Christ makes us one, eliminating all distinctions and prejudices.

"There is neither Jew nor Greek, there is neither bond nor free, there is neither male nor female: for ye are all one in Christ Jesus" (v.28).

This is a startling truth: Jesus Christ is the answer to all the prejudice, bitterness, hatred, oppression, and inequalities of the world. How can He solve the divisions among men? Note the phenomenal statement: "Ye are all one in Christ Jesus." What is there about Jesus Christ that makes us one?

1. Every believer stands on an equal footing before Jesus Christ: the footing of faith. No person is accepted for any reason other than faith. All persons who come to Jesus Christ come because...

- they are ever so short of Christ.
- they are ever so different from Christ.
- they are ever so imperfect.

Yet, Jesus Christ accepts them. Jesus Christ reaches out to embrace all believers despite their being so much less and so different from Him. Therefore, when we look at another believer who differs from us, we do just what Jesus Christ did for us. We love, accept, and embrace him; differences do not matter. All that matters is love, acceptance, and brotherhood in Christ.

2. Every true believer loves and stands *in Jesus Christ*. Therefore, when we look at another believer, we see him *in Christ*. We are not to see the believer but to see Christ covering the believer. We are to pay no attention to his color, nationality, sex, social status, or any other differences. Differences just do not matter. All that matters is that we all grow into the image of Christ—love, accept, and become more and more the brothers and sisters of God.

"For there is no difference between the Jew and the Greek: for the same Lord over all is rich unto all that call upon him" (Ro.10:12).

ILLUSTRATION:

If we walk with Christ, we will notice that petty things that divide us will fade away. How is this possible? By the cross. At the foot of the cross, all the ground is level. Listen to this humorous, yet sad discussion between two brothers. Comedian Emo Philips tells this story:

"In conversation with a person I had recently met, I asked, 'Are you Protestant or Catholic?' My new acquaintance replied, 'Protestant.' I said, 'Me too! What franchise?'

"He answered, 'Baptist.'

"'Me too,' I said. 'Northern Baptist or Southern Baptist?'

"'Northern Baptist,' he replied.

"'Me too!' I shouted.

"We continued to go back and forth. Finally I asked, 'Northern conservative fundamentalist Baptist, Great Lakes Region, Council of 1879 or Northern conservative fundamentalist Baptist, Great Lakes Region, Council of 1912?'

"He replied, 'Northern conservative fundamentalist Baptist, Great Lakes Region, Council of 1912.'

"I said, 'Die, heretic!'"[2]

Too many churches and too many relationships are split over insignificant matters! In Christ, we are brothers and sisters. We must focus on our oneness in Christ, not on our differences. We have too many things which unite us with other Christian believers to let the petty things divide us from His Body.

QUESTIONS:
1. What are some of the petty things which divide the body of Christ?
2. What part does spiritual pride play in dividing true Christians? What kind of role does God want you to play to bring unity to your church?
3. How hard is it to accept Christians who are of a different race? Why is racism such a problem in some churches? What is God's answer to this sin?

4. FAITH IN CHRIST MAKES US HEIRS OF THE PROMISE (v.29).

How do we know that we are justified by faith instead of by the law and by doing the best we can? Because faith in Christ makes us heirs of the promise.

⇒ Remember the promise made to Abraham: the promise of God's blessing, of God's presence and leadership, of being accepted by God and given the privilege of living forever in the land of Canaan (the type and symbol of heaven, of the new heavens and earth).

The point is this: Jesus Christ is the heir of Abraham; therefore, if a person is in *Christ*, then he inherits the promise made to Abraham. He inherits the promise of God's acceptance, of righteousness, and of living forever in the new heavens and earth as a son of God.

"For ye have not received the spirit of bondage again to fear; but ye have received the Spirit of adoption, whereby we cry, Abba, Father. The Spirit itself beareth witness with our spirit, that we are the children of God: and if children, then heirs; heirs of God, and joint-heirs with Christ; if so be that we suffer with him, that we may be also glorified together" (Ro.8:15-17).

QUESTIONS:
1. According to Scripture, who is the heir of Abraham's promise? How does this inheritance apply to the Christian believer?
2. What guarantees has God given to the Christian believer that make His promises available today?

GALATIANS 3:23-29

SUMMARY:

As you picture your life on a road map, are you on course, trusting and living for God? Or have you focused your eyes on the things of this world?

God is the supreme, all-knowing Guide who will never lead you astray. Listen to these lyrics from the pen of Christian song writer Michael Card:

> *To hear with my heart,*
> *To see with my soul,*
> *To be guided by a hand that I cannot hold,*
> *To trust in a way that I cannot see,*
> *That's what faith must be.*[3]

How do you lay hold of the benefits of faith in Christ? Remember that...

1. Faith in Christ was before the law.
2. Faith makes us children of God.
3. Faith in Christ makes us one: eliminates all distinctions and prejudices.
4. Faith in Christ makes us heirs of the promise.

PERSONAL JOURNAL NOTES
(Reflection & Response)

1. The most important thing that I learned from this lesson was:

2. The area that I need to work on the most is:

3. I can apply this lesson to my life by:

4. Closing Statement of Commitment:

---

[1] Selected from *Leadership*, Summer '93, vol.XIV #3, p.60.
[2] From *New Republic*. Selected from *Leadership,* Fall '92, vol.13 #4, p.47.
[3] Written by Michael Card. *That's What Faith Must Be* (Birdwing Music [a division of The Sparrow Corporation] and BMG Songs, Inc./ Mole End Music [ASCAP], 1988).

1. There was a time when the world was in bondage
- a. A child: An illustration
  - 1) Is under tutors
  - 2) Inherits the estate at the appointed time
- b. The world: In bondage because of its elementary approach to God

CHAPTER 4

F. The Proof of Christ & the Fulness of Time, 4:1-7

Now I say, that the heir, as long as he is a child, differeth nothing from a servant, though he be lord of all;
2 But is under tutors and governors until the time appointed of the father.
3 Even so we, when we were children, were in bondage under the elements of the world:
4 But when the fulness of the time was come, God sent forth his Son, made of a woman, made under the law,
5 To redeem them that were under the law, that we might receive the adoption of sons.
6 And because ye are sons, God hath sent forth the Spirit of his Son into your hearts, crying, Abba, Father.
7 Wherefore thou art no more a servant, but a son; and if a son, then an heir of God through Christ.

2. There was an appointed time when God delivered the world
- a. How? God sent His own Son as a man, under the law
- b. Why? To redeem the world
- c. Results
  - 1) We are adopted as God's sons
  - 2) We receive assurance of acceptance by the Spirit
  - 3) We become heirs of God

Section III
THE PROOF THAT A MAN IS JUSTIFIED BY FAITH ALONE & NOT BY WORKS, Galatians 3:1-4:7

Study 6: **THE PROOF OF CHRIST AND THE FULNESS OF TIME**

Text: **Galatians 4:1-7**

Aim: To rest assured that God's time is the right time in all things.

Memory Verse:

"But when the fulness of the time was come, God sent forth His Son, made of a woman, made under the law" (Galatians 4:4).

INTRODUCTION:

Have you ever watched and waited for a pot of water to boil? It seems to take forever! In the same sense, we sometimes look at God and wonder *when is He going to do this or do that*? No matter how impatient we get, God will do things in His time--the right time.

Just as water boils at the right temperature, God sent His Son into the world at the right time. God was not early. God was not late. He was right on time…just in time!

Some in the churches of Galatia were teaching that a person is saved by law; that is, he is saved by being good and religious and by doing the best he can. Of course, every person…
- should be good, ever striving to be better and better.
- should be faithful in worshipping God *in church*.
- should do the best he can--always.

However, Scripture is clear and forceful: a person is not saved by these things, for no amount of effort or energy or work can make a person perfect. And to be acceptable to God--to be given the right to live with God--a person must be perfect.

GALATIANS 4:1-7

How then can man be saved--be justified and made acceptable to God? This passage deals with the issue; it gives the answer. It shows how Christ and the fulness of time prove that a man is justified by faith and not by law nor by works.

OUTLINE:

1. There was a time when the world was in bondage (v.1-3).
2. There was a fulness of time when God delivered the world (v.4-7).

1. THERE WAS A TIME WHEN THE WORLD WAS IN BONDAGE (v.1-3).

The illustration is brief, yet descriptive: an heir who is a young child is under the care of guardians and trustees until the time appointed for him to receive his inheritance. Until the appointed time arrives, he has no more right to the inheritance than a slave.

The point is striking: there was a time when man was in bondage under the elementary things of the world. What is meant by the *elements* or *elementary things* of the world? Very simply, it means man's *elementary notions and ideas about God and the various ways he tries to approach God*. Letting Scripture interpret Scripture:

⇒ It means the first principles (the ABC's) of the Word of God, that is, the sacrifices, observances, rituals, and ceremonies of the Old Testament (Heb.5:12).
⇒ It means philosophy, the traditions of men, and the rudimentary or elementary teachings of men--the ABC approaches of men to God (Col.2:8).
⇒ It means the elements, the heavenly bodies of the universe (2 Pt.3:10). (There have always been men who tried to rule their lives by the heavenly bodies or astrology and the signs of the zodiac.)
⇒ It means the ordinances, rules, and regulations of men (Col.2:20).
⇒ It means the ceremonial laws, the legal yoke placed upon men as they try to approach God (Acts 15:10).
⇒ It means the law of the Old Testament, the yoke of bondage (Gal.5:1; cp. 4:3).
⇒ It means the observances of religious days, months, and years (Gal.4:9).

Very simply, the elements of the world refers to all the things that men use to get right with God and to secure the favor and approval of God. It refers to anything that man uses to justify himself before God, any approach to God that is taken by man through his own energy and effort...

- law or works
- ritual or ceremony
- church membership or ordinance
- astrology or science
- philosophy or religion

The point is this: before Christ, all approaches to God were only elementary approaches. No approach was the right approach, for man had only little knowledge of God--an elementary knowledge that required the *discipline and guidance of the law*.

However, when everything was ready for the world to come of age and to gain an adult knowledge of God, Christ came to release men from the law and to reveal that man was intended to have a father-son relationship with God. In Christ, men are no longer to be slaves to the law, they are to be sons of God. In Christ, they are to enter into their inheritance.

"Brethren, be not children in understanding: howbeit in malice be ye children, but in understanding be men" (1 Cor.14:20).

ILLUSTRATION:

How often have you heard someone in your church say this: "We've always done it this way before"? People tend to be creatures of habit. Often, to our own detriment, we voluntarily give ourselves over to bondage. Instead of depending on God's divine creativity (the power of the cross), there is the tendency to get stuck on what is familiar, on what we can create. Listen to this scenario:

> The school's talent show was filled with young children who were more than willing to dazzle the proud parents in the audience. Of all the talent on display that night, one 1st grader had the most *unique talent*. Standing on the stage, he held his accordion and played *one* note. After a few seconds, he played the same note again. For his big finish, he played that same note a third time. With his shoulders held erect and his head held high, he stated to the amused audience that he had written that song--*"all by myself!"*
>
> Like this little boy, there are many Christians who get stuck on one note--and then brag about how wonderful they are doing. But it takes more than one note to make up a song. And it takes more than your best efforts to become free from the bondage of your fallen nature. It took Jesus Christ, the New Song, and His completed work on the cross to release believers from the power and bondage of the law.

Are you stuck on one note or has Christ freed you and added spiritual harmony to your life?

QUESTIONS:
1. In what ways does man attempt to approach God?
2. Why do these ways always fail?
3. How are you tempted to approach God when your faith seems to be weak? What can you do to guard yourself from wrongly approaching God?

2. THERE WAS A FULNESS OF TIME WHEN GOD DELIVERED THE WORLD (v.4-7).

This is one of the great passages of Scripture dealing with the mission or work of God's Son, the Lord Jesus Christ. Note several significant points.

1. Note that God had prepared the world for the coming of Christ (see **A CLOSER LOOK:** Fulness of Time--Gal.4:4 for discussion).

2. Note that God sent His own Son into the world to deliver men. It was not an angel nor some other creature that God sent--nor was it some great leader from among men. It was God's very Son that He sent. God cared for and loved men so much that He would send no less than His own Son to deliver men from the terrible condemnation of the law: the bondage of sin and death.

> **"For I came down from heaven, not to do mine own will, but the will of him that sent me" (Jn.6:38).**
>
> **"But I know him: for I am from him, and he hath sent me" (Jn.7:29).**

3. Note that God sent His Son "made of a woman," that is "born out of a woman." He came into the world just as all men do, through a woman. But note the most glorious truth: He was "sent forth" by God. Jesus Christ was "His Son," the Son of God. God spoke the Word and the woman conceived miraculously. The Virgin Birth did take place: God's very own Son has been sent into the world *as a man* to save men.

> **"And, behold, thou shalt conceive in thy womb, and bring forth a son, and shalt call his name JESUS" (Lk.1:31).**

4. Note that God sent His Son born under the law. Jesus Christ had to live under the law in order to secure the perfect righteousness of the law for man. He had to obey the law in every single precept and stand before God as the Perfect and Ideal Man--the Ideal Embodiment of Righteousness. As stated, He had to do what no other person had ever done: secure the Ideal Righteousness and Perfection so that He could stand for all men.

> **"For what the law could not do, in that it was weak through the flesh, God sending his own Son in the likeness of sinful flesh, and for sin, condemned sin in the flesh: that the righteousness of the law might be fulfilled in us, who walk not after the flesh, but after the Spirit" (Ro.8:3-4).**

5. Note why God sent His Son: to redeem men from the curse of the law. The law convicts us of sin.
6. Note the result of God's sending His Son to redeem men.
   a. Believers are adopted as sons of God. When a person believes in *Jesus Christ*, God takes his faith and counts the person as being in *Jesus Christ*. Since Christ is God's Son, the believer is counted as a son of God--all because he is seen as being in *Jesus Christ*. His faith in *Jesus Christ* causes God to adopt him as a son of God.

   > **"But as many as received him, to them gave he power to become the sons of God, even to them that believe on his name" (Jn.1:12).**

   b. Believers receive assurance of being accepted by God through the Spirit of His Son. The Spirit of Christ is sent by God to dwell in our hearts and to give us a personal relationship with God. The Spirit of Christ, that is, the Holy Spirit, gives us a fellowship of communication and communion with God: He stirs our hearts to cry out to God as our Father: "Father, Father."

   > **"The Spirit itself beareth witness with our spirit, that we are the children of God" (Ro.8:16).**

   c. Believers are made heirs of God. But note: they are heirs because they are sons of God. Both sonship and heirship are "through Christ"--through faith in Him.

   > **"The Spirit itself beareth witness with our spirit, that we are the children of God: and if children, then heirs; heirs of God, and joint-heirs with Christ; if so be that we suffer with him, that we may be also glorified together" (Ro.8:16-17).**

ILLUSTRATION:

There is an old missionary tale that describes in a simple fashion why Jesus Christ's coming was so important.

> The missionary was becoming frustrated over his inability to communicate the gospel to his lost friend. There was a very real mental and spiritual block. One day while walking in a field they came upon an ant hill. The missionary and his friend were struck by how hard these ants were working. As they were observing this wonder of nature, they suddenly looked up to see an ant-eater lumbering toward them.
>
> "*Well, this looks like the end of this ant hill,*" remarked the missionary in a casual tone. Sorry that their study of this ant hill was coming to a close he said, "*I wish I could warn them about the ant-eater.*"
>
> "*That's it!*" said the missionary. "*My friend, God saw man as ants who were working as hard as they knew how to. But sin was killing them. The only way to*

warn them was to become one of them. Then they would understand and take action to save themselves."

God sent His Son into the world as a man to save you from destruction. The choice is yours: listen to Christ and be saved, or shut your ears to Christ and be doomed to death!

QUESTIONS:
1. What is the real reason God sent His Son into the world?
2. Do you sometimes forget the great price God the Father and His Son paid for you?
3. What are some of the results of God's sending His Son to redeem men?
4. What is the secret to becoming an heir of God?
5. What kind of relationship did Jesus have with the law? What is your relationship to be?

A CLOSER LOOK:

Fulness of Time: the coming of Christ upon the world scene was not by chance. His coming was under the strategic timing providentially set aside by God. His coming was not one day before or behind the appointed time. A child who is placed under the control of guardians is under their control until "the date fixed by his father" (Gal.4:2). God and God alone decided the fulness of time for the coming of Christ. Christ was born of a particular person, at a particular time, in a particular way (incarnation), under a particular system (the law). He shared the frustration and agony of being subjected to the very system from which He came to save men. The world had been wonderfully prepared for His coming.

1. The law had done its educational work. It had shown through the Jewish nation that men are terrible transgressors, and despite all of God's favor and blessings, men still failed to worship God in love. The world now had a picture of the depraved heart of man. (Cp. Ro.3:10-18 for a clear description of man's sinfulness.)
2. The world was full of people spiritually starved. The worship of self, pleasure, gods, philosophical ethics--all had left many empty and barren. The soul was now ready to have its hunger met.
3. The world was at peace under Roman rule. The world was an open door for the spread of the gospel--without any restraint.
4. The world spoke Greek as a basic language, making communication possible with many from all over the world.
5. The world had a system of roads for mass travel which allowed Christian missionaries to reach the farthest parts of the earth. It also brought commercial travelers to metropolitan centers where Christian believers were concentrated.

"And saying, The time is fulfilled, and the kingdom of God is at hand: repent ye, and believe the gospel" (Mk.1:15).

QUESTIONS:
1. What did God do to prepare the world for the coming of His Son?
2. God is always on time. When do you feel most <u>uncertain</u> of that fact? Why?
3. How can you learn to wait on God's timing, to become more patient?

A CLOSER LOOK:

Adoption: the word "adoption" means *to place as a son*. The picture of adoption is a beautiful picture of what God does for the Christian believer. In the ancient world, the family was based on a Roman law called "patria potestas," the father's power. The law gave the father absolute authority over his children so long as the father lived. He could work, enslave, sell, and if he wished, he could pronounce the death penalty. Regardless of the child's adult age, the father held all power over personal and property rights.

Therefore, adoption was a serious matter. Yet, it was a common practice to ensure that a family would not become extinct by having no male children. And when a child was adopted, three legal steps were taken.

1. The adopted son was adopted permanently. He could not be adopted today and disinherited tomorrow. He became a son of the father--forever. He was eternally secure as a son.
2. The adopted son immediately had all the rights of a legitimate son in the new family.
3. The adopted son completely lost all rights in his old family. The adopted son was looked upon as a new person--so new that old debts and obligations connected with his former family were cancelled and abolished as if they never existed.

The Bible says several things about the believer's adoption as a son of God.

1. The believer's adoption establishes a new relationship with God--forever. He is eternally secure as a child of God. But the new relationship is established only when a person comes to Christ through faith (Gal.3:26; 4:4-5).
2. The believer's adoption establishes a new relationship with God as father. The believer has all the rights and privileges of a genuine son of God (Ro.8:16-17; 1 Jn.3:1-2).
3. The believer's adoption establishes a new dynamic experience with God as father, a moment by moment access into His very presence (Ro.8:14, 16; Gal.4:6).
4. The believer's adoption gives him a very special relationship with other children of God--a family relationship that binds him with others in an unparalleled spiritual union.
5. The believer's adoption makes him a new person. The believer has been taken out from under the authority and power of the world and its sin. The believer is *placed as a son* into the family and authority of God. The old life with all of its debts and obligations are cancelled and wiped out (2 Cor.5:17; Gal.3:23-27; 2 Pt.1:4).
6. The believer's adoption is to be fully realized in the future at the return of Jesus Christ (Ro.8:19; Eph.1:14; 1 Th.4:14-17; 1 Jn.3:2).
7. The believer's adoption and its joy will be shared by all creation on a cosmic scale (Ro.8:21). There is to be a new heavens and earth (2 Pt.3:12-14; Rev.21:1-7).

ILLUSTRATION:

The single red rose placed at the front of the church was there to honor the newest member of the church family. A little boy had been born and would be raised by parents who would raise him in a loving, Christian home.

But this little boy was fortunate, for he was almost aborted. His nine months in his mother's womb were spent in great uncertainty. He was conceived in sin and his mother did not want to care for him. Her options ranged from abortion to adoption. Thankfully, she chose to give the gift of life to this little baby boy.

While she was waiting to deliver, adoptive parents were sought out and secured. These willing parents wanted this little boy to become their own. He would be given their name. He would become an heir to the parents. He would become a legal member of their family--and would not be given away to anyone else again.

Our heavenly Father did the same thing for us. He has given each Christian believer His name. We have become joint-heirs with Jesus. We are in the family of God--and He will never give us away again.

Have you been adopted into His family?

QUESTIONS:

1. Have you ever doubted God's willingness to keep you as His child? What kind of assurances does the Scripture give you concerning this?
2. Do you know anyone who has been adopted? What kind of life would they have had if they had not been adopted? If God had not adopted you, what kind of life would you have?
3. What special traits did you have that caused God to adopt you?

GALATIANS 4:1-7

SUMMARY:

God sent His Son to save us--He did it at the right time and it was a once-for-all act. We can be adopted as God's sons through Jesus Christ alone. Have you taken that leap of faith to accept Jesus Christ as Savior? Remember:

1. There was a time when the world was in bondage.
2. There was a fulness of time when God delivered the world.

PERSONAL JOURNAL NOTES
(Reflection & Response)

1. The most important thing that I learned from this lesson was:

2. The area that I need to work on the most is:

3. I can apply this lesson to my life by:

4. Closing Statement of Commitment:

GALATIANS 4:8-11

	IV THE FIVEFOLD APPEAL TO BE JUSTIFIED BY FAITH ALONE, 4:8-5:12	9 But now, after that ye have known God, or rather are known of God, how turn ye again to the weak and beggarly elements, whereunto ye desire again to be in bondage?	**2. Look at your present life: You know God & are known by God**
			3. Consider your turning back a. What you turn to: Beggarly elements
	A. Appeal One: Do Not Turn Back, 4:8-11	10 Ye observe days, and months, and times, and years.	b. What the results of backsliding are: 1) Bondage (v.9) 2) A wasted life
1. Remember your former life a. You did not know God b. You served false gods	8 Howbeit then, when ye knew not God, ye did service unto them which by nature are no gods.	11 I am afraid of you, lest I have bestowed upon you labour in vain.	

Section IV
THE FIVEFOLD APPEAL TO BE JUSTIFIED BY FAITH ALONE
Galatians 4:8-5:12

Study 1: APPEAL ONE: DO NOT TURN BACK

Text: Galatians 4:8-11

Aim: To forge ahead in our Christian walk: to never turn back.

Memory Verse:

"But now, after that ye have known God, or rather are known of God, how turn ye again to the weak and beggarly elements, whereunto ye desire again to be in bondage?" (Galatians 4:9).

SECTION OVERVIEW:

A person is justified by faith and not by law nor by works. It does not matter how many good works a person does nor how good he may become; he can never secure perfection. Therefore, a man can never earn or win the right to live in God's presence. A man cannot make God accept him--put God in debt--by being good and doing good. God is perfect; therefore, if a man is ever going to live in God's presence, it will be because God loves man enough to provide some way for man to become perfect. Glorious news! God has provided the way through His very own Son, the Lord Jesus Christ. When a man believes in the Lord Jesus Christ, God takes His belief and counts it as righteousness, as perfection. God accepts the man on the basis of faith, the kind of faith that says, "Lord God, I believe that your Son died for me. He took my imperfection, my shame, my sin, my being short of your glory; and He died for it all. I honor Him. I give my life, *all I am and have*, to serve Him. Save me--accept me in Him."

When a man approaches God in such a spirit, he honors God's Son, Jesus Christ. And God honors any person who honors His Son. He honors the person by doing the very thing the man believes or asks. If a man believes in Jesus Christ for righteousness, then God counts that man's belief (commitment to Christ) as righteousness. This is justification; this is the way a person becomes acceptable to God.

Justification by faith in Jesus Christ has been proven. This has been the point of the last six passages in the Book of Galatians. Now Paul launches a fivefold appeal to the church: a fivefold appeal to be justified by faith.

GALATIANS 4:8-11

SECTION OUTLINE:

A. Appeal One: Do Not Turn Back (4:8-11).
B. Appeal Two: Restir Affection for the Minister of God (4:12-20).
C. Appeal Three: Listen to What the Law Really Says (v.4:21-31).
D. Appeal Four: Stand Firm in the Liberty of Christ (v.5:1-6).
E. Appeal Five: Obey the Truth (5:7-12).

INTRODUCTION:

Are you the kind of person who is willing to take a risk? The true Christian knows that following Christ is well worth any risk. But think for a moment:

⇒ How many experiences meant for the Christian believer have you missed out on because you turned your back?
⇒ Why is turning back so appealing at times?

Maybe it is fear or just being perfectly content to keep things like they are. Or maybe your excuse is a complete lack of faith.

If you are thinking about turning back, or if you have already started down the backward journey, listen closely to this first appeal: Do not turn back!

OUTLINE:

1. Remember your former life (v.8).
2. Look at your present life: you know God and are known by God (v.9).
3. Consider your turning back (v.9-11).

1. REMEMBER YOUR FORMER LIFE (v.8).

Remember what you were when you were an unbeliever, before you ever believed in Jesus Christ and experienced salvation. The unbeliever is characterized by two significant traits.

1. The unbeliever does not know God. This means that he does not know God in a personal way; God's Spirit does not dwell in the unbeliever filling the unbeliever with the fulness of God. The unbeliever does not experience God's...

- divine nature (2 Pt.1:4)
- presence
- assurance
- care
- love
- life
- power
- confidence
- provision

The unbeliever does not have the day-by-day experience of knowing God, of experiencing the presence, fellowship, communion, care, and provision of God--of experiencing the abundance of life with God. And as tragic as any of his shortcomings, the unbeliever does not have the absolute assurance of living forever with God.

2. The unbeliever serves false gods. Even before their conversion, the Galatians had sensed their need for God. They had not been atheists or agnostics. They had been a religious people seeking to become acceptable to God. Their worship had been the worship of *many gods* including both Jupiter (Zeus) and Mercury (Hermes). This, of course, meant that they had been enslaved to heathen gods, religion and worship, rituals and ceremonies, rules and regulations, superstitions and idols.

Note what is said about the unbeliever: he serves gods which *by nature are not gods*. By their very nature, the objects of man's worship are not gods. How could they be, for they are only a creation of the unbeliever's mind. He may count them as gods, but they are no more than ideas in his own mind.

GALATIANS 4:8-11

ILLUSTRATION:

Have you ever wondered what it would be like to stumble upon a community of idolaters? What kinds of things would offend you? Take a glimpse into one such community:

As we peek into one of their homes, several things strike us as *unChristian-like*. It seems that their worship is centered in their main living area. The entire room has been arranged to give honor to this inanimate object (which makes all kinds of noises and appeals to the senses of those who worship it). All of the available seating in this room is angled in order to provide the best seating and viewing arrangement possible.

Upon further investigation in this house, the closets are full of sewn materials which are hung on metal hanging ornaments. One can only guess about this culture, but there seems to have been a lot of value placed upon this area of the living quarters.

Seeing their bookkeeping records might give some insight on what they valued, you find the only entry on the ledger is entitled "self."

Let's leave this uncivilized culture behind. What kind of people are they anyhow? Sad to say, but it looks a lot like our culture. The inanimate object displayed in the main living area is a television. For many, it has become an object of worship as its pull has overcome many a Christian.

The closet represents the value our culture places on apparel--especially the trendy and expensive type. Many are judged for what they wear on the outside and not for what dresses the heart.

Finally, how we invest our financial resources tells a lot about what we consider important. Our culture is one that promotes "me first" and then others if anything is left over (by accident).

Some would respond and say, "But we don't have idols. We are civilized." However, the evidence is clear: anything that is placed before Jesus Christ is an idol. Let this rule of thumb keep you from the sin of idolatry.

APPLICATION 1:

What most people worship is only a creation of their own mind's. They have an idea of god, who he is and what he is like, and they worship that idea. Few ever seek God's revelation of Himself in Jesus Christ. If men really believed that Jesus Christ was the living revelation of God, then they would study Him and His life, seeking to know Him with every ounce of energy they had. But few ever do, and this failure is a clear indication that they do not believe, not really.

The point is this: since the unbeliever does not believe in Jesus Christ, the One who came to reveal God to the world, then whatever it is that he worships is false--a false god. It is a figment of his imagination, only an idea in his mind. Whether a man bows to an idol or not, he is merely worshipping his own idea, thought, concept, and imagination.

> **"For as I passed by, and beheld your devotions, I found an altar with this inscription, TO THE UNKNOWN GOD. Whom therefore ye ignorantly worship, him declare I unto you" (Acts 17:23).**
>
> **"That at that time ye were without Christ, being aliens from the commonwealth of Israel, and strangers from the covenants of promise, having no hope, and without God in the world" (Eph.2:12).**

APPLICATION 2:

Every believer needs to remember where he came from before he came to know God. God has been most merciful to us all; therefore, we must never forget that Jesus Christ has purged us from our sins.

> **"According as his divine power hath given unto us all things [God and His blessings] that pertain unto life and godliness, through the knowledge of him that hath called us to glory and virtue" (2 Pt.1:3).**

QUESTIONS:
1. What advantages does a believer have over an unbeliever? Do you make the most of these advantages, or do you slip back into the same patterns of your former life?
2. Why do people create gods? In what way is this also a temptation to you?
3. Where is the Christian believer to go in order to know who God really is? Do you make it a regular habit of doing this? Why or why not?

2. LOOK AT YOUR PRESENT LIFE: YOU KNOW GOD AND ARE KNOWN BY GOD (v.9).

You are given the most wonderful privilege of knowing God, or more accurately stated, you are known by God. Think about the glorious privilege of knowing God and being known by God Himself!

As R.A. Cole points out, when a person accepts Jesus Christ as His Savior, he comes to know God personally not just intellectually--but in a much deeper way, for in the Bible "to know" means far more than just intellectual knowledge. It means an intimate relationship; that is why the Bible uses the word "know" to express the most intimate relation between man and wife: "And Adam knew Eve his wife; and she conceived" (Gen.4:1).[1]

However, note a critical point. When a person *turns away and separates himself* from the world to know God, the most wonderful thing happens: God accepts him, becoming a Father to him and knowing him as His son or daughter. The person becomes known by God. This is exactly what Scripture says:

> **"Wherefore come out from among them, and be ye separate, saith the Lord, and touch not the unclean thing; and I will receive you, and will be a Father unto you, and ye shall be my sons and daughters, saith the Lord Almighty" (2 Cor.6:17-18).**

Again, imagine the glorious privilege of such a precious relationship! Not only to know God as Father but to be *known by God* as His son or daughter!

> **"...I have redeemed thee, I have called thee by thy name; thou art mine" (Is.43:1).**

APPLICATION:

Believers should constantly look at their present lives--the glorious salvation God has given them: the privilege of knowing Him and of being known by Him. But note: we must always remember that we do not come to know God by our own efforts or works, not by doing the best we can and obeying the law, as important as all these are. We come to know God through justification, that is, by faith in Jesus Christ and by faith in Him alone.

QUESTIONS:
1. What does it mean to "know God"?
2. What can you do in order to know God better?
3. Who do you know personally who knows God well? What qualities does he have which strike you? How did that person come to have those character traits?

3. CONSIDER YOUR TURNING BACK (v.9-11).

1. Note a critical point: the Galatians were about to turn back to the elementary things or notions about God. Does this mean they were about to turn back to their pagan, idolatrous wor-

ship? No, that was not what they were about to do. What were they turning back to? The false teachers (Judaizers) in Galatia were teaching that a man was to approach God by the law and works--that a man became acceptable to God by his own efforts, by working and doing as much good as he could.

Of course, this is exactly what all religious people do, no matter their religion: they try to please their god, to secure the god's approval by doing what pleases him. This means that all religions (except Christianity) are religions of works and of law. Therefore, if the Galatians subjected themselves to the law and to a religion of works, they would be *returning* to a life of bondage--the bondage of working to get God to pay attention to them and to receive and accept them.

The crucial point is this: there is no difference between seeking God through the law and seeking God through pagan worship. The foundation of all religious seeking (except Christianity) is the same: that of working to keep the laws that please a person's god--that of doing good so that a person's *god* will accept him.

Note that Paul calls man's elementary notions of God weak and beggarly.

a. The law and other approaches to God are weak in that they are helpless in saving man. The law itself could only point out man's sin, but it could never justify and make him acceptable to God.
b. The law and other approaches to God are beggarly, that is, worthless in saving man. The law itself is meaningless, of no use whatsoever in justifying and making man acceptable to God. It is not the law nor man's works and attempts to be good that saves him.

Note also that Paul illustrates his point by referring to special religious holidays. The point is that ritual, ceremony, and the keeping of religious days will not justify and make a person acceptable before God. Christ and Christ alone--faith in Him--saves a person.

2. Note the results of backsliding, of turning back to the world and seeking to please God by self-effort and self-righteousness.

a. A person becomes enslaved in that he tries to please God by keeping the rules of the law, but he finds he cannot. But he still slavishly tries and tries again. However, it is all to no avail, for the man finds himself still in the bondage of sin and death. He still sins and he still dies, and there is no absolute assurance within of eternal life. And it is the lack of assurance, of knowing that one is acceptable to God, that is so enslaving. The question and doubt of living with God gnaws and gnaws at man--always without the sure knowledge and assurance of God's love. Perfect assurance, confidence, and security come only through faith in Jesus Christ.
b. A person lives a wasted life. Every approach to God fails except faith in Jesus Christ. Every approach leads to death and condemnation; therefore, every life that approaches God by any other means than faith in Jesus Christ is a wasted life.

"And Jesus said unto him, No man, having put his hand to the plough, and looking back, is fit for the kingdom of God" (Lk.9:62).

"Now the just shall live by faith: but if any man draw back, my soul shall have no pleasure in him" (Heb.10:38).

ILLUSTRATION:

What things would cause a Christian believer to backslide? Perhaps some illumination will come through this story.

The boy scout was really excited about going on the annual winter camperee. With a couple feet of snow on the ground, the setting was perfect for a great weekend.

His was one of the first troops to hike in and set up camp. The boy scout, along with his troop, forged into the wilderness. Upon arrival, they set up camp and prepared for their weekend adventure.

GALATIANS 4:8-11

After pitching his tent, the boy scout realized that he had left something in the bus. So, he proceeded to take the long walk back to the bus which was a few miles away. Feeling confident in his "retriever skills," he did not take care to look for the important landmarks which would show him the way back to camp.

Coming back from the bus proved to be an unplanned adventure. The confusion from other scouts setting up their own camps caused him to question which paths to take. After awhile, every path looked the same. To say that he was getting worried would be an obvious observation. "How could I have missed it? If only I could find something (or someone) familiar."

The backslider is a lot like this confused boyscout. They forget to set familiar landmarks in place to keep themselves on track. What are those landmarks? Regular time in God's Word, frequent prayer, and accountable fellowship with other believers.

Whatever happened to that backslidden boyscout you might be wondering? Every approach to his camp ended in failure. Hours later, his scoutmaster found him and brought him back to camp. That is exactly what the Great Scoutmaster, the Good Shepherd, does for wayward sheep. He finds them and brings them to Himself.

QUESTIONS:

1. What insights can you gain from the experiences of this boy scout?
2. What sort of attitude are you to have in regards to backsliding?
3. What are some of the results of backsliding? What have you done to prevent becoming a backslider?

SUMMARY:

You have come too far to turn back now. Go ahead and take the risk: follow hard after God! As a matter of review, remember the three main points:

1. Remember your former life.
2. Look at your present life: you know God and are known by God.
3. Consider your turning back.

PERSONAL JOURNAL NOTES
(Reflection & Response)

1. The most important thing that I learned from this lesson was:

2. The area that I need to work on the most is:

3. I can apply this lesson to my life by:

4. Closing Statement of Commitment:

---

[1] R.A. Cole. *The Epistle of Paul to the Galatians*. "Tyndale New Testament Commentaries," Edited by RVG Tasker (Grand Rapids, MI: Eerdmans, 1965), p.118.

	B. Appeal Two: Restir Affection for the Minister of God, 4:12-20	have plucked out your own eyes, and have given them to me. 16 Am I therefore become your enemy, because I tell you the truth?	d. In the truth they proclaim
1. Treat the minister of God as a brother a. Identify with all b. Hold no grievances	12 Brethren, I beseech you, be as I am; for I am as ye are: ye have not injured me at all.	17 They zealously affect you, but not well; yea, they would exclude you, that ye might affect them.	**3. Guard against and reject false ministers**
2. Welcome true ministers of God a. In their witness	13 Ye know how through infirmity of the flesh I preached the gospel unto you at the first.	18 But it is good to be zealously affected always in a good thing, and not only when I am present with you.	**4. Receive true ministers—always** a. They seek after believers for good
b. In their infirmities of the flesh	14 And my temptation which was in my flesh ye despised not, nor rejected; but received me as an angel of God, even as Christ Jesus.	19 My little children, of whom I travail in birth again until Christ be formed in you,	b. They hold to believers as dear children c. They agonize over the believer's growth
c. In empathy & identification	15 Where is then the blessedness ye spake of? for I bear you record, that, If it had been possible, ye	20 I desire to be present with you now, and to change my voice; for I stand in doubt of you.	d. They watch over error

Section IV
THE FIVEFOLD APPEAL TO BE JUSTIFIED BY FAITH ALONE
Galatians 4:8-5:12

Study 2: APPEAL TWO: RESTIR AFFECTION FOR THE MINISTER OF GOD

Text: Galatians 4:12-20

Aim: To strongly support your minister in word and deed.

Memory Verse:

"Obey them that have the rule over you, and submit yourselves: for they watch for your souls, as they that must give account, that they may do it with joy, and not with grief: for that is unprofitable for you" (Hebrews 13:17).

INTRODUCTION:

Contrary to popular opinion, your minister does not get dressed in a phone booth and come out with a large "S" on his shirt and a flowing cape tied at the base of his neck. Instead of leaping buildings with a single bound, he is usually trying to keep the building which contains the congregation from flying apart.

What is one of the most important missions of the ministers of God? One of the most vital duties is to restore sheep that have strayed away from the Lord.

Backsliding people need appeal after appeal, for they are walking a dangerous course when they turn their backs upon God. Also, a backsliding person is usually alienated from his minister: he wants little to do with the minister when he is turning away from God. The Galatian churches went even further. False teachers and critics of Paul had begun to attack Paul personally, both his person and his ministry. They were tearing down his character every way they could. There was great danger that the churches would reject his ministry; therefore, Paul had to do all he could to stop the mess and save the churches from destruction and apostasy. The present passage is an appeal for the believers to *remember and restir their* affection for the minister of God.

OUTLINE:

1. Treat the minister of God as a brother (v.12).
2. Welcome true ministers of God (v.13-16).
3. Guard against and reject false ministers (v.17).
4. Receive true ministers--always (v.18-20).

1. TREAT THE MINISTER OF GOD AS A BROTHER (v.12).

Remember that some in the churches of Galatia were criticizing and attacking Paul. But note several significant facts.

1. Paul called them brothers: he did not treat them as enemies, not even as antagonists. He did not murmur, gripe, complain, or even attack them. The very opposite is true: he sensed and expressed deep brotherly affection for them.
2. Paul *beseeched* them; that is, he was not commanding or instructing, but he was begging and pleading from the heart of a true minister of God.
3. Paul begged them to be as he was, for he had become one of them. He had always loved and cared and shown affection for them, and he wanted them to do the same for him--not to abandon and turn against him and his ministry.

It should be noted that many commentators understand Paul to be saying that he had become as they were, that is, a Gentile; therefore, he wanted them to remain as he was, a Gentile who trusted Christ, and not to turn to Jewish law in seeking God's approval.

4. Paul assured them that what they had done had not injured him: he held no bitterness, anger, or malice against them.

APPLICATION 1:

The heart of a true minister is clearly seen in verse twelve: love, affection, kindness, and care for a people who had become critics of the minister of God.

APPLICATION 2:

Believers must heed the appeal of the minister of God: "Be as I am in affection and love--do not abandon and turn away from me."

ILLUSTRATION:

Several Christian men who had been touched by the Lord decided to do something practical for their pastor: pray for him. What is so unusual about that, you might ask. Well, for one particular pastor, it was a brand new sensation.

These few laymen had just returned from a Bible study that encouraged them to approach their pastor and tell him that they were committing to pray for him on a regular basis. They liked their pastor but had never thought that such a "great man of God" needed their awkward prayers. After all, they were just laymen and *he* was the pastor.

During their appointment with their pastor, they shared with him what God had led them to do. In response to their offer, the pastor took a deep breath and told them a sad truth: "In all of my fifteen years of being in the ministry, no group of men have ever come to me to tell me that they were praying for me." He was truly touched by their Christian love; and make no mistake about it, from that day forward he preached, pastored, and prayed with a greater confidence knowing that he was not in the battle alone.

Does your pastor know that you are praying for him?

QUESTIONS:
1. Do you think of your pastor as a brother? Do you treat him as a brother?
2. Do you need to change your attitude toward your pastor? If yes, in what way?
3. What can you do for your pastor to show him your love and appreciation?

2. WELCOME TRUE MINISTERS OF GOD (v.13-16).

There are three areas in which true ministers should be welcomed.

1. True ministers should be welcomed in their witness. Note: the Galatians had welcomed Paul when he first preached the gospel to them, and they had readily responded to his message. They did not question his call to preach nor the message he preached. There was no criticism nor censoring of his person or preaching. Their arms were wide open and their hearts were receptive.

Note that Paul was appealing for the same spirit of welcome and receptivity now. No other spirit should ever characterize God's people--not toward the minister of God--not toward any child of God.

2. True ministers should be welcomed even in the infirmities and weaknesses of their flesh. Too often, this is not true. Churches and believers sometimes abandon and ignore the minister of God when he is stricken in body or spirit. When Paul first went to the Galatian churches, he was stricken with some infirmity. Just what the infirmity was is not known, although the best guess seems to be some serious eye problem (v.15). The point is that the Galatians...

- did not despise him.
- did not reject him.
- received him as an angel or messenger from God Himself.

This last fact stresses just how wide open the welcome was to Paul. There was no lack in receiving and caring for the minister of God. They would have even plucked out their own eyes and given them to Paul if they had been able.

3. True ministers should be welcomed in the truth they proclaim. Paul had been proclaiming the truth: a person is justified by faith and not by law nor by works--not by trying to earn God's acceptance by doing good deeds here and there. Was the church going to treat Paul as an enemy because he had told them the truth?

APPLICATION:

How many churches turn against the minister of God because he preaches and tells the truth? The church must always welcome the minister who speaks and proclaims the truth.

> **"Receive him therefore in the Lord with all gladness; and hold such in reputation" (Ph.2:29).**

ILLUSTRATION:

If the minister of God tells the truth, will he be exempt from persecution? John wished it were so. Let's hear his painful story:

John was a man of God who had forsaken all to follow Christ. He was willing to go wherever God wanted. It looked like a golden opportunity for a young minister. This congregation wanted him, and he felt led to the church. Right up front he told the congregation that he would never compromise the truth. And they replied, "Pastor, that's great! We're sure glad to have you with us."

As the years went by, the truth from God's Word put the congregation in the fork of the road. There is an old saying that the truth hurts. Instead of responding in repentence to the Lord, many in the church began to shift the blame for their guilty hearts to the pastor's sermons.

The result was tragic. John was spiritually tarred and feathered. The people were looking for something that would tickle their ears. To his credit, John refused to give in to the pressure, counting the truth more important than acceptance by man.

QUESTIONS:

1. What responsibilities do you have to your minister? Are you satisfied that you are doing all you can and should for him?
2. Put yourself in your minister's shoes for a moment. Have you given him the freedom to speak the truth? What things in your life could be barriers to enhancing your relationship with him?
3. Have you made a commitment to pray for your pastor in areas where he might be weak? When he asks you to pray for him, do you?

3. GUARD AGAINST AND REJECT FALSE MINISTERS (v.17).

Note that the false teachers (Judaizers, religionists) were zealous in their teaching, and they were out to secure as large a following as possible. Note how they went about it: by excluding the people, trying to cut them off from the minister of God. They not only sought people through the merits of their own teaching, but they attacked and tore down the minister in order to alienate the people from him.

Note the difference between what the Christian minister (Paul) was doing and what the false teachers were doing. Or, to put it in the form of a question: What is the difference between the evangelistic efforts of the true minister of God and false teachers?

⇒ False teachers seek to focus people upon law, works, effort, ritual, ceremony, observances, sacrifice, rules, and regulations--upon something that requires man to work at being good or doing good in order to become acceptable to God.

⇒ The true minister of God seeks to focus people upon God Himself: His love, honor, and praise--upon the fact that God Himself has provided the way for man to become acceptable to Him, and that way is through His Son Jesus Christ.

> **"Beware of false prophets, which come to you in sheep's clothing, but inwardly they are ravening wolves" (Mt.7:15).**
>
> **"Now the Spirit speaketh expressly, that in the latter times some shall depart from the faith, giving heed to seducing spirits, and doctrines of devils; speaking lies in hypocrisy; having their conscience seared with a hot iron" (1 Tim.4:1-2).**

QUESTIONS:

1. What things does a false teacher focus upon? What does a genuine Christian teacher focus on?
2. Would you consider yourself to be "easy prey" for a crafty false teacher? Why or why not?
3. What sort of protective barriers does your church have in place in order to protect the sheep from wolves (false teachers)?

4. RECEIVE TRUE MINISTERS--ALWAYS (v.18-20).

Paul said that the church should always welcome ministers who seek to do well, ministers who labor for the church's welfare. Note that he was encouraging the church not only to accept his ministry but the ministry of other true ministers. They must reject false ministers and have nothing to do with them, but they must receive the ministry of true ministers in order to grow in Christ. Paul himself demonstrated three reasons why the church is to receive true ministers of God.

1. True ministers hold believers within their hearts as *dear children*. The minister's heart is ever so tender, warm, caring, protecting, and providing toward the church.

2. True ministers agonize over the growth of believers. They seek "Christ to be formed" in the believers. They want them living as Christ lived and conformed into the image of Christ.

> **"O Jerusalem, Jerusalem, thou that killest the prophets, and stonest them which are sent unto thee, how often would I have gathered thy children together, even as a hen gathereth her chickens under her wings, and ye would not" (Mt.23:37).**

3. True ministers guard the church against error. Note: if there is any doubt about the matter, he warns the church.

> **"For many walk, of whom I have told you often, and now tell you even weeping, that they are the enemies of the cross of Christ" (Ph.3:18).**

APPLICATION:

No believer or church should ever reject the ministry of a minister who seeks to help them and to grow them in Christ.

ILLUSTRATION:

How open is your church's pulpit to visiting ministers? Does your pastor have every gift in the Bible and a resume that lists every possible spiritual experience? Of course not. A healthy church wants and needs input from other parts of the body of Christ. Without an extended vision, a church will never grow; eventually it will dry up and die.

> *"About 350 years ago a shipload of travelers landed on the northeast coast of America. The first year they established a town sight. The next year they elected a town government. The third year the town government planned to build a road five miles westward into the wilderness.*
>
> *"In the fourth year the people tried to impeach their town government because they thought it was a waste of public funds to build a road five miles westward into a wilderness. Who needed to go there anyway?*
>
> *"Here were people who had the vision to see three thousand miles across an ocean and overcome great hardships to get there. But in just a few years they were not able to see even five miles out of town. They had lost their pioneering vision.*
>
> *"With a clear vision of what we can become in Christ, no ocean of difficulty is too great. Without it, we rarely move beyond our current boundaries."*[1]

Without a vision from outside our walls of comfort, we'll never know what God is doing in His world. Don't you want to know?

QUESTIONS:

1. Who has come to your church recently that gave you a bigger picture of what God is doing in the world?
2. Does your church support any missionaries, evangelists, mission churches, or student ministers? Do they come and share their experiences with your congregation? What does your congregation do for them? What can you do?
3. Is Christ being formed in you? If yes, in what way?

GALATIANS 4:12-20

SUMMARY:

Do you have a better understanding of how to relate to the minister of God? You must realize that they are all human just like you, and they need your prayers and support as they follow God's will for their lives. God's will for you is to...

1. Treat the minister of God as a brother.
2. Welcome true ministers of God.
3. Guard against and reject false ministers.
4. Receive true ministers--always.

PERSONAL JOURNAL NOTES
(Reflection & Response)

1. The most important thing that I learned from this lesson was:

2. The area that I need to work on the most is:

3. I can apply this lesson to my life by:

4. Closing Statement of Commitment:

[1] Craig B. Larson, Editor. *Illustrations for Preaching & Teaching*, p.276.

GALATIANS 4:21-31

1. Understanding 1: A person must hear the law, grasp its implications **2. Understanding 2: Abraham had two sons** a. One was born a slave b. One was born free c. The first was born naturally—by man's efforts d. The second was born by promise **3. Understanding 3: The two mothers represent two covenants** a. Hagar: A type of the law 1) It enslaves 2) It represents the very center of legal religion—Jerusalem of that day	**C. Appeal Three: Listen to What the Law Really Says, 4:21-31** 21 Tell me, ye that desire to be under the law, do ye not hear the law? 22 For it is written, that Abraham had two sons, the one by a bondmaid, the other by a freewoman. 23 But he who was of the bondwoman was born after the flesh; but he of the freewoman was by promise. 24 Which things are an allegory: for these are the two covenants; the one from the mount Sinai, which gendereth to bondage, which is Agar. 25 For this Agar is mount Sinai in Arabia, and answereth to Jerusalem which now is, and is in bondage with her children.	26 But Jerusalem which is above is free, which is the mother of us all. 27 For it is written, Rejoice, thou barren that bearest not; break forth and cry, thou that travailest not: for the desolate hath many more children than she which hath an husband. 28 Now we, brethren, as Isaac was, are the children of promise. 29 But as then he that was born after the flesh persecuted him that was born after the Spirit, even so it is now. 30 Nevertheless what saith the scripture? Cast out the bondwoman and her son: for the son of the bondwoman shall not be heir with the son of the freewoman. 31 So then, brethren, we are not children of the bondwoman, but of the free.	b. Sarah: A type of grace 1) It represents heavenly Jerusalem—the spiritual 2) It sets men free, v.26 3) It results in joy & far more children c. The point: Believers are children of promise **4. Understanding 4: Legalism persecutes & enslaves believers** **5. Understanding 5: Legalism is to be cast out—have no inheritance** **6. Understanding 6: Legalism has no claim upon the children of grace**

Section IV
THE FIVEFOLD APPEAL TO BE JUSTIFIED BY FAITH ALONE
Galatians 4:8-5:12

Study 3: APPEAL THREE: LISTEN TO WHAT THE LAW REALLY SAYS

Text: Galatians 4:21-31

Aim: To fine-tune our spiritual hearing and understanding.

Memory Verse:
"Now we, brethren, as Isaac was, are the children of promise (Galatians 4:28).

INTRODUCTION:
Noted radio announcer Paul Harvey is known for this famous phrase: "And now, for the rest of the story." This was the Apostle Paul's exact point to the churches of Galatia. There were some church members who did not fully understand all that the law was saying. What they

needed was an adjustment to their spiritual hearing. Once that adjustment was made, then they too would come to know the rest of the story.

The way to heaven is not by works nor by the law. A person cannot do enough works nor keep enough laws to become *perfectly good*. And for a person to live in God's presence, he has to be perfect. What, then, is the way to heaven? If a person cannot be good enough nor do enough works to make it to heaven, how can he get there? By faith in the promise of God. God has promised heaven to those who believe in His Son--to those who genuinely trust Jesus Christ to save them.

However, most people in the world do not believe the promise of God. They still think they have to earn and work their way into the favor of God--that they have to build up a long list of *good works* that will force God to accept them. They think that they have to make themselves righteous by being good and doing religious things in order to enter heaven. Therefore, they place themselves under the rules and regulations of the law and of religion, and they do the best they can to make it to heaven. This is the appeal of this passage; the person who approaches God through the works of religion and law must listen to *what the law really says*.

OUTLINE:

1. Understanding 1: a person must hear the law, grasp its implications (v.21).
2. Understanding 2: Abraham had two sons (v.22-23).
3. Understanding 3: the two mothers represent two covenants (v.24-28).
4. Understanding 4: legalism persecutes and enslaves believers (v.29).
5. Understanding 5: legalism is to be cast out--have no inheritance (v.30).
6. Understanding 6: legalism has no claim upon the children of grace (v.31).

1. UNDERSTANDING 1: A PERSON MUST HEAR THE LAW, GRASP ITS IMPLICATIONS (V.21).

The legalist and religionist are the persons who approach God by the law or by the works of goodness or religion. The legalist and religionist need to hear and really understand what they are doing, just how they are approaching God. They need to understand the implication of what they are doing.

QUESTIONS:

1. What reasons would a legalist give for his approach to God?
2. Why is it important for the legalist and religionist to understand the implication of what they are doing?
3. In what ways are you tempted to be a legalist or religionist?

2. UNDERSTANDING 2: ABRAHAM HAD TWO SONS (v.22-23).

Remember that the way to become acceptable to God and to enter heaven is not by law nor by the works of goodness but by the promise of God. Paul uses the illustration of Abraham to prove the point (cp. Genesis Chapters 16, 17, and 21). Briefly and simply, Abraham had two sons. One son had been promised by God to Abraham through his wife, Sarah; however, many years passed without Sarah's having a child. She seemed incapable. She became discouraged; so she sent a slave girl, Hagar, in to Abraham. Hagar bore a son, Ishmael. Sometime later, however, God kept His promise and the impossible happened: Sarah, well beyond childbearing years, bore a son and his name was Isaac (Ro.4:10).

1. Note the facts about Ishmael. He was...
    - born through a natural process.
    - born into slavery, being born of a slave girl.
    - born because of the work, effort, and will of Sarah.
    - born because of the fleshly impulses, urges, and attraction of Abraham.

2. Note the facts about Isaac. He was...
   - born as a free man, born of a free woman, Sarah.
   - born by the promise of God alone. God had promised Abraham that Sarah would bear a son, and when Isaac was born, Abraham and Sarah were both well beyond the years of childbearing--one hundred years old. Isaac was a miracle-child, born miraculously by the working of God--all because God had promised Abraham a son. Isaac was, therefore, a promised child.

The point is this, and it must be remembered: Ishmael, the child born by human ingenuity, energy, and effort, was born into slavery. But Isaac, the child promised by God, was born miraculously by the promise of God--by His love and power alone--all because He had made the promise. Isaac was born by the grace of God and by the grace of God alone.

ILLUSTRATION:

We must remember that even our best efforts fall short of gaining a place in heaven. It has to be grace and grace alone. Listen to this humorous story that illustrates the point well.

"In his mission field, a certain missionary had to do many things for himself and his family. When the baby grew too big for the carriage he started to build a bed for the child. After he prepared the wood, he glued the mortised pieces and was ready to complete the bed. His wife thought it too cold to work in the shed so he brought the materials into the kitchen and started to work. When the bed was finished, the baby was brought to the kitchen and placed in it while his parents gazed admiringly. Suddenly the father had a disquieting thought. Suppose the bed would not go through the door! Quickly he measured bed and door and found the bed one inch too wide to pass through.

"There are many people who spend their time building their lives according to the plan of this world. They take great pride in their work....The day will come when they suddenly realize the measurements will not allow [them] to pass Heaven's door."[1]

QUESTIONS:

1. Do you believe God is going to accept you because of your own ingenuity ? Your own energy and effort? Your own goodness? Because you keep the commandments of God and do the best you can? Why or why not?
2. Was there a time when you made a choice between being like Ishmael (man's way) or being like Isaac (God's way)? Which one did you choose and why?

3. UNDERSTANDING 3: THE TWO MOTHERS REPRESENT TWO COVENANTS (v.24-28).

Note: Paul says that these things are an allegory, that is, an illustration of truth can be seen and drawn from the event. When looking closely at the story, we can see how the mothers, Hagar and Sarah, represent the two covenants--the covenant of law and the covenant of God's grace or promise.

1. Hagar was a type of the old covenant between God and man--the law. Two things are said about the law.
   a. Hagar, that is, the law, bears children to slavery. The law says do this and do not do that. It demands and insists on obedience. It enslaves a person to do exactly what it says. Therefore, if a person hopes to approach God in his own goodness, merit, virtue, morality, and righteousness, he is in bondage to the law. He must keep it in order to be good and moral and righteous and to earn the favor of God. The law, the rules and regulations of goodness and righteousness, enslaves him. (Keep in mind, Paul is not saying the law is not good. We are to live righteously

and morally, but we are not acceptable to God because of our goodness and self-efforts. We do not save ourselves; we are not to be praised because of our works and goodness. Praise belongs to God. God is the One who saves us. This is what is being discussed.)

b. Hagar, the law, represents the very center of a religion of law and works which was Jerusalem of that day (v.25). Note that Paul makes two connections to stress the point:
   - ⇒ Hagar stands for Mt. Sinai, the Mount in Arabia where the law was given.
   - ⇒ Hagar and Mt. Sinai both picture the very center of a religion of law and works, the Jerusalem of that day. Of course, Hagar also pictures any religion, church, people, or person who seeks to be righteous and acceptable to God and heaven through works and law.

2. Sarah was a type of the new covenant between God and man, the covenant of grace or of promise. Two things are said about the grace and promise of God to man.

a. Sarah, that is, grace, is seen in the Jerusalem which is above, the heavenly Jerusalem. Heavenly Jerusalem is the spiritual and eternal city which God has promised to those who approach Him through faith.

b. Sarah and grace and the promise of a heavenly city are all free. Any person who accepts God's promise of a heavenly city which is eternal--who accepts His promise enough to believe it with all his heart, basing all he is and has upon that promise--is acceptable to God. God takes the man's sheer faith--the faith that has cast itself totally upon the promise of God--and counts it as the man's righteousness. Therefore, the man becomes acceptable to God: he is given the promise of God freely--without price--without having to work for it by keeping rules and laws.

c. Note a second result as well: the covenant of grace ends up with more children than the Jewish legalist. This is a prophecy which simply predicted that more Gentiles would believe the grace of God than Jews (Is.55:1).

3. The point is forcefully stated: "Now we, brothers, as Isaac was, are the children of promise." Believers--all those who have believed in Jesus Christ--have been given birth by God--a spiritual birth. We receive the promise of God. God freely takes our faith and counts it as righteousness.

- ⇒ Our faith is credited, imputed, counted as the righteousness which we lack within ourselves.

This is the glorious promise of God's grace, the covenant of grace which God has now made with man. Man can now inherit the promised land (Canaan, the heavenly Jerusalem or city of God) and live eternally with God.

> **"For the promise, that he should be the <u>heir of the world</u>, was not to Abraham, or to his seed, through the law, but through the righteousness of faith. For if they which are of the law be heirs, faith is made void, and the promise made of none effect" (Ro.4:13-14).**

<u>QUESTIONS:</u>
1. What are the two covenants that Paul is referring to in these Scriptures?
2. Give some examples of how some people seek God through the law. What are some of the natural results of this choice?
3. Who are the children of promise? How does this affect your day-to-day life?

4. UNDERSTANDING 4: LEGALISM PERSECUTES AND ENSLAVES BELIEVERS (v.29).

Ishmael ridiculed, mocked, and persecuted Isaac. Paul draws upon this fact to show why believers are persecuted. It is because men try to approach God in the flesh, that is, by their own energy and effort in trying to be good and righteous.

1. The person in the flesh consciously or subconsciously is trying to secure credit, recognition, esteem, approval, acceptance, and praise from God--all by his own energy and effort. Therefore, he mocks, ridicules, and persecutes the believer who says that self-effort and self-righteousness are not enough and will not make a person acceptable to God.

2. The person in the flesh has to confess human weakness and inadequacy--that he cannot make himself acceptable to God because he is...

- too sinful
- too short of God's glory
- too unrighteous
- too unholy
- too polluted
- too hopeless
- too helpless
- too undeserving

The person in the flesh refuses to accept this fact. He wants to think highly of himself and place himself on a level close to God. Therefore, when a believer comes along and says that a person has to be born again by the Spirit of God, the natural man reacts. He refuses to accept the fact that his flesh, his own energy and effort, is unable to earn, win, and merit God's approval.

> **"Blessed are ye, when men shall revile you, and persecute you, and shall say all manner of evil against you falsely, for my sake" (Mt.5:11).**

ILLUSTRATION:

There are few things sadder in life than that of a Christian believer who has been bound up by legalism. Charles Simpson, in Pastoral Renewal, writes:

> *"I met a young man not long ago who dives for exotic fish for aquariums. He said one of the most popular aquarium fish is the shark. He explained that if you catch a small shark and confine it, it will stay a size proportionate to the aquarium. Sharks can be six inches long yet fully matured. But if you turn them loose in the ocean, they grow to their normal length of eight feet.*
>
> *"That also happens to some Christians. I've seen the cutest little six-inch Christians who swim around in a little puddle. But if you put them into a larger arena--into the whole of creation--only then can they become great."*[2]

Where are you swimming...in the tank of legalism or in the joyful sea of freedom?

QUESTIONS:

1. Why are believers persecuted?
2. Why does a person who lives by the flesh persecute believers?
3. What motivates a person who lives by the flesh?
4. What barriers does a person who lives by the flesh have to overcome?
5. What can you do to earn God's approval?

5. UNDERSTANDING 5: LEGALISM IS TO BE CAST OUT--HAVE NO INHERITANCE (v.30).

The law cannot co-exist with the grace of God. The son of Hagar, the law, shall not be heir with the son of Sarah, that is, grace. The fact of coming judgment could not be illustrated any clearer: Ishmael was cast out so that he would not share in the inheritance with Isaac (Gen.21:10f).

God never will accept anyone who approaches Him by law or by works. Why? Because the person has to stand before God saying, "God, here are my works, my goodness, my righteousness, a list of laws I have kept, a list of my contributions." Such a claim is merely deceptive boasting. Such a profession presents to God only human effort and energy, works and deeds. God is perfect; therefore, only perfection can exist with Him. No matter how much good and how many good works a person presents to God, they are not enough, for they do not make him perfect. Therefore, he must be cast from God's presence. But not the person of promise. The person of promise approaches God saying:

> *"Father, you are my Savior and Lord. You have loved me so much that you sent your Son to die for me. I believe with all my heart that Christ died for me, and I surrender all I am and have into His keeping. I cast myself totally upon His righteousness and His death for my sins."*

God has promised that the person who sincerely believes in His Son shall never perish but shall have everlasting life. He shall inherit the promise of God. God will accept his belief, counting it as righteousness, and the man shall inherit the promise.

> **"For the promise, that he should be the heir of the world, was not to Abraham, or to his seed, through the law, but through the righteousness of faith" (Ro.4:13).**

QUESTIONS:

1. Why can grace and law not co-exist together? Have you ever tried to mix them together? If so, what happened?
2. Did God have a right to cast out Ishmael? Why?
3. Exactly what is it that qualifies you to inherit the promise of God?

6. UNDERSTANDING 6: LEGALISM HAS NO CLAIM UPON THE CHILDREN OF GRACE (v.31).

Believers are the children of grace, not of law. The fact is clearly seen in all that has been stated above. Believers-- all men if they would only accept the fact--have so much for which to thank God. God has loved the world and demonstrated His love beyond anything any person could ever ask.

> **"For God so loved the world, that he gave his only begotten Son, that whosoever believeth in him should not perish, but have everlasting life" (Jn.3:16).**

ILLUSTRATION:

God gives each one of His children an eternal assurance of His care for them. Legalism cannot have us anymore--we are now children of grace. This reality gives the Christian believer peace of mind. This story illustrates the truth:

> *"Two brethren who differed on the question of the believer's safety in Christ were discussing the question, and one said to the other:*
>
> *"'I tell you a child of God is safe only so long as he stays in the lifeboat. He may jump out, and if he jumps out he is lost.'*
>
> *"To this the other person replied, saying: 'You remind me of an incident in my own life. I took my little son out with me in a boat. I realized, as he did not, the danger of his falling or even jumping, into the water. So I sat with him all the time, and all the time I held him fast, so he could neither fall out, nor jump out, of the boat.'*
>
> *"'But,' said the first speaker, 'he could have wriggled out of his coat and got away in spite of you.'*
>
> *"'Oh,' said the other, 'you misunderstood me if you supposed I was holding his coat; I was holding him.'"*[3]

GALATIANS 4:21-31

Do you understand that your heavenly Father is holding you tightly? That He has a grip on your life, not just your hand? You can rest assured that once you have genuinely placed your faith in Christ, you have eternal life. But you must take that step of faith!

QUESTIONS:

1. Who has the better grip on your life: you or God?
2. What would life be like if you lived every day like a child of grace? What things keep you from doing this?
3. Why is it important for you to know the difference between the law and grace?

SUMMARY:

And now, you do know the rest of the story. If you slip from a life of grace back to the bondage of legalism, remember your need for some understanding:

1. Understanding 1: a person must hear the law, grasp its implications.
2. Understanding 2: Abraham had two sons.
3. Understanding 3: the two mothers represent two covenants
4. Understanding 4: legalism persecutes and enslaves believers.
5. Understanding 5: legalism is to be cast out--have no inheritance.
6. Understanding 6: legalism has no claim upon the children of grace.

PERSONAL JOURNAL NOTES
(Reflection & Response)

1. The most important thing that I learned from this lesson was:

2. The area that I need to work on the most is:

3. I can apply this lesson to my life by:

4. Closing Statement of Commitment:

---

[1] Donald Grey Barnhouse. *Let Me Illustrate*. (Grand Rapids, MI: Fleming H. Revell, 1967), p.359-360.
[2] Craig B. Larson, Editor. *Illustrations for Preaching & Teaching*, p.93.
[3] *Christian Courier*. Walter B. Knight. *3,000 Illustrations for Christian Service*, p.324.

CHAPTER 5

D. Appeal Four: Stand Fast in the Liberty of Christ, 5:1-6

Stand fast there-
fore in the liberty
wherewith Christ hath
made us free, and be
not entangled again
with the yoke of
bondage.
2 Behold, I Paul say
unto you, that if ye be
circumcised, Christ
shall profit you noth-
ing.
3 For I testify again to
every man that is cir-
cumcised, that he is a
debtor to do the whole
law.
4 Christ is become of
no effect unto you,
whosoever of you are
justified by the law;
ye are fallen from
grace.
5 For we through the
Spirit wait for the
hope of righteousness
by faith.
6 For in Jesus Christ
neither circumcision
availeth any thing, nor
uncircumcision; but
faith which worketh
by love.

1. **Stand fast because Christ has freed the believer**
2. **Stand fast because the law is not God's way for man to be justified**
   a. If *ritualized*, Christ profits nothing
   b. If *ritualized*, a person is bound to do the whole law
   c. If a person seeks to be justified by law, Christ can have no effect upon him: He is cut off, fallen from grace
3. **Stand fast because the hope of righteousness is by faith**
   a. It comes through the Spirit
   b. It comes through Jesus Christ alone—not by law
   c. It comes by faith—stirred by God's love

Section IV
THE FIVEFOLD APPEAL TO BE JUSTIFIED BY FAITH ALONE
Galatians 4:8-5:12

Study 4: APPEAL FOUR: STAND FAST IN THE LIBERTY OF CHRIST

Text: Galatians 5:1-6

Aim: To stand fast and live victoriously in the liberty given by Christ.

Memory Verse:

"Stand fast therefore in the liberty wherewith Christ hath made us free, and be not entangled again with the yoke of bondage" (Galatians 5:1).

INTRODUCTION:

It was the American patriot Patrick Henry who said "Give me liberty or give me death." Henry knew what it was like to live under the thumb of a tyrant. Along the way, he had the good fortune to get a small taste of liberty. And once he tasted liberty, his tastebuds exploded with flavor. The bland taste of bondage would never satisfy him again.

In the same sense, the law serves as a tyrant. It shows no mercy and hates anything related to freedom. Anyone who weds himself to the law will be entangled in the chains of bondage. What is the alternative for the Christian believer? Liberty in Christ. But *why* and *how*? The purpose of this session is to answer those questions.

Straightforward and direct, a much needed appeal is given to backsliding churches and their people—stand fast in the liberty of Christ.

OUTLINE:

1. Stand fast because Christ has freed the believer (v.1).
2. Stand fast because the law is not God's way for man to be justified (v.2-4).
3. Stand fast because the hope of righteousness is by faith (v.5-6).

GALATIANS 5:1-6

1. STAND FAST BECAUSE CHRIST HAS FREED THE BELIEVER (v.1).

Note two points.

1. When a person believes in Jesus Christ, he is freed from the law and its enslaving power. He no longer has to worry if he is good enough or if he has done enough good works or kept enough laws to be acceptable to God. Why? Because Christ has fulfilled the law for him. When Christ was on earth, He was sinless; He obeyed the law perfectly, never violating it a single time. Therefore, He secured the Ideal Righteousness and stood before God as the Perfect Man. But Christ did something else much more wonderful. It was not enough for the Ideal Righteousness to be secured for man. There was also the problem of the penalty of the law; once the law had been broken, the penalty had been enacted; it had to be paid. This is the glorious message of the cross—what the death of Jesus Christ is all about. Jesus Christ not only secured the ideal righteousness for us, He took the penalty for our trespassing upon Himself and bore it. Jesus Christ bore our judgment and punishment for having broken the law which was death.

If righteousness has been secured for us and if the punishment for our transgressions has been paid, then we stand before God perfect—absolutely righteous and free from transgression—and acceptable to Him. Does this mean everyone is accepted by God and covered by the life and death of Jesus Christ? No! And the reason is easily seen: not everyone accepts what Jesus Christ has done for him—not everyone *believes* in Jesus Christ. Jesus Christ has set us free; we do stand in liberty free from the bondage of sin and death wrought by the law—but only if we believe it. Naturally—it is as obvious as can be—if we do not believe and accept a gift freely given, then the Giver still possesses it. We do not receive the gift; therefore, we do not have it.

The point is this: Christ has freed the believer from the bondage of the law. Therefore, we must stand fast in the liberty He has provided for us.

2. The Galatians were about to become entangled again with the yoke of bondage. False teachers had arisen who were teaching that the basic work of Christ was to live as a great example and to bring us the great teachings of God. That is, they accepted Jesus Christ as the Son of God, but they did not accept the message of salvation by grace (the righteousness and death of Jesus Christ). They taught that Jesus Christ had not come to give us a new approach to God; He came to add new teachings to the law. Therefore, a person was still to approach God...

- by undergoing the basic ritual of Jewish religion (circumcision, baptism, church membership, etc.).
- by committing himself to the law.
- by observing all the rituals and ceremonies of Jewish religion.

All of this of course sounds familiar to every generation, for if we simply omit the word *Jewish*, the three stipulations are seen to be present in so many teachings, religions, and churches of society.

Again, the exhortation is that a person must not become entangled with approaching God by law or works, for no person can ever do enough good to become perfect before God. Our perfection and acceptance before God has already been secured for us—in Christ Jesus our Lord. Therefore, we must stand fast in the liberty that Christ has given us. For the only person who will ever be acceptable to God is the person who stands before God *free of sin and condemnation*, a person who has been set free by God's very own Son.

> **"For the law of the Spirit of life in Christ Jesus hath made me free from the law of sin and death. For what the law could not do, in that it was weak through the flesh, God sending his own Son in the likeness of sinful flesh, and for sin, condemned sin in the flesh" (Ro.8:2-3).**

ILLUSTRATION:

Christ has freed the Christian believer from the power of the law. With that truth stated, keep yourself free. In Who Will Deliver Us?, Paul F.M. Zahl writes:

"A duck hunter was with a friend in the wide-open land of southeastern Georgia. Far away on the horizon he noticed a cloud of smoke. Soon he could hear cracking as the wind shifted. He realized the terrible truth: a brushfire was advancing, so fast they couldn't outrun it.

"Rifling through his pockets, he soon found what he was looking for—a book of matches. He lit a small fire around the two of them. Soon they were standing in a circle of blackened earth, waiting for the fire to come.

"They didn't have to wait long. They covered their mouths with handkerchiefs and braced themselves. The fire came near—and swept over them. But they were completely unhurt, untouched. Fire would not pass where fire had already passed.

"The law is like a brushfire. I cannot escape it. But if I stand in the burned-over place, not a hair of my head will be singed. Christ's death is the burned-over place. There I huddle, hardly believing yet relieved. The law is powerful, yet powerless: Christ's death has disarmed it."[1]

QUESTIONS:

1. What things could become potential entanglements of bondage to you? What protective barriers have you put in place in order to stay free?
2. What is Christ's relationship with the law?
3. Can rituals sometimes become yokes of bondage? What can you do to keep rituals from enslaving you, from becoming the focus of attention instead of Christ Himself?

2. STAND FAST BECAUSE THE LAW IS NOT GOD'S WAY FOR A MAN TO BE JUSTIFIED (v.2-4).

Three significant warnings are strongly issued.

1. If a person is *ritualized*, Christ shall profit him nothing. *Ritualized* means a person is depending upon some religious thing to make him acceptable to God. In the case of the Galatians, it was the ritual of circumcision; but it can apply to anything: ritual, ceremony, works, law, goodness, church membership, baptism, last rites, prayer, religious services, ministry, even religion itself. If a person approaches God and tries to secure God's acceptance by any means other than Christ, then Christ shall profit him nothing. This means that what Christ has done for man is of no benefit to the person. What Christ has done for man will have no effect upon the man whatsoever. The righteousness and death of Jesus Christ will be of no avail to the man, for the man is trusting his own works and goodness, not the righteousness and death of Jesus Christ.

2. If a person is ritualized, he has to do the whole law. Think for a moment: if a person trusts a ritual to save him, really depends upon a ritual to make him acceptable to God, then he had better keep the whole law. Why? Because he is accepting the law (works, religion) as the way to approach God. He is subjecting himself to ritual, walking the way of law in order to approach God. Therefore, he must continue to approach God by law. He must keep the *whole* law.

In a summary statement: if a person approaches God by ritual, any ritual, he assumes responsibility for doing the whole law.

3. If a person seeks to be justified by law, Christ can have no effect upon him—he is fallen from grace. What does this mean?

Remember: Paul is warning the Galatian believers by issuing a strong warning. False teachers were saying this: a person could be saved only by obeying the law and by doing as much good as possible. They were teaching that the righteousness and death of Jesus Christ was not what it took to approach God and to receive eternal life. They said more than Christ was needed: one's own righteousness and goodness, works and effort, were also needed.

Keep this in mind: we can readily see why Paul issued such a severe warning to the Galatian believers. They must not follow the false teachers, must not turn away from Christ and become apostates.

The point is this: not only the Galatians, but we also, must heed the warning lest we begin to deny Christ. To deny Christ, His righteousness and death, is bound to lead to the doom of the apostate. We must always remember: Paul himself said that he was to be accursed if he ever preached any other gospel than that of God's glorious love in His Son, the Lord Jesus Christ. Eternal security is not the issue here, as it is so often made to be. The issue is God's own dear Son, His righteousness and death—His very life and work—His honor and Person. No person is living or ever will live who will be allowed to tamper with the righteousness and death of God's dear Son. We are *fools* to think so, even if we are trying to defend and explain a doctrinal position. This was certainly the thought and position of Paul when he said he was to be cursed if he became apostate.

> **"Many will say to me in that day, Lord, Lord, have we not prophesied in thy name? and in thy name have cast out devils? and in thy name done many wonderful works? And then will I profess unto them, I never knew you: depart from me, ye that work iniquity" (Mt.7:22-23).**
>
> **"Therefore by the deeds of the law there shall no flesh be justified in his sight: for by the law is the knowledge of sin" (Ro.3:20).**

ILLUSTRATION:

Accepting the grace of God at face-value is difficult for many Christians: "How can God be that good to us? What is the catch? Surely, we have to add something to what God has done to be saved." J. Vernon McGee illustrates this point for us:

> *"Years ago a tonic called Hadacol was advertised. I don't think it is sold any more. I am not sure of the details, but they found it was about seventy-five percent alcohol. A lot of people were using it. The company that made it was giving out glowing testimonials about its product.*
>
> *"Now suppose a testimonial read something like this: 'I took 513 bottles of your medicine. Before I began using Hadacol, I could not walk. Now I am able to run....I really have improved. But I think you ought to know that during that time I also concocted a bottle of my own medicine and used it also.'*
>
> *"Now, my friend, that final sentence certainly muddied the water. There is no way to tell if it was the 513 bottles of Hadacol that cured him or his own concoction. The minute you put something else into the formula, you are not sure.*
>
> *"Now notice carefully what Paul is saying. If you trust Christ plus something else you are not saved...How can He profit you anything when you have made up a bottle of your own concoction rather than trusting Him alone for your salvation?"*[2]

QUESTIONS:

1. What warnings does Paul issue in these verses? Why is it important for you to heed these warnings also?
2. What does it mean to "fall from grace"?
3. Can you remember a time when you fell from grace? How did you recover?
4. What practical things can you do to prevent a future fall from grace?

3. STAND FAST BECAUSE THE HOPE OF RIGHTEOUSNESS IS BY FAITH (v.5-6).

The hope of the believer is for righteousness. *Hope* does not mean the uncertainty of worldly hope, that the believer might—but then again he might not—secure righteousness before God. The believer's hope is in Jesus Christ, and it is as assured as God exists. Hope in the Bible means the focus, the concentration, the longing, the craving, the desire for righteousness—the privilege of being redeemed and spending eternity with God. Note the source of such an assurance and secured hope.

GALATIANS 5:1-6

1. The hope for righteousness comes through the Spirit of God. It is the presence of the Spirit who dwells within the believer that stirs the hope. The Holy Spirit stirs hope and gives *absolute assurance* that God will take His faith and count it for righteousness.

2. The hope for righteousness comes through Jesus Christ alone, not by a ritual (circumcision, law) nor by the lack of a ritual. Note exactly what this is saying:

⇒ neither undergoing a ritual (circumcision) nor being without a ritual brings hope.
⇒ neither having and keeping the law nor being without law brings hope.
⇒ neither working for righteousness nor not working for righteousness brings hope.

Nothing, absolutely nothing, can provide the sure hope of righteousness within a person except Jesus Christ: His righteousness and His death alone can offer hope to man.

3. The hope for righteousness comes by faith wrought by love. It was God's love that sent His Son to secure our righteousness to die for us. When a person *really sees* this, it breaks him; and he bows and surrenders his own love, faith, life, and loyalty to Christ. The love of God stirs us to love Him and to believe Him. We love Him because He has loved us.

> **"For we are saved by hope: but hope that is seen is not hope: for what a man seeth, why doth he yet hope for?" (Ro.8:24).**

QUESTIONS:

1. What is the difference between faith and hope?
2. Upon what is your hope to be focused?
3. What difference does hope make in your Christian journey?
4. What did Paul mean when he said "faith...worketh by love"? Does your faith work like this? What adjustments do you need to make?

SUMMARY:

"Give me liberty or give me death." These were the words of a great patriot. They are to be the words of a Christian believer also. We have been challenged to...

1. Stand fast because Christ has freed the believer.
2. Stand fast because the law is not God's way for man to be justified.
3. Stand fast because the hope of righteousness is by faith.

PERSONAL JOURNAL NOTES
(Reflection & Response)

1. The most important thing that I learned from this lesson was:

2. The area that I need to work on the most is:

3. I can apply this lesson to my life by:

4. Closing Statement of Commitment:

---

[1] Craig B. Larson, editor. *Illustrations for Preaching & Teaching*, p.127.
[2] J. Vernon McGee. *Thru The Bible, Vol.5*, p.183-184.

	E. Appeal Five: Obey the Truth, 5:7-12		
1. Obey the truth, for the Christian life is a race	7 Ye did run well; who did hinder you that ye should not obey the truth?	that ye will be none otherwise minded: but he that troubleth you shall bear his judgment, whosoever he be.	**the Minster of God has confidence in you**
2. Obey the truth, for God called you to freedom	8 This persuasion cometh not of him that calleth you.	11 And I, brethren, If I yet preach circumcision, why do I yet suffer persecution? then is the offence of the cross ceased.	**5. Obey the truth, for false teachers will be judged** a. Bc. they trouble believers b. Bc. they spread falsehood about the minister of Christ c. Bc. they stumble over the cross
3. Obey the truth, for a little untruth corrupts the whole	9 A little leaven leaveneth the whole lump.	12 I would they were even cut off which trouble you.	d. Bc. they deserve condemnation
4. Obey the truth, for	10 I have confidence in you through the Lord,		

Section IV
THE FIVEFOLD APPEAL TO BE JUSTIFIED BY FAITH ALONE
Galatians 4:8-5:12

Study 5: APPEAL FIVE: OBEY THE TRUTH

Text: Galatians 5:7-12

Aim: To stop backsliding: obey the truth.

Memory Verse:
"Ye did run well; who did hinder you that ye should not obey the truth?" (Galatians 5:7).

INTRODUCTION:

A constant frustration for sailboat owners is barnacles. These tiny sea creatures attach themselves to the hull of the boat. For the sailor who wants to keep his boat in "ship-shape" condition, the barnacles must be removed.

If the Christian believer wants to be in the best shape, he too must be free of worldly attachments. How is this done? He must stop backsliding by scraping away the barnacles of sin until he sees the surface of the truth. Paul gives us specific instructions on how to do this needful chore.

The Galatian churches had backslidden. They were turning away from the truth, from Jesus Christ Himself. In this passage, Paul makes one last appeal to them: obey the truth. The only hope for the backslider is to turn back to Christ and obey the truth.

OUTLINE:

1. Obey the truth because the Christian life is a race (v.7).
2. Obey the truth because God called you to freedom (v.8).
3. Obey the truth because a little untruth corrupts the whole (v.9).
4. Obey the truth because of the confidence others have in you (v.10).
5. Obey the truth because false teachers will be judged (v.10-12).

1. OBEY THE TRUTH, FOR THE CHRISTIAN LIFE IS A RACE (v.7).

The phrase "you did run well" is a picture of athletes running in a race.

GALATIANS 5:7-12

1. The Galatians had been running and running well. When they first heard the gospel, they believed…

- in God's love—that God loved the world so much that He sent His Son into the world to save it.
- in the righteousness of Christ—that Jesus Christ lived a perfect and righteous life, securing righteousness for them.
- in the death of Christ—that Jesus Christ died for their sins—that He actually bore the punishment for their transgressions.

As stated, the Galatians had been running the Christian race *well*. Having believed in Christ, they had been living for Christ: living clean and pure lives and bearing testimony for Him. They had been worshipping and serving Him with zeal. They had been living what they were professing. There had been no false profession about them: no counterfeit and no hypocrisy. They had not been *Sunday only Christians*; they had been busy for Christ seven days a week, and people from all over the city were coming to know Christ.

But note: some person had stepped in and had begun to hinder their running the Christian race. We know from the previous four chapters that some false teachers had arisen in the churches of Galatia. However, the present reference is to a single individual. Apparently one person had taken charge, becoming a ringleader of the trouble and false teaching. The word "hinder" means to cut in, to edge in, to interfere, to obstruct. The picture is still that of the running track. While the Galatians had been running the Christian race, some had edged in on them and begun to hinder and interfere with their running. They were no longer obeying the truth. They were now trying to approach God by some way other than Christ. They were now thinking…

- that God accepted them because they had been *ritualized*: circumcised and baptized.
- that God accepted them because they tried to keep the law: tried to be as good as they could and did good deeds as opportunity arose.
- that God approved them because they were faithful to the church: its rituals, ceremonies, services, rules and regulations.

They were no longer running well. They had allowed some false teacher to hinder them and to turn them from the truth. They had a need to think about the matter, a desperate need…

- to think about the race they had been running.
- to think about who it was that was now hindering their running.

> **"Know ye not that they which run in a race run all, but one receiveth the prize? So run, that ye may obtain" (1 Cor.9:24).**
>
> **"Wherefore, seeing we also are compassed about with so great a cloud of witnesses, let us lay aside every weight, and the sin which doth so easily beset us, and let us run with patience the race that is set before us" (Heb.12:1).**

ILLUSTRATION:

Has anyone tried to hinder you in your spiritual race? Listen to this illustration about a little boy who knew how to keep on course.

Dennis wasn't a big fellow, but as he played Little League Baseball, his knowledge of the game made up for any lack of size. On a particular summer day he swung at the ball with all his might, and to his amazement, the ball rocketed off his bat in the general direction of left field.

Off he ran! As he rounded first base, his head was down. In doing so, he failed to see whether or not the ball had landed in fair or foul territory. Before he arrived at second base, the second baseman on the other team flagged Dennis down and said, "Go back. It was a foul ball."

Without hesitation, Dennis ignored the second baseman and slid safely into second base. The umpire, whose opinion mattered the most, signaled that the ball was fair.

What is the lesson for us here? Keep on running until the Umpire of our souls, the Lord Jesus Christ, tells us to go back. We need to ignore any other voice that would hinder our running ahead to the next base.

Fair or foul? Fair ball—keep on running to the Lord. In Him, you'll always be called safe!

QUESTIONS:

1. What types of things represent the "second basemen" in your life? Who or what hinders you from being faithful in your Christian race?
2. How do you feel when you have listened to the advice of someone who hinders you in your spiritual race? What could you do differently the next time?
3. Why do you fail to obey the truth? What changes do you need to make to become more faithful?

2. OBEY THE TRUTH, FOR GOD CALLED YOU TO FREEDOM (v.8).

Note how concise and forceful this statement is; it is direct and to the point: "This persuasion does not come from him who calls you!" The Greek word *is persuasion*. Any persuasion, any position, any teaching that leads away from the truth of Jesus Christ is not of God. God and God alone determines how He can be approached, and He has determined it. A person approaches Him through the righteousness and death of His Son Jesus Christ. There is no other way to be justified and saved other than by His Son. There is absolutely no other way to approach God. Therefore, any person who teaches otherwise is teaching a false doctrine; the person's persuasion or teaching is not the persuasion of God.

"Neither is there salvation in any other: for there is none other name under heaven given among men, whereby we must be saved" (Acts 4:12).

QUESTIONS:

1. Who tends to be easily persuaded by false doctrines? Why?
2. How can you know the truth? What can you do to protect yourself from false teachers?
3. Has your knowledge of the truth helped you to resist temptation? If you had not known the truth, what would have been the result?

3. OBEY THE TRUTH, FOR A LITTLE UNTRUTH CORRUPTS THE WHOLE (v.9).

Leaven stands for evil and corruption, fermentation and infection. It takes only a little leaven to permeate and influence the whole lump of dough. So it is with false teachers. (Remember, Paul was referring only to the ringleader in this present passage.) One false teacher can inject his false teaching into the church, and it will soon permeate and influence the whole church. This is what Paul and Scripture are proclaiming. If the Galatians did not root out the false teaching, the whole church would soon be corrupted and the truth would be destroyed. Jesus Christ would no longer be the focus of attention. The church and its people would be focusing upon their rituals, ceremonies, and good works instead of upon Christ.

They would be trying to approach God through their own goodness and merit. Jesus Christ would soon be placed on the back burner, de-emphasized, and lost sight of by many. His prominence and the absolute necessity of His righteousness and death would be diminished and downplayed. This always happens when false teaching is allowed in a church. The only answer to false teaching is what has been stated: root it out.

"Then understood they how that he bade them not beware of the leaven of bread, but of the doctrine of the Pharisees and of the Sadducees" (Mt.16:12).

"Beware lest any man spoil you through philosophy and vain deceit, after the tradition of men, after the rudiments of the world, and not after Christ" (Col.2:8).

ILLUSTRATION:

Is there any way you can avoid the corruption that falsehood brings to your culture?

There once was an 'old fashioned' prophet who came to a large city. His agenda was pretty simple, *"Repent or perish!"* At first glance, many of the city's residents listened to his sermons. But after a few days, they went back to doing what they wanted to do. Listening to this prophet was not on their list of things to do.

The prophet did not stop preaching. Every day he would stand in the market place and preach to those within the sound of his voice. A shop-keeper approached the prophet and asked, "Why are you still preaching? No one is paying any attention to you." The prophet narrowed his eyes and responded, "I'm preaching so their hardness to the gospel will not change me!"

Are you allowing a little evil into your life each day? Or do you bind yourself to God so closely that it has no room to get in? Don't compromise and allow the leaven of the world to water down the gospel. Keep on preaching the truth. The more you speak it and hear it, the more you will live like a Christian believer ought to live.

QUESTIONS:

1. What secret sins do you need to confess to the Lord right now? Remember, He wants to cleanse you and forgive you (1 Jn.1:9).
2. We cannot hide our sins from God. Why do some people think they can fool God?
3. What kind of advice would you give to someone like the above illustration describes?

4. OBEY THE TRUTH, FOR THE MINISTER OF GOD HAS CONFIDENCE IN YOU (v.10).

What an amazing statement! When you think about all that has been written in the Book of Galatians (the terrible attacks against Paul himself and the seriousness of the false teaching that had threatened the church), Paul's confidence in the Galatians is shocking.

However, note exactly what he said: his confidence is "through the Lord"; that is, the Galatians could overcome the false teaching only through the Lord. Through Christ they could conquer the situation and come out victorious. In fact, Paul had confidence that the churches would heed his warnings and turn back to the Lord and begin to obey the truth.

APPLICATION:

The only way false teaching or any other difficulty in the church can be handled is "through the Lord."

"Now unto him that is able to keep you from falling, and to present you faultless before the presence of his glory with exceeding joy, to the only wise God our Saviour, be glory and majesty, dominion and power, both now and ever" (Jude 24-25).

QUESTIONS:
1. Paul had an amazing confidence in the Galatian's ability to do what was right. What was the secret to his confidence? Do you have the same confidence in other Christians that you know? Why or why not?
2. Is it easier for you to confront someone with the truth or easier to ignore people who are being deceived? Why?
3. What can you do to build your minister's confidence in you? What can any Christian believer do to build confidence in one another?

5. OBEY THE TRUTH, FOR FALSE TEACHERS WILL BE JUDGED (v.10-12).

The fact is stated in no uncertain terms: the false teacher who was troubling the church would bear the judgment of God. Paul gave four reasons why false teachers will be judged.

1. False teachers shall be judged because they trouble the church and its believers. By *trouble* is meant to unsettle and disturb. The false teachers were loosening the cords of faith in Christ, disturbing the security and lives of the believers and the ministry of the churches. They were misleading believers and defiling the church of God with false teaching.

> **"If any man defile the temple of God, him shall God destroy; for the temple of God is holy, which temple ye are" (1 Cor.3:17).**

2. False teachers shall be judged because they spread falsehood about the minister of Christ. Paul did not preach that ritual was necessary for salvation (circumcision, baptism, church membership, etc.); but the false teachers were saying that he did. However, the fact that Paul did not preach circumcision was the main reason the Jews persecuted him so much. That is the reason Paul simply asks: Why am I persecuted by the Jews so much if I preach salvation by ritual (circumcision, baptism, church membership, etc.)?

The point is this: the false teachers had attacked Paul, attempting to discredit him and his ministry among the believers. And one thing God does not tolerate is an attack on His anointed.

> **"Who art thou that judgest another man's servant? to his own master he standeth or falleth. Yea, he shall be holden up: for God is able to make him stand" (Ro.14:4).**

3. False teachers shall be judged because they are offended by the cross. Paul preached the cross, that a person was justified and acceptable to God *only by the cross of Jesus Christ*. The false teachers (Judaizers) were offended by this. The word "offense" means stumbling or staggering. It was the cross that had caused the false teachers to stumble in their approach to God. They had taught that the death of Jesus Christ was not enough to make a person acceptable to God. The cross was not sufficient by itself; more was needed. A person had to be *ritualized* (circumcised, baptized) and subject himself to the law of God and keep all the rituals, ceremonies, and rules of the church. If he did, then he was a true Christian.

Salvation by works and law, of course, is false. Salvation is through God's Son, Jesus Christ, and through Him alone. Scripture is clear: anyone who follows or teaches any other salvation shall be severely judged by God.

4. False teachers shall be judged because they deserve condemnation. Paul is gripped with intense emotion here: he wishes the false teachers would just go and castrate themselves—cut themselves completely off. This is a repulsive thought to some and rightly so, for false teaching is the most serious offense. Nothing surpasses it, in particular when it adds or takes away from the cross of Christ. God gave His Son to die for men, and if men miss Him, they miss the righteousness necessary to live in God's presence. There is no other righteousness than the righteousness of Jesus Christ, and there is no other death that can stand as the Ideal substitute for man's death—not to God. God will not accept any death other than Christ's death—not to cover the death of man. If a man wishes to approach God, he must come through the cross, through the

death of Jesus Christ. God accepts no other way. Therefore, if a person takes any other way to God, it would be best if he just went ahead and went all the way with whatever he teaches—better if he just went all the way and cut himself off and got out of the way—much better than to continue destroying the people of God.

The point is this: a false teacher deserves to be judged. There is no punishment too good for him. As stated above, "He shall bear his judgment."

> **"For the son of man shall come in the glory of his Father with his angels; and then he shall reward every man according to his works" (Mt.16:27).**
>
> **"For we must all appear before the judgment seat of Christ; that every one may receive the things done in his body, according to that he hath done, whether it be good or bad" (2 Cor.5:10).**

QUESTIONS:

1. What consequences do false teachers face?
2. Some would say that God is too harsh in His dealing with false teachers. Would you agree or disagree? Why?
3. What would happen to your church if a false teacher had an opportunity to teach your people?

SUMMARY:

Are you in the best shape you can be in your Christian life? Are the barnacles of sin, of worldly attachments, scraped away? If you are having a difficult time, remember the instructions given on how to become "ship-shape":

1. Obey the truth because the Christian life is a race.
2. Obey the truth because God called you to freedom.
3. Obey the truth because a little untruth corrupts the whole.
4. Obey the truth because of the confidence others have in you.
5. Obey the truth because false teachers will be judged

PERSONAL JOURNAL NOTES
(Reflection & Response)

1. The most important thing that I learned from this lesson was:

2. The area that I need to work on the most is:

3. I can apply this lesson to my life by:

4. Closing Statement of Commitment:

1. **Love is necessary: Liberty vs. license** a. License is the danger	**V. THE BELIEVER'S LIFE & WALK: FREE & SPIRITUAL, 5:13-6:18** **A. The Believer's Great Law of Life: Love, 5:13-15** 13 For, brethren, ye have been called unto liberty; only use	not liberty for an occasion to the flesh, but by love serve one another. 14 For all the law is fulfilled in one word, even in this; Thou shalt love thy neighbour as thyself. 15 But if ye bite and devour one another, take heed that ye be not consumed one of another.	b. The restraint: love **2. Love is serving others** **3. Love is not offending but caring for one's neighbor** **4. Love is not biting & devouring one another**

Section V
THE BELIEVER'S LIFE AND WALK: FREE AND SPIRITUAL
Galatians 5:13-6:18

Study 1: THE BELIEVER'S GREAT LAW OF LIFE: LOVE

Text: Galatians 5:13-15

Aim: To demonstrate the love of God on a daily basis.

Memory Verse:
"For all the law is fulfilled in one word, even in this; Thou shalt love thy neighbor as thyself" (Galatians 5:14).

SECTION OVERVIEW:

This passage begins the last section of Galatians. Up until now everything has dealt with doctrine; now Paul begins to deal with the practical day-to-day affairs of the believer. Paul has six very practical subjects to discuss. Bunching all six subjects together, a simple title would be: "The Believer's Life and Walk: Free and Spiritual."

SECTION OUTLINE:
1. The Believer's Great Law of Life: Love (5:13-15)
2. A Walk Combating the Great Enemy in Life: The Lusts of the Flesh (5:16-21).
3. A Walk Bearing God's Nature: The Fruit of the Spirit (5:22-26).
4. A Walk Restoring the Man Who Slips (6:1-5).
5. A Walk Doing Good to One's Teacher (6:6-10).
6. A Walk Boasting in the Cross of Christ (6:11-18).

INTRODUCTION:
Have you ever received a letter in the mail that informed you of some great news: "*Congratulations! You have been pre-approved to use our credit card. We think so much of you, that we have extended your limit to $7,500.00!*" At once, your spending motor turns on as you begin to visualize all those things you cannot afford--but that does not matter--just charge it! All of a sudden you are tempted to cross the line between liberty and license. You are in a dilemma: Where do you draw the line? How can you control yourself?

GALATIANS 5:13-15

Jesus Christ has set the believer free from having to make decisions over and over again. You face the same temptations in your Christian life day after day. But fortunately, the believer no longer has to work and work in order to secure God's approval and acceptance. The believer is accepted by God through the work of Jesus Christ. However, there is a critical fact that must always be remembered: Christian liberty is not license, that is, being free to sin, to do as a person likes. Christian liberty is being free ***not to sin***. It is being free to overcome the passions and urges of the flesh that unceasingly wage war against the better judgment of man. The believer is a person who is so conscious of the indwelling Holy Spirit and His power that he is able to purge and cleanse himself and to love his neighbor as himself.

The point is this: the believer is not to walk in sin, for he loves God and loves his neighbor. The believer is to walk and live under the greatest of laws--the law of love. Love is the guiding law of the believer's life and walk.

OUTLINE:

1. Love is necessary: liberty vs. license (v.13).
2. Love is serving others (v.14).
3. Love is not offending, but caring for one's neighbor (v.14).
4. Love is not biting and devouring one another (v.15).

1. LOVE IS NECESSARY: LIBERTY VS. LICENSE (v.13).

It has been well established that the believer does not live by the law nor by some work or act of goodness. The believer knows that he can never become perfect, no matter how much good he does. He knows that he cannot keep enough laws nor can he work to make himself like God. He knows that he is short, far short, of God. If he is ever to be acceptable to God, it has to be because God loves him enough...

- to provide an Ideal Righteousness for him.
- to provide Someone to bear his punishment for having violated the law.

The believer knows that God has loved him and everyone else that much. He knows that God has loved the world so much that he sent His Son, Jesus Christ, into the world to do both things for him and for all the people of the earth. He knows...

- that Jesus Christ lived a sinless life and secured the Ideal Righteousness for him.
- that Jesus Christ died for him--died bearing the judgment of the law for him.

The point is this: when a person believes this about Christ--that Christ is His Savior--God takes that man's belief and counts it as righteousness. The man becomes acceptable to God. This is what the believer knows: he is not acceptable to God because he works and becomes better by keeping some law or rule or ritual. He is acceptable to God because Christ has set him free from having to struggle to be good enough to be saved and always wondering if he has done enough good. Man no longer has to work to keep laws to be saved. Living by law was always a hopeless task that left man lost and helpless. Man is saved by the grace of God in giving His Son for the world: by believing that Jesus Christ is his Savior--that Jesus Christ died for him. However, having said this, note two things.

1. There is the danger of license. A question needs to be asked: if Christ sets us free from the law, does this mean that a person can *believe in Christ* and then live as he wants, doing his own thing? Can he use his liberty as an occasion to satisfy the flesh, knowing that God will forgive him? Can a person continue to seek the things of the world and give way to the desires and lusts of his flesh? Can he believe in Christ and still live in worldliness? No! A thousand times no, Scripture declares!

A person who thinks and declares such an idea fails to understand belief--true belief. In the Bible belief does not mean intellectual belief, to just believe something in the mind. Belief means a *committed belief*, to believe something with one's life. To believe Christ is to commit one's life to Christ. Just think about it for a moment, and it becomes perfectly clear: if a person is not willing to commit his life to Christ, he does not believe in Christ. He could not believe, not really; for if he really believed, he would beyond all question give all he is and has to the Son of God. (Cp. Ro.6:16; Heb.5:9.)

2. There is the restraint of love. A person who thinks that belief in Christ frees him and gives him license to sin does not understand what love is. This is the subject of the present passage. The true believer is freed from having to secure God's approval by law, but love is the one restraint that is placed upon him. The believer needs no restraint but love. There are at least two reasons for this.

⇒ God has loved him, so the person who truly sees the love of God is drawn to love God and to love all God's creatures.

> **"For the love of Christ constraineth us; because we thus judge, that if one died for all, then were all dead: and that he died for all, that they which live should not henceforth live unto themselves, but unto him which died for them, and rose again" (2 Cor.5:14-15).**

⇒ Love embraces all the commandments of God. Jesus Himself said so, and the fact is clearly seen in the points of this passage.

> **"Master, which is the great commandment in the law? Jesus said unto him, Thou shalt love the Lord thy God with all thy heart, and with all thy soul, and with all thy mind. This is the first and great commandment. And the second is like unto it, Thou shalt love thy neighbour as thyself. On these two commandments hang all the law and the prophets" (Mt.22:36-40).**

ILLUSTRATION:

There is an old saying which says, "give him enough rope and he'll hang himself." Somehow, some Christians feel that God's love gives them enough rope (license) to explore the sins of the world. Listen to this example of one who took advantage of God's love.

"My name is Sidney the Sheep. I had the good fortune of belonging to the Good Shepherd. He treated me with great respect and provided me with the finest care.

"I really had it made. He made me to lie down in green pastures. And when I got thirsty, He led me beside quiet waters. When I felt bad inside, He restored my soul. I could always count on Him to lead me in the right path--a path of righteousness.

"Sometimes, life got really scary as I faced the shadows of death. But my Good Shepherd stayed with me and brought comfort to my troubled heart. He kept me secure against the enemies who surrounded me. Life with Him has been wonderful.

"He has promised to help me--even when I stray from His side. I could kick myself (with each of my four legs) when I allow myself to be drawn to the other side of the fence. The grass just looks greener at times. But as I sample the grass, I quickly realize that I have been deceived! When will I ever learn to trust Him for everything that I need?"

Have you tried the world's green pastures? Then you have also come to realize, or will shortly, what Sidney did: looks can be deceiving!

QUESTIONS:

1. What circumstances tempt you to wander from the Good Shepherd?
2. Give some examples of abusing the liberty that God has given you. What is needed in your life in order to correct this problem?
3. What restraints has God provided for you to stay true to Him?

2. LOVE IS SERVING OTHERS (v.14).

A believer is *free* in Christ: he is set free of all law, restraints, and works. He is under nothing, absolutely nothing but Christ. He lives in Christ, moves and has his being in Christ. The love of Christ is his law and restraint. Why? Because Christ loved the believer, served and gave Himself for the believer, and the believer knows it. Therefore, the believer loves Christ with all his heart and life. He wants to please Christ and do all he can to serve Him. And this is just the point: how can the believer serve Christ? By doing exactly what Christ did: loving and serving others.

"By love serve one another" (Gal.5:13^b^).

A person who loves does not act like a *lord over people*; he...

- serves and helps
- shows kindness and gentleness
- expresses concern and care
- demonstrates sympathy and empathy

The person who truly loves identifies with a person, gets down where he is, even below where he is, and ministers to him. Love serves--always reaches out to do whatever it can for the other person. Love never withdraws from the other person, feeling that he or she...

- does not deserve the effort or help.
- is not worth the effort or help.
- is less than what he should be.
- is too derelict, immoral, uneducated, unrecognized, below others.

"Even as the Son of man came not to be ministered unto, but to minister, and to give his life a ransom for many" (Mt.20:28).

ILLUSTRATION:

What motivates your service to others? Keep your thoughts close to the heart as you listen to this story:

"A young woman in New York held what was considered a splendid position in a school attended by children from wealthy homes. Suddenly she gave it up and went to teach in one of the most squalid districts on East Side.

"'These East Side kiddies have so little,' she explained. 'School is the one bright spot in their lives. I feel almost like a fairy godmother when in their midst. The children in my other school had everything. They even were [brought] to the schoolroom door by nurses and chauffeurs. There was no 'kick' in it for me.'

"Such confessions as this prove that Jesus was right when He stressed the fact that the joy that comes from helping others is the richest reward one can experience in life."[1]

QUESTIONS:

1. When is it easiest for you to serve? Is it supposed to be easy to serve? Why or why not?
2. What motivates you to serve others? Are there wrong motives for serving? What are they?
3. Who are some people who serve you? What motivations do they have to serve you?

3. LOVE IS NOT OFFENDING, BUT CARING FOR ONE'S NEIGHBOR (v.14).

It must be admitted:

⇒ If a person cared for everyone else as much as he cared for himself, he would need no law. He would be living and doing exactly what he should.

This is the reason love fulfills all the law. Love does not take advantage of other people. Love will not use other people to fulfill one's own purpose, greed, or lust. Love will not hurt someone else any more than we would want someone to hurt us.

Love involves some very practical acts that are clearly spelled out in Scripture (1 Cor.13:4-7).

⇒ Love suffers long (endures long and is patient).
⇒ Love is kind.
⇒ Love envies not (is not jealous).
⇒ Love vaunts not itself (does not brag; does not boast).
⇒ Love is not puffed up (vainglorious, arrogant, prideful).
⇒ Love does not behave itself unseemingly (unbecomingly, rudely, indecently, unmannerly).
⇒ Love seeks not her own (is not selfish or self-seeking; does not insist on its own right and way).
⇒ Love is not easily provoked (not touchy, angry, fretful, resentful).
⇒ Love thinks no evil (harbors and plans no evil thought; takes no account of a wrong done it).
⇒ Love rejoices not in iniquity (wrong, sin, evil, injustice), but rejoices in the truth (justice and righteousness).
⇒ Love bears all things.
⇒ Love believes all things (exercises faith in everything; is ready to believe the best in everyone).
⇒ Love hopes all things (keeps up hope in everything and under all circumstances).
⇒ Love endures all things (without weakening; it gives power to endure).

> **"Owe no man any thing, but to love one another: for he that loveth another hath fulfilled the law. For this, Thou shalt not commit adultery, Thou shalt not kill, Thou shalt not steal, Thou shalt not bear false witness, Thou shalt not covet; and if there be any other commandment, it is briefly comprehended in this saying, namely, Thou shalt love thy neighbour as thyself. Love worketh no ill to his neighbour: therefore love is the fulfilling of the law" (Ro.13:8-10).**

QUESTIONS:

1. Why are we to love others? When? Are there exceptions to this commandment from God?
2. How does trusting God help you to love others?
3. Are you satisfied with your current level of love for others? In what areas does God need to help you?

4. LOVE IS NOT BITING AND DEVOURING ONE ANOTHER (v.15).

A.T. Robertson says that the picture of biting and devouring is that of a fight between a dog and cat or a fight between wild animals (*Word Pictures in the New Testament*, Vol.4, p.311). Biting and devouring refers to much more than just feuding and fighting. Men bite and devour each other when they violate each other. For example, nothing takes a hunk out a person any more than the biting or devouring that takes place between a wife and husband. However, love respects the other person--no matter who he is or what he has done. Love does not bite or devour others in any way whatsoever. Love does not…

- snap
- condemn
- expose
- hurt
- slander
- censor
- covet
- abuse
- criticize
- accuse
- misuse
- gossip
- exploit
- take

> **"From whence come wars and fightings among you? come they not hence, even of your lusts that war in your members? Ye lust, and have**

not: ye kill, and desire to have, and cannot obtain: ye fight and war, yet ye have not, because ye ask not" (Jas.4:1-2).

"Hatred stirreth up strifes: but love covereth all sins" (Pr.10:12).

ILLUSTRATION:

There is an old Indian story told about two wolves; one black and one white. As the story is told, a man was describing to his chief the vicious battle which was taking place inside of him:

> "*Old and wise chief, help me to understand those things which trouble me.*" Taking a deep breath, the chief shared his insightful wisdom. "*My son, inside each man are two wolves: one good and one bad. They will be in continual conflict for as long as you live. Your responsibility in this inner-struggle is to feed the good one and to starve the bad one. Your life will become an open record based upon your ability to do this.*"

How about you? Everyone has a war between the good and the bad. Which one do you tend to feed the most? Are gossip, criticizing, accusing, hurting, and so on a part of your daily diet? If so, then the bad in you will continue to win the battle. It is only as you starve the bad and overcome it with good (love, care, concern) that the good will take over!

QUESTIONS:

1. In response to the above illustration, what kinds of things feed the bad wolf inside of you?
2. What practical things can you do in order to not bite and devour someone else?
3. What are some ways you can feed the good inside you?

SUMMARY:

Love must be your guide in all that you do. When you choose to follow this great law of life, you will discover that...

1. Love is necessary: liberty vs. license.
2. Love is serving others.
3. Love is not offending, but caring for one's neighbor.
4. Love is not biting and devouring one another.

PERSONAL JOURNAL NOTES
(Reflection & Response)

1. The most important thing that I learned from this lesson was:

2. The area that I need to work on the most is:

3. I can apply this lesson to my life by:

4. Closing Statement of Commitment:

[1] Walter B. Knight. *3,000 Illustrations for Christian Service*, p.614.

GALATIANS 5:16-21

	B. A Walk Combating the Great Enemy In Life: Lusts of the Flesh, 5:16-21	19 Now the works of the flesh are manifest, which are these; Adultery, fornication, uncleanness, lasciviousness,	**2. The works or acts of the flesh are listed**
1. The answer to conquering the lusts of the flesh: The Holy Spirit a. The flesh fights for dominance b. The flesh is contrary to the Spirit c. The flesh keeps a person from doing what he should d. The flesh fails to keep the law	16 This I say then, Walk in the Spirit, and ye shall not fulfil the lust of the flesh. 17 For the flesh lusteth against the Spirit, and the Spirit against the flesh: and these are contrary the one to the other: so that ye cannot do the things that ye would. 18 But if ye be led of the Spirit, ye are not under the law.	20 Idolatry, witchcraft, hatred, variance, emulations, wrath, strife, seditions, heresies, 21 Envyings, murders, drunkenness, revellings, and such like: of the which I tell you before, as I have also told you in time past, that they which do such things shall not inherit the kingdom of God.	**3. The judgment of those who live by the flesh**

Section V
THE BELIEVER'S LIFE AND WALK:
FREE AND SPIRITUAL
Galatians 5:13-6:18

Study 2: A WALK COMBATING THE GREAT ENEMY IN LIFE: LUSTS OF THE FLESH

Text: Galatians 5:16-21

Aim: To crush the lusts of the flesh.

Memory Verse:
"This I say then, Walk in the Spirit, and ye shall not fulfil the lust of the flesh" (Galatians 5:16).

INTRODUCTION:
Do you experience the victorious Christian life? Or would you compare your life to that of a prisoner of war? Can your life be described by this graphic testimony?

"I lost my freedom while fighting in this spiritual war. Years ago, the enemy surrounded me and forced me to surrender unconditionally. And now, I stare through the fence of bondage and long for the freedom that was once mine. Every day I listen to propaganda from the enemy. Its message is pounded into my mind that there is no hope for escape."

Can you relate to any of this man's testimony? Often we forget how to escape from the clutches of the flesh and its lusts. Through this session, God will remind us once again how to escape as well as how to stay free!

This and the next passage are two critical passages for the believer's walk. They deal with walking in the Spirit of God and conquering the flesh. The lessons being taught need to be diligently followed by the believer.

GALATIANS 5:16-21

OUTLINE:

1. The answer to conquering the lusts of the flesh: the Holy Spirit (v.16-18).
2. The works or acts of the flesh are listed (v.19-21).
3. The judgment of those who live by the flesh (v.21).

1. THE ANSWER TO CONQUERING THE LUSTS OF THE FLESH: THE HOLY SPIRIT (v.16-18).

The believer is to walk in the presence and power of the Holy Spirit. This is the only conceivable way he can keep from fulfilling the lusts of the flesh. No person has the power to control the lusts of his flesh—not within himself. The reason why is clearly seen in the four reasons given by Scripture.

1. The flesh fights for dominance. It lusts against the Spirit, struggles and fights to control the man. The picture is that of a tug of war[1]. The flesh stands contrary to the Spirit—toe to toe, face to face—and it seeks to control man.

The word "lusts" means *a yearning passion for*. Every person has experienced the flesh...

- yearning
- pulling
- desiring
- wanting
- craving
- hungering
- thirsting
- longing
- grasping
- grabbing
- taking

Every person knows what it is to have his flesh lusting after something, to have it yearning to lay hold of something. The flesh is very strong and difficult to control. This is the first reason why a believer's only hope to control the flesh is the Spirit of God.

> **"But I see another law in my members, warring against the law of my mind, and bringing me into captivity to the law of sin which is in my members" (Ro.7:23).**

2. The flesh is contrary to the Spirit. The flesh has within itself base and unregulated urges and passions. A man senses the desire to do what he likes, to lift the restraints and follow his own inclinations, desires, passions, and emotions. This is what the Bible means when it speaks of the "lust of the flesh."

However, the genuine believer has another force within his life—the force of the Holy Spirit. When the believer feels *the constraint* and *the pressure* between the flesh and the Holy Spirit, the Holy Spirit is giving the power to overcome the flesh. The constraint *is the power*. The believer who listens to the constraint and walks away from the object of the pressure and calls upon God for the courage to stay away is the believer who walks in the Spirit. The believer is to know no such thing as peaceful co-existence between the flesh and the Spirit.

QUESTIONS:

1. What is the secret to conquering the lusts of the flesh?
2. What things can you do to control the power of the flesh in your life?

3. The flesh keeps a person from doing what he should. Every person has experienced the power of the flesh; everyone has caved in to the flesh and done something that he did not want to do. He fought against doing it—knew it was harmful or hurtful—yet he did not resist the flesh. He gave in to the power of the flesh and did it. He...

- overate
- became angry
- began smoking
- got drunk
- did evil
- lusted
- became prideful
- cursed
- acted selfishly
- committed immorality
- cheated, lied, or stole

Note another fact as well. All of us have been tempted, and we have known how to combat and overcome the temptation. However, the flesh was so strong we did not overcome it. The struggle we experienced involved that of...

- controlling
- reaching out
- loving
- being patient
- showing kindness
- giving
- giving in
- helping
- sacrificing

The point is this: the flesh is so strong that it often keeps us from doing what we should. The only hope of ever controlling the flesh is to walk in the Spirit of God—in His presence and power.

> **"For that which I do I allow not: for what I would, that do I not; for what I hate, that do I. If then I do that which I would not, I consent unto the law that it is good. Now then it is no more I that do it, but sin that dwelleth in me. For I know that in me (that is, in my flesh,) dwelleth no good thing: for to will is present with me; but how to perform that which is good I find not. For the good that I would I do not: but the evil which I would not, that I do. Now if I do that I would not, it is no more I that do it, but sin that dwelleth in me" (Ro.7:15-20).**

4. The flesh fails to keep the law. This has been clearly shown in the previous point. No person keeps the law all the time: the flesh causes us to fail, and no matter how much we try, we cannot do everything the law says—not all the time. What then is the answer?

The Spirit of God is the answer; being led by the Holy Spirit will free us from the flesh and from the condemnation of the law. What does this mean? It means that the Holy Spirit frees us to live as Christ lived. The *active energy* of life, the dynamic force and being of life—all that is in Christ Jesus—is given to the believer. The believer actually lives *in* Christ Jesus. And the Spirit of life which is in Christ frees the believer from the fate (law) of sin and death. This simply means that the believer lives in a *consciousness of being free*. He breathes and senses a depth of life, a richness, a fulness of life that is indescribable. He lives with power—power over the pressures, strain, impediments, and bondages of life—even the bondages of sin and death. He lives now and shall live forever. He senses this and knows this. Life to him is a *spirit, a breath, a consciousness* of being set free through Christ. Even when he sins and guilt sets in, there is a tug, a power (the Holy Spirit) that draws him back to God. He asks forgiveness and removal of the guilt (1 Jn.1:9), and immediately upon asking, the same power (the Holy Spirit) instills an instantaneous assurance of cleansing. He feels free again, and he feels full of life in all its liberating power and freedom. He is full of the "Spirit of life"--a life that is now and forever.

> **"For the law of the Spirit of life in Christ Jesus hath made me free from the law of sin and death. For what the law could not do, in that it was weak through the flesh, God sending his own Son in the likeness of sinful flesh, and for sin, condemned sin in the flesh" (Ro.8:2-4).**

ILLUSTRATION:

With a little imagination, we can take a peek into our hearts and see the struggle between the flesh and Spirit being acted out:

> *The scene is a field with two opposing teams tightly gripping a rope. On one side is a team that could pass for sumari wrestlers. On the other end of the rope is you; yes, just you. In the middle of the rope is a smelly pit of slime. As you begin to survey the situation, it doesn't take long to reach this conclusion: You will not be able to resist the pit which lies before you. The opposing team, or the temptation to go it alone, is ready to pull you in. You need help and you need it now. "Holy Spirit! Fill me now. Hold this rope with me as I hold onto You!"*

Put a real face on what we have just seen. Fred was a fine Christian man. He had a wife and a child who were gifts from God. In a weak moment, Fred was tempted to break his word to his wife and child. A woman where he worked "needed" him. Fred was such a good listener, so every time she got a chance, she filled his ear with her problems. The more Fred listened, the more dangerous the situation became. Before he knew what was happening, the snares were set and every step Fred took was presented a threatening temptation, a temptation that could devastate him and his dear family.

Fred felt trapped! The more he struggled with this, the deeper he sank in despair. "Lord, I feel so weak. Please help me to resist—for the sake of my family. For Your sake, give me the strength to resist." At that very moment, a vibrant light entered Fred's heart and a strength that was not his own took over. In a very dramatic moment, Fred jerked the rope in his heart and pulled temptation into the pit and walked away a free man—a man who walked away in the Spirit.

Don't be left holding your rope alone. Walk in the Spirit...and pull!

QUESTIONS:

1. Can you think of an example when you lost the tug of war and were pulled into the pit? What were some of the results of your losing that tug of war? What would you do differently today?
2. Do you think it is possible to control the power of the flesh in your life without God's help? What kind of help does God offer you?

2. THE WORKS OR ACTS OF THE FLESH (v.19-21).

The works or acts of the flesh show just how strong the flesh is. Note a fact of extreme importance: the flesh in itself is not sinful. The flesh or human body is given by God; it is for God's use. In fact, when a person is converted to Christ, his body becomes a temple for God to dwell in through the Holy Spirit. The Christian is not told to cleanse himself from the flesh but from "the lust of the flesh" (Gal.5:16), "the filthiness of the flesh" (2 Cor.7:1), and from "the works of the flesh" (Ro.13:12; Gal.5:19). The works of the flesh are the 'fruit' of sin within us, and sin originates in the heart not in the flesh. The sins of the flesh listed in this passage are clearly seen all throughout society; and tragically they are seen not only on the daily newscasts of every city, but within every community, home, and life on planet earth. The very presence of such fleshly sins shows just how strong the flesh is and how helpless man is to control his flesh.

1. *Adultery*: sexual unfaithfulness to husband or wife. It is also looking at a woman or a man to lust after her or him. Looking at and lusting after the opposite sex--whether in person, magazines, books, on beaches or anywhere else--is adultery. Imagining and lusting within the heart is the very same as committing the act.

"But I say unto you, that whosoever looketh on a woman to lust after her hath committed adultery with her already in his heart" (Mt.5:28).

2. *Fornication*: a broad word including all forms of immoral and sexual acts. It is premarital sex and adultery; it is abnormal sex, all kinds of sexual vice.

"Flee fornication. Every sin that man doeth is without the body; but he that committeth fornication sinneth against his own body" (1 Cor.6:18).

3. *Uncleanness*: moral impurity; doing things that dirty, pollute, and soil life.

"Wherefore God also gave them up to uncleanness through the lusts of their own hearts, to dishonour their own bodies between themselves" (Ro.1:24).

4. *Lasciviousness*: filthiness, indecency, shamelessness. A chief characteristic of the behavior is open and shameless indecency. It means unrestrained evil thoughts and behavior. It is giving in to brutish and lustful desires, a readiness for any pleasure. It is a man who knows no restraint, a man who has sinned so much that he no longer cares what people say or think. It is something far more distasteful than just doing wrong. A man who misbehaves usually tries to hide his wrong, but a lascivious man does not care who knows about his exploits or shame. He wants; therefore, he seeks to take and gratify. Decency and opinion do not matter. Initially when he began to sin, he did as all men do: he misbehaved in secret. But eventually, the sin got the best of him—to the point that he no longer cared who saw or knew. He became the subject of a master—the master of habit, of the thing itself. Men become the slaves of such things as unbridled lust, wantonness, licentiousness, outrageousness, shamelessness, insolence (Mk.7:22); wanton manners, filthy words, indecent body movements, immoral handling of males and females (Ro.13:13); public display of affection, carnality, gluttony, and sexual immorality (1 Pt.4:3; 2 Pt.2:2, 18). (Cp. 2 Cor.12:21; Gal.5:19; Eph.4:19; 2 Pt.2:7.)

> **"And likewise also the men, leaving the natural use of the woman, burned in their lust one toward another; men with men working that which is unseemly, and receiving in themselves that recompense of their error which was meet" (Ro.1:27).**

5. *Idolatry*: the worship of idols, whether mental or made by man's hands; the worship of some idea of what God is like, of an image of God within a person's mind; the giving of one's primary devotion (time and energy) to something other than God.

> **"For this ye know, that no whoremonger, nor unclean person, nor covetous man, who is an idolater, hath any inheritance in the kingdom of Christ and of God" (Eph.5:5).**
>
> **"Mortify therefore your members which are upon the earth; fornication, uncleanness, inordinate affection, evil concupiscence, and covetousness, which is idolatry: for which things' sake the wrath of God cometh on the children of disobedience" (Col.3:5-6).**

6. *Witchcraft*: sorcery; the use of drugs or of evil spirits to gain control over the lives of others or over one's own life. In the present context, it would include all forms of seeking the control of one's fate including astrology, palm-reading, seances, fortune telling, crystals, and other forms of witchcraft.

> **"So Saul died for his transgression which he committed against the LORD, even against the word of the LORD, which he kept not, and also for asking counsel of one that had a familiar spirit, to inquire of it" (1 Chron.10:13).**
>
> **"And when they shall say unto you, Seek unto them that have familiar spirits, and unto wizards that peep, and that mutter: should not a people seek unto their God? for the living to the dead? To the law and to the testimony: if they speak not according to this word, it is because there is no light in them" (Is.8:19-20).**

7. *Hatred*: enmity, hostility, animosity. It is the hatred that lingers and is held for a long, long time; a hatred that is deep within.

> **"He that saith he is in the light, and hateth his brother, is in darkness even until now" (1 Jn.2:9).**

8. *Variance*: strife, discord, contention, fighting, struggling, quarreling, dissension, wrangling. It means that a man fights against another person in order to get something: position,

promotion, property, honor, recognition. He deceives, doing whatever has to be done to get what he is after.

> **"As coals are to burning coals, and wood to fire; so is a contentious man to kindle strife" (Pr.26:21).**

9. *Emulations*: jealousy, wanting and desiring to have what someone else has. It may be material things, recognition, honor, or position.

> **"For jealousy is the rage of a man: therefore he will not spare in the day of vengeance" (Pr.6:34).**

10. *Wrath*: bursts of anger; indignation; a violent, explosive temper; quick-tempered explosive reactions that arise from stirred and boiling emotions. But it is anger which fades away just as quickly as it arose. It is not anger that lasts.

> **"Wherefore, my beloved brethren, let every man be swift to hear, slow to speak, slow to wrath: for the wrath of man worketh not the righteousness of God" (Jas.1:19-20).**

11. *Strife*: conflict, struggle, fight, contention, faction, dissension; a party spirit, a cliquish spirit.

> **"Let nothing be done through strife or vainglory; but in lowliness of mind let each esteem other better than themselves" (Ph.2:3).**

12. *Seditions*: division, rebellion, standing against others, splitting off from others.

> **"For rebellion is as the sin of witchcraft, and stubbornness is as iniquity and idolatry. Because thou hast rejected the word of the LORD, he hath also rejected thee from being king" (1 Sam.15:23).**
>
> **"But chiefly them that walk after the flesh in the lust of uncleanness, and despise government. presumptuous are they, selfwilled, and they are not afraid to speak evil of dignities" (2 Pt.2:10).**

13. *Heresies*: rejecting the fundamental beliefs of God, Christ, the Scriptures, and the church; believing and holding to some teaching other than the truth.

> **"But in vain they do worship me, teaching for doctrines the commandments of men" (Mt.15:9).**

14. *Envyings*: this word goes beyond jealousy. It is the spirit...
   - that wants not only the things that another person has, but begrudges the fact that the person has them.
   - that wants not only the things to be taken away from the person, but wants him to suffer through the loss of them.

> **"A sound heart is the life of the flesh: but envy the rottenness of the bones" (Pr.14:30).**

15. *Murders*: to kill, to take the life of another person. Murder is sin against the sixth commandment.

> **"Whosoever hateth his brother is a murderer: and ye know that no murderer hath eternal life abiding in him" (1 Jn.3:15).**

16. *Drunkenness*: taking drink or drugs to affect one's senses for lust or pleasure; becoming tipsy or intoxicated; partaking of drugs; seeking to loosen moral restraint for bodily pleasure.

> **"Nor thieves, nor covetous, nor drunkards, nor revilers, nor extortioners, shall inherit the kingdom of God" (1 Cor.6:10).**

17. *Revellings*: carousing; uncontrolled license, indulgence, and pleasure; taking part in wild parties or in drinking parties; lying around indulging in feeding the lusts of the flesh; orgies.

> **"For the time past of our life may suffice us to have wrought the will of the Gentiles, when we walked in lasciviousness, lusts, excess of wine, revellings, banquetings, and abominable idolatries" (1 Pt.4:3).**

QUESTIONS:
1. Do you worry about being a slave to your flesh?
2. Which one of these works of the flesh has the greatest influence in your life? You may not be able to confess it publicly, but answer the question in your own heart: which work of the flesh does give you the most problem? What can be done to free you from its power over you?
3. Is it easier for you to fight the works of the flesh or to surrender to their influence over you? Why?
4. Why does God want you to be aware of the works of the flesh?

3. THE JUDGMENT OF THOSE WHO LIVE BY THE FLESH (v.21).

Very simply, those who live by the flesh shall not inherit the kingdom of God. This can be clearly seen: if God is righteous, then people must live righteous lives in order to be accepted by Him. However, people ignore the fact of God's righteousness and His demand for righteousness. People divorce their behavior from religion. People...

- profess religion
- practice religion
- talk religion
- defend their beliefs about religion

However, they go ahead and live like they want regardless of their religion. If they want to do something, they do it feeling that God will forgive them. There are few people who really think that God will reject them. They feel that they will have done enough good to be acceptable to God...

- enough kindness
- enough religion
- enough works
- enough service

In the final analysis, most people just think that God will accept them. This attitude comes from a false concept of God, a concept that looks upon God as a father who is indulgent and who gives his children the license to do *some wrong*.

This is a fatal mistake. It was the mistake that some of the Galatian church members were making, and it is the same mistake that teeming multitudes of religious people have made down through the centuries.

> **"Know ye not that the unrighteous *shall not inherit* the kingdom of God?" (1 Cor.6:9).**

Believers are to inherit a kingdom, a new heavens and earth where God will rule and reign. They are to be given eternal life and given the glorious privilege of being citizens in God's kingdom and world. They are to live with Him and serve Him in *perfection* for all eternity. But this glorious privilege is to be given only to genuine believers, those men and women who have truly given their lives to the Lord Jesus Christ—given their lives to live as Jesus Christ says to live. No matter how religious a person is—no matter how much zeal a person may have in keeping religious rituals and in attending services and in giving to charity—if he does not live a pure and righteous life, he "shall not inherit the kingdom of God."

> **"Know ye not that the unrighteous shall not inherit the kingdom of God?" (1 Cor.6:9).**
>
> **"For I say unto you, That except your righteousness shall exceed the righteousness of the scribes and Pharisees, ye shall in no case enter into the kingdom of heaven" (Mt.5:20).**
>
> **"For without [the Kingdom of God] are dogs, and sorcerers, and whoremongers, and murderers, and idolaters, and whosoever loveth and maketh a lie" (Rev.22:15).**

ILLUSTRATION:

The love of God should always be balanced with the judgment of God. Listen to this story from Warren Wiersbe's *Meet Yourself in the Psalms*.

> *"[He] tells about a frontier town where a horse bolted and ran away with a wagon carrying a little boy. Seeing the child in danger, a young man risked his life to catch the horse and stop the wagon.*
>
> *"The child who was saved grew up to be a lawless man, and one day he stood before a judge to be sentenced for a serious crime. The prisoner recognized the judge as the man who, many years before, had saved his life; so he pled for mercy on the basis of that experience.*
>
> *"But the words from the bench silenced his plea, 'Young man, then I was your savior; today I am your judge, and I must sentence you to be hanged.'*
>
> *"One day Jesus will say to rebellious sinners, 'During that long day of grace, I was the Savior, and I would have forgiven you. But today I am your Judge. Depart from me, ye cursed, into everlasting fire!'"*[2]

If you play with fire, you will get burned. Allow Christ to be your Savior, so you will not have to face Him as the Judge in the terrible day of judgment that is coming upon all the world.

QUESTIONS:

1. Why do some believers take their salvation lightly?
2. What are some specific things you can do in order to keep your relationship with the Lord alive?
3. What inheritance are you expecting to receive from the Lord? On what basis do you make these claims?
4. For what will we be judged when we face the Lord?

SUMMARY:

Christ has done all that He needed to do in order to make you free. Have you done all that you need to do? Remember His Word to us in this session:

1. The answer to conquering the lusts of the flesh is the Holy Spirit.
2. The works or acts of the flesh are listed.
3. Those who live by the flesh will be judged.

GALATIANS 5:16-21

PERSONAL JOURNAL NOTES
(Reflection & Response)

1. The most important thing that I learned from this lesson was:

2. The area that I need to work on the most is:

3. I can apply this lesson to my life by:

4. Closing Statement of Commitment:

---

[1] A.T. Robertson. *Word Pictures in the New Testament*, Vol.4, p.311.
[2] Craig B. Larson, editor. *Illustrations for Preaching & Teaching*, p.100.

	C. A Walk Bearing God's Nature: The Fruit of the Spirit, 5:22-26	is no law.	fleshly works
		24 And they that are Christ's have crucified the flesh with the affections and lusts.	2. The believer is to walk bearing a crucified flesh
1. The believer is to walk bearing God's nature	22 But the fruit of the Spirit is love, joy, peace, longsuffering,	25 If we live in the Spirit, let us also walk in the Spirit.	3. The believer is to walk consistent with his position in Christ
a. Source: The Holy Spirit b. Purpose: To stand strongly against	gentleness, goodness, faith, 23 Meekness, temperance: against such there	26 Let us not be desirous of vain glory, provoking one another, envying one another.	4. The believer is to walk free from super-spirituality & envy

Section V
THE BELIEVER'S LIFE AND WALK: FREE AND SPIRITUAL
Galatians 5:13-6:18

Study 3: **A WALK BEARING GOD'S NATURE: THE FRUIT OF THE SPIRIT**

Text: **Galatians 5:22-26**

Aim: To produce a life that is marked with the Fruit of the Spirit.

Memory Verse:

> **"But the fruit of the Spirit is love, joy, peace, longsuffering, gentleness, goodness, faith, meekness, temperance: against such there is no law" (Galatians 5:22-23).**

INTRODUCTION:

When was the last time you took a bite from a beautiful orange only to be disappointed by its flavor? Instead of enjoying a sweet, juicy taste, you only tasted dry fruit. It looked like an orange, smelled like an orange, and even felt like an orange. But it did not taste like an orange should taste: sweet and juicy. Instead, it was sour and dry. The Christian life can at times be likened to an orange that is sweet and juicy, producing as expected. However, many believers are offering a life that is the exact opposite: sour and dry.

The believer is to walk bearing God's nature: a life that is marked by the Fruit of the Spirit. A life that is *sweet* and *juicy*.

Note that the fruit which is produced in the believer is the fruit of the Spirit. God is in the business of producing top-quality fruit which is abundant and eternal. The believer has done nothing to deserve this kind of fruit. The Fruit of the Spirit is an act of the mercy and grace of a loving God.

A genuine believer stands before God approved and acceptable. He is embraced and loved by God, looked after and cared for by God. And he is the recipient of eternal life and of the absolute assurance of eternal life. The believer has been accepted by God because of Jesus Christ. Jesus Christ died to pay the penalty for man's transgressions of the law. He died to free men from the law, from its judgment and condemnation. Therefore, standing before God, the believer is not there because he has kept laws and has earned the right to stand there. He is there because of his faith in Jesus Christ. His faith honors God's Son, and God loves His Son so much that He honors anyone who believes in His Son. Therefore, the man who believes that Jesus Christ makes him acceptable to God becomes acceptable to God.

The point is this: since the believer has to approach God through Jesus Christ and not through the law, he is freed from the law. He is under Jesus Christ, not under the law. Does this mean, then, that the believer has no restraint upon his life and behavior—that he is free to live like he wants? Is he free to follow the desires and lusts of his flesh—to seek the things of the world and give in to the urges to look, think, touch, taste, and do?

The answer is no! A thousand times no! For the believer has been given God's nature; he walks through life bearing God's nature (2 Pt.1:4; Eph.4:24; Col.3:10; 1 Cor.6:19-20). God has absolutely nothing to do with sin, not within His nature. Therefore, the believer is not to cave in to the lusts of the flesh; he is to walk bearing the fruit of God's nature, that is, the fruit of God's Spirit.

OUTLINE:

1. The believer is to walk bearing God's nature (v.22-23).
2. The believer is to walk bearing a crucified flesh (v.24).
3. The believer is to walk consistent with his position in Christ (v.25).
4. The believer is to walk free from selfishness, super-spirituality, and envy (v.26).

1. THE BELIEVER IS TO WALK BEARING GOD'S NATURE (v.22-23).

Note that the word "fruit" is singular, not plural. The Holy Spirit has only *one fruit*. It is broken down into a list of traits in order to help us understand His nature. However, the Spirit has only one nature, one fruit. Therefore, when He lives within a person, all these traits are present. The genuine believer does not experience and bear just some of them: the Spirit of God produces them all in the life of the believer. Whether or not a believer displays all the traits of the Holy Spirit depends on whether the believer suppresses the Holy Spirit or calls on Him to live actively through and in his life.

1. There is the fruit of *love* (agape). Agape love is the love of the mind, of the reason, of the will. It is the love that goes so far...
   - that it loves regardless of feelings—whether a person feels like loving or not.
   - that it loves a person even if the person does not deserve to be loved.
   - that it actually loves the person who is utterly unworthy of being loved.

Note four significant points about agape love.

a. Selfless or agape love is the love of God, the very love possessed by God Himself. It is the love demonstrated in the cross of Christ.

⇒ It is the love of God for the *ungodly*.

> **"For when we were yet without strength, in due time Christ died for the ungodly" (Ro.5:6).**

⇒ It is the love of God for *unworthy sinners*.

> **"But God commendeth his love toward us, in that, while we were yet sinners, Christ died for us" (Ro.5:8).**

⇒ It is the love of God for *undeserving enemies*.

> **"For if, when we were enemies, we were reconciled to God by the death of his Son, much more, being reconciled, we shall be saved by his life" (Ro.5:10).**

b. Selfless or agape love is a gift of God. It can be experienced only if a person knows God *personally*—only if a person has received the love of God, that is, Christ Jesus, into his heart and life. Agape love has to be shed abroad (poured out, flooded, spread about) by the Spirit of God within the heart of a person.

"And hope maketh not ashamed; because the love of God is shed abroad in our hearts by the Holy Ghost which is given unto us" (Ro.5:5).

c. Selfless or agape love is the greatest thing in all of life according to the Lord Jesus Christ.

"And Jesus answered him, The <u>first of all the commandments</u> is, Hear, O Israel; The Lord our God is one Lord: and thou shalt love the Lord thy God with all thy heart, and with all thy soul, and with all thy mind, and with all thy strength: this is the <u>first commandment</u>. And the second is like, namely this, Thou shalt love thy neighbour as thyself. There is <u>none other commandment</u> greater than these" (Mk.12:29-31).

d. Selfless or agape love is the greatest possession and gift in human life according to the Scripture (1 Cor.13:1-13).

"And now abideth faith, hope, charity, these three; but the greatest of these is charity" (1 Cor.13:13).

<u>QUESTIONS:</u>
1. What is the "fruit of love?" Does this trait often express itself in your life? Why or why not?
2. What are the special aspects of agape love which makes it different from what the world calls "love?"

2. There is the fruit of *joy*: an inner gladness; a deep seated pleasure. It is a depth of assurance and confidence that ignites a cheerful heart. It is a cheerful heart that leads to cheerful behavior.

3. There is the fruit of *peace*: it means to bind together, to join, to weave together. It means that a person is bound, woven and joined together with himself and with God and others.

The Hebrew word is *shalom*. It means freedom from trouble and much more. It means experiencing the highest good, enjoying the very best possible, possessing all the inner good possible. It means wholeness and soundness. It means prosperity in the widest sense, especially prosperity in the spiritual sense of having a soul that blossoms and flourishes.

a. There is the peace of the world. This is a peace of escapism, of avoiding trouble, of refusing to face things, of unreality. It is a peace that is sought through pleasure, satisfaction, contentment, absence of trouble, positive thinking, or denial of problems.

b. There is the peace of Christ and of God.

⇒ The peace of God is, first, a *bosom peace*, a peace deep within. It is a tranquillity of mind, a composure, and a restfulness that is undisturbed by circumstances and situations. It is more than feelings—even more than attitude and thought.

⇒ The peace of God is, second, the *peace of conquest* (cp. Jn.16:33). It is the peace that is independent of conditions and environment; the peace which no sorrow, danger, suffering, or experience can take away.

"These things I have spoken unto you, that in me ye might have peace. In the world ye shall have tribulation: but be of good cheer; I have overcome the world" (Jn.16:33).

⇒ The peace of God is, third, the *peace of assurance* (cp. Ro.8:28). It is the peace of unquestionable confidence; the peace with a sure knowledge that one's life is in the hands of God and that all things will work out for good to those who love God and are called according to His purpose.

> **"And we know that all things work together for good to them that love God, to them who are the called according to his purpose" (Ro.8:28).**

⇒ The peace of God is, fourth, the *peace of intimacy with God* (cp. Ph.4:6-7). It is the peace of the highest good. It is the peace that settles the mind, strengthens the will, and establishes the heart.

c. There is the source of peace. Peace is always born out of reconciliation. Its source is found only in the reconciliation wrought by Jesus Christ. Peace always has to do with personal relationships: a man's relationship to himself, to God, and to his fellow men.
   ⇒ A man must be bound, woven, and joined together with himself in order to have peace.
   ⇒ A man must be bound, woven, and joined together with God in order to have peace.
   ⇒ A man must be bound, woven, and joined together with his fellow man to have peace.

> **"But now in Christ Jesus ye who sometimes were far off are made nigh by the blood of Christ. For he is our peace, who hath made both one [both Jew and Gentile, all men], and hath broken down the middle wall of partition between us" (Eph.2:13-14).**

QUESTIONS:
1. In what ways does "joy" affect how you live? If joy were not a part of your life, what would replace it?
2. What is the "fruit of peace"?
3. Why is the world unable to duplicate God's peace?

4. There is the fruit of *longsuffering*: patience, bearing and suffering a long time, perseverance, being constant, stedfast, and enduring. Long-suffering never gives in; it is never broken no matter what attacks it.
   ⇒ Pressure and hard work may fall upon us, but the Spirit of God helps us suffer long under it all.
   ⇒ Disease or accident or old age may afflict us, but the Spirit of God helps us to suffer long under it.
   ⇒ Discouragement and disappointment may attack us, but the Spirit of God helps us to suffer long under it.
   ⇒ Men may do us wrong, abuse, slander, and injure us; but the Spirit of God helps us to suffer long under it all.

Two significant things need to be noted about longsuffering.

a. Longsuffering never strikes back. Common sense tells us that a person who is attacked by others could strike back and retaliate. *But* the Christian believer is given the power of longsuffering—the power to suffer the situation or person for a long, long time.
b. Longsuffering is one of the great traits of God. As pointed out in this verse, it is a fruit of God's very own Spirit, a fruit that is to be in the life of the believer.
   ⇒ God and Christ are long-suffering toward sinners.

"Or despisest thou the riches of his goodness and forbearance and longsuffering; not knowing that the goodness of God leadeth thee to repentance?" (Ro.2:4).

⇒ God saves believers so that they may be examples of longsuffering.

"Howbeit for this cause I obtained mercy, that in me first Jesus Christ might show forth all longsuffering, for a pattern to them which should hereafter believe on him to life everlasting" (1 Tim.1:16).

⇒ God withholds His judgment from the world because He is longsuffering, waiting for more and more to be saved.

"And account that the longsuffering of our Lord is salvation; even as our beloved brother Paul also according to the wisdom given unto him hath written unto you" (2 Pt.3:9; cp. 1 Pt.4:20).

William Barclay says that if God had been a man, He would have long ago wiped man off the face of the earth because of his terrible disobedience.[1] But God loves and cares for man; therefore, God is longsuffering toward man. God is suffering a long, long time with man, allowing more and more men to be saved.

"Strengthened with all might, according to his glorious power, unto all patience and long-suffering with joyfulness" (Col.1:11).

QUESTIONS:
1. What makes the fruit of longsuffering such an important possession for the believer?
2. Do you know anyone who has mastered longsuffering as a part of his or her nature? What kinds of things can you glean from his or her example?

5. There is the fruit of *gentleness*: it is being kind and good, useful and helpful, gentle and sweet, considerate and gracious through all situations no matter the circumstances. A person who is gentle does not act...

- hard
- indifferent
- harsh
- unconcerned
- too busy
- bitter

Gentleness cares for the feelings of others and feels with them. It experiences the full depth of sympathy and empathy. It shows care and gets right into the situation with a person. Gentleness suffers with those who suffer, and struggles with those who struggle, and works with those who work.

⇒ God is kind.

"But love ye your enemies, and do good, and lend, hoping for nothing again; and your reward shall be great, and ye shall be the children of the Highest: for he is kind unto the unthankful and to the evil" (Lk.6:35).

⇒ Believers are to be kind to one another.

"Be kindly affectioned one to another with brotherly love; in honour preferring one another" (Ro.12:10).

6. There is the fruit of *goodness*: it is being full of virtue and excellence, kindness and helpfulness, peace and consideration. It means that a person is full of all good and he does all good. It means...

- that he has a good heart and good behavior.
- that he is good and does good.
- that he is a quality person.

Note that a good person lives and treats everyone just as they should be treated. He does not take advantage of any person nor does he stand by and let others take advantage. He stands up and lives for what is right and good and just. This means that goodness involves discipline and rebuke, correction and instruction as well as love and care, peace and conciliation. A good person will not give license to evil, will not let evil run rampant. He will not allow evil to indulge itself and treat others unjustly. He will not allow others to suffer evil. Goodness steps forward and does what it can to stop and control evil.

⇒ God is full of goodness.

> **"He loveth righteousness and judgment: the earth is full of the goodness of the LORD" (Ps.33:5).**

⇒ Believers are to be full of all goodness.

> **"And I myself also am persuaded of you, my brethren, that ye also are full of goodness, filled with all knowledge, able also to admonish one another" (Ro.15:14).**

QUESTIONS:

1. Why do some people consider "gentleness" as a weakness of character? What makes "gentleness" a strength? Would you consider yourself to be gentle according to God's definition? Why or why not?
2. What kind of impact does the "fruit of goodness" have in the world today? When "goodness" is absent, what are some of the consequences?

7. There is the fruit of *faith* or faithfulness: it means to be faithful and trustworthy, to be loyal and stedfast in devotion and allegiance. It means to be constant, staunch, and enduring. A faithful person denies and sacrifices himself—all he is and has—and trusts God. He believes God and knows that God will work all things out for good. Therefore, he casts himself totally upon God and becomes faithful to God.

⇒ Faithfulness does not doubt God—not His salvation, provision, or strength to help.
⇒ Faithfulness does not begin with God then back off and give up.
⇒ Faithfulness does not walk with God then give in to the lusts of the flesh.

Faithfulness begins with God and continues with God. Faithfulness continues on and on; it never slackens or surrenders.

⇒ God is faithful.

> **"God is faithful, by whom ye were called unto the fellowship of his Son Jesus Christ our Lord" (1 Cor.1:9).**
>
> **"I will sing of the mercies of the Lord for ever: with my mouth will I make known thy faithfulness to all generations" (Ps.89:1).**

⇒ Believers are to be faithful.

> **"Moreover it is required in stewards [believers], that a man be found faithful" (1 Cor.4:2).**

QUESTIONS:
1. What does faithfulness not do? According to this definition, are you being faithful?
2. In what ways can you cultivate faithfulness in your life?

8. There is the fruit of *meekness*: it means to be gentle, tender, humble, mild, considerate, but strongly so. Meekness has the strength to control and discipline, and it does so at the right time.

a. Meekness has *a humble state of mind*. But this does not mean the person is weak, cowardly, and bowing. The meek person simply loves people and loves peace; therefore, he walks humbly among men regardless of their status and circumstance in life. Associating with the poor and lowly of this earth does not bother the meek person. He desires to be a friend to all and to help all as much as possible.

b. Meekness has *a strong state of mind*. It looks at situations and wants justice and right to be done. It is not a weak mind that ignores and neglects evil and wrong-doing, abuse and suffering.
   ⇒ If someone is suffering, meekness steps in and does what it can to help.
   ⇒ If evil is being done, meekness does what it can to stop and correct it.
   ⇒ If evil is running rampant and indulging itself, meekness actually strikes out in anger. However, note a crucial point: the anger is always at the right time and against the right thing.

c. Meekness has *strong self-control*. The meek person controls his spirit and mind. He controls the lusts of his flesh. He does not give way to ill-temper, retaliation, passion, indulgence, or license. The meek person dies to himself, to what his flesh would like to do, and he does the right thing—exactly what God wants done.

In summary, the meek man walks in a humble, tender, but strong state of mind; he denies himself, giving utmost consideration to others. He shows a control and righteous anger against injustice and evil. A meek man forgets and lives for others because of what Christ has done for him.

⇒ God is meek.

> **"But the fruit of the Spirit is love, joy, peace, longsuffering, gentleness, goodness, faith, meekness, temperance: against such there is no law" (Gal.5:22-23).**

⇒ Jesus Christ was meek.

> **"Take my yoke upon you, and learn of me; for I am meek and lowly in heart: and ye shall find rest unto your souls" (Mt.11:29).**

⇒ Believers are to be meek.

> **"Brethren, if a man be overtaken in a fault, ye which are spiritual, restore such an one in the spirit of meekness; considering thyself, lest thou also be tempted" (Gal.6:1).**

QUESTIONS:
1. What are some specific qualities of the "fruit of meekness"?
2. What challenges do you face when you need to possess the fruit of meekness? In what ways can you overcome these challenges?

9. There is the fruit of *temperance*: to master and control the body or the flesh with all of its lusts. It means self-control, the master of desire, appetite and passion, especially sensual

urges and cravings. It means to be strong and controlled and restrained. It means to stand against the lust of the flesh and the lust of the eye and the pride of life (1 Jn.2:15-16).

⇒ Self-control is of God, a fruit of the Holy Spirit.

> **"But the fruit of the Spirit is love, joy, peace, longsuffering, gentleness, goodness, faith, meekness, <u>temperance</u>: against such there is no law" (Gal.5:22-23).**

⇒ The believer is to proclaim self-control to the lost.

> **"And as he reasoned of righteousness, <u>temperance</u>, and judgment to come, Felix trembled, and answered, Go thy way for this time; when I have a convenient season, I will call for thee" (Acts 24:25).**

⇒ The believer is to control his sexual desires.

> **"But if they cannot contain [control], let them marry: for it is better to marry than to burn" (1 Cor.7:9).**

⇒ The believer is to strenuously exercise self-control, just as an athlete controls himself.

> **"And every man that striveth for the mastery is temperate in all things. Now they do it to obtain a corruptible crown; but we an incorruptible" (1 Cor.9:25).**

⇒ The believer is to grow in self-control.

> **"And to knowledge <u>temperance</u>; and to temperance patience; and to patience godliness" (2 Pt.1:6).**

⇒ The aged believer is especially to be on guard to control himself.

> **"That the aged men be sober, grave, temperate, sound in faith, in charity, in patience" (Tit.2:2).**

In concluding our discussion, we should remember that the fruit of the Spirit is the very nature of God (Gal.2:20; Eph.5:18). The believer is to walk in the Spirit; that is, he is to walk in such a consciousness of God and in such open confession that he is kept constantly clean from sin. God keeps him clean and pure and acceptable as though he were perfect. As the believer so walks in such an awareness of God, he assimilates the very nature of God and the Holy Spirit's fruit is produced. No law can stand against such things.

<u>QUESTIONS:</u>

1. What is the secret to having temperance or self-control as a part of your character?
2. Which trait of the fruit of the Spirit would others say is the strongest in your life? Why?
3. Which trait of the fruit of the Spirit would others say is the least noticed in your life? What things can you do to improve this trait in your life?
4. Are you comfortable with the quality of fruit being produced in your life? Why or why not?

5. If the fruit which is being produced in your life were displayed in a grocery store, where would it be located:
________In the fresh produce section.
________In the dated, soon to spoil section.
________In the frozen food section.
________In the garbage can—the fruit is spoiled.
Are you making any effort to improve the quality and production of fruit in your life?

2. THE BELIEVER IS TO WALK BEARING A CRUCIFIED FLESH (v.24).

This is a striking verse. Note several points.

1. Note the words, "they that are Christ's." A person becomes the *property and the possession* of Christ when he first trusts Christ as his Savior. When a person comes to Jesus Christ to save him, he is coming because he wants to be delivered from the enslavement and bondage of sin, death, and judgment. He wants to live forever with God. He does not want to continue being the slave of the flesh, subjected to its lusts, death and sure judgment. He wants to be saved from the flesh of a corruptible world. Therefore, when a person comes to Christ, he is turning away from the flesh to God; he is turning his back upon the mastery of the flesh and all that it stands for. He is turning to Jesus Christ as his new master. Consequently...

- the believer no longer belongs to the flesh; he belongs to Jesus Christ.
- the flesh no longer possesses the believer; Jesus Christ possesses him.
- the believer no longer serves the flesh; he serves the Lord Jesus Christ.

2. Note that the believer has crucified the flesh with the affections (passions) and lusts. How? By dying with Jesus Christ. How can a person die with Jesus Christ? By an act of God. Only God can count a person to have died with Jesus Christ and *it be true, an actual occurrence*. This is exactly what God does. When a person genuinely believes in Jesus Christ, God takes that person's belief and counts it as his death with Jesus Christ. God honors his faith by identifying him with Christ. God counts and considers the person...

- to have died in Christ's death.
- to be placed into Christ's death.
- to be identified with Christ's death.
- to be a partaker of Christ's death.
- to be in union with Christ's death.
- to be bound in Christ's death.

Now, note the point: if the believer is counted by God as having been crucified with Christ, then the believer...

- has died to the flesh.
- has died to the passions of the flesh.
- has died to the lusts of the flesh.
- is freed from the flesh.
- is freed from the passions of the flesh.
- is freed from the lusts of the flesh.

Once a person has died, he is dead. The rule and reign and the habits and desires of the flesh no longer have control over him. The flesh ceases to have a place or a position in his life. He is free from the flesh, free from...

- fleshly habits
- fleshly control
- fleshly bondage
- fleshly judgment
- fleshly enslavement
- fleshly condemnation
- fleshly death

To be crucified with Christ means that we no longer live *in the flesh*, in the place and position of the flesh. We cannot live *apart* from the flesh, for we are in this body upon this earth. But we are free from living *after* the flesh. We no longer follow the passions and lusts of the flesh. We desire and follow righteousness, seeking to please God in all that we do.

> **"God forbid. How shall we, that are dead to sin, live any longer therein?" (Ro.6:2).**
>
> **"I am crucified with Christ: nevertheless I live; yet not I, but Christ liveth in me: and the life which I now live in the flesh I live by the faith of the Son of God, who loved me, and gave himself for me" (Gal.2:20).**

ILLUSTRATION:

The Christian believer belongs to Jesus. When your flesh rises up and wants to rebel against Him, remember this soldier's example:

> *"At a dinner given by a Grand Army Post, a veteran soldier was introduced as one of the speakers. In making the introduction, the presiding officer referred to the fact that the man who was to speak had lost a leg in the war, and the veteran was greeted with loud cheering as he arose to make the address.*
>
> *"He began by disavowing the introduction. 'No,' he said, 'that is a mistake. I lost nothing in the war, for, when we went into the war, we gave our country all that we had, and all we brought back was so much clear gain."*[2]

The closer that you walk with Jesus, the farther away you will be from fulfilling the lusts of the flesh. What have you crucified lately…or is it crucifying you?

QUESTIONS:

1. What things do you need to crucify in your life? Why are these things such a struggle for you?
2. What are you told to do in this verse?
3. This verse says that you are to crucify the flesh with its affections and lusts. What will it take for you to obey God, to actually do this?

3. THE BELIEVER IS TO WALK CONSISTENT WITH HIS POSITION IN CHRIST (v.25).

To be in Christ is to be in God's Spirit. When the believer trusts Jesus Christ as his Savior, God places His Spirit in the heart of the believer. The Spirit is placed there to guide and direct the believer day by day. Therefore, the believer is to walk in the Spirit; he is to live just as the Spirit of God directs. This is the point of this verse. If we live by the Spirit, let us also walk by the Spirit. The Spirit gives us life, the life of God; therefore, let us *walk and live out* the life He gives us.

> **"Therefore we are buried with him by baptism into death: that like as Christ was raised up from the dead by the glory of the Father, even so we also should walk in newness of life" (Ro.6:4).**

QUESTIONS:

1. What does it mean to live in the Spirit?
2. What barriers do you have to overcome in order to consistently walk in the Spirit?
3. What kind of advice would you give a Christian who was trying to live a life out of and not in the Spirit? Would your life be an example for them to imitate? Why or why not?

4. THE BELIEVER IS TO WALK FREE FROM SUPER-SPIRITUALITY AND ENVY (v.26).

When believer's are challenged to live spiritual lives, there is always the danger that some will become super-spiritual and others will begin to envy the spiritual gifts of those who are genuinely spiritual and greatly blessed by God.

1. There is the danger of super-spirituality. There is the temptation of pride and of showing superiority. It is the attitude that says, "I have it, and you don't." This attitude, of course, irritates and provokes people. It causes division within the church.

> **"Woe unto you that are full [who say they are full]! for ye shall hunger. Woe unto you that laugh now! for ye shall mourn and weep" (Lk.6:25).**

2. There is the danger of envy.

ILLUSTRATION:

There is a fine line to walk between living in the Spirit and in the flesh. One of the things that will trip us up is pride. Pride comes when we forget the Cross. Listen to this practical illustration and see how you relate to its point:

"The growth chart had slipped from the playroom wall because the tape on its corners had become dry and brittle. Five-year-old Jordan hung it up again, meticulously working to get it straight. Then he stood his sister against the wall to measure her height.

"'Mommy! Mommy! Anneke is forty inches tall!' he shouted as he burst into the kitchen. 'I measured her.'

"His mom replied, 'That's impossible, Sweetheart. She's only 3 years old. Let's go see.' They walked back into the playroom, where the mother's suspicions were confirmed. Despite his efforts to hang the chart straight, Jordan had failed to set it at the proper height. It was several inches low.

"We easily make Jordan's mistake in gauging our spiritual growth or importance. Compared to a shortened scale, we may appear better than we are. Only when we stand against the Cross, that 'Great leveler of men' as A. T. Robertson called it, can we not think of ourselves '...higher than we ought to think.' Christ, Himself, must be our standard."[3]

QUESTIONS:

1. In what ways does spiritual pride cause you to stumble? What is your role in preventing pride from controlling your life?
2. What are some of the consequences of becoming "super-spiritual"? Do you know anyone like this? How do people respond to the person?
3. How can you become aware of pride in your life? Through others pointing it out? Through God's Word? How?

SUMMARY:

How fruitful are you? God wants you to bear His fruit increasingly, growing in Him day by day. From this session, He has told you how it is to be done:

1. The believer is to walk bearing God's nature.
2. The believer is to walk bearing a crucified flesh.
3. The believer is to walk consistently with his position in Christ.
4. The believer is to walk free from selfishness, super-spirituality and envy.

It is harvest time. Do you have any fruit to offer to God and to others?

GALATIANS 5:22-26

PERSONAL JOURNAL NOTES
(Reflection & Response)

1. The most important thing that I learned from this lesson was:

2. The area that I need to work on the most is:

3. I can apply this lesson to my life by:

4. Closing Statement of Commitment:

---

[1] William Barclay. *The Letters to the Galatians and Ephesians*, p.56.
[2] Walter B. Knight. *Knight's Master Book of 4,000 Illustrations*, p.111.
[3] Craig B. Larson, editor. *Illustrations for Preaching & Teaching*, p.246.

	CHAPTER 6		
1. **First, let the spiritual believers handle the matter** 2. **Second, approach the brother in a spirit of meekness** 3. **Third, consider yourself** 4. **Fourth, bear one another's burden**	**D. A Walk Restoring the Man Who Slips, 6:1-5** Brethren, if a man be overtaken in a fault, ye which are spiritual, restore such an one in the spirit of meekness; considering thyself, lest thou also be tempted. 2 Bear ye one another's burdens, and so fulfil the law of Christ.	3 For if a man think himself to be something, when he is nothing, he deceiveth himself. 4 But let every man prove his own work, and then shall he have rejoicing in himself alone, and not in another. 5 For every man shall bear his own burden.	5. **Fifth, confess your own nothingness** 6. **Sixth, examine your own work** 7. **Seventh, realize your own responsibility**

Section V
THE BELIEVER'S LIFE AND WALK:
FREE AND SPIRITUAL
Galatians 5:13-6:18

Study 4: **A WALK RESTORING THE MAN WHO SLIPS**

Text: **Galatians 6:1-5**

Aim: To learn how to help fallen and hurting believers.

Memory Verse:
"For if a man think himself to be something, when he is nothing, he deceiveth himself" (Galatians 6:3).

INTRODUCTION:

The Christian army is the only one that shoots its wounded This is a saying that is often stated. But is this really true? Are Christians really guilty of shooting their wounded? Sadly, Christians do often put other believers down when they fail or fall. For too often, believers become judgmental and critical when others slip and are wounded by the effects of sin.

But note: the issue is not to be why was a believer wounded by sin but how can a believer be restored? We have been given an opportunity that has been birthed in the heart of God. God is a God of restoration. He does not hold a grudge. Just ask the Prodigal Son...just look into the mirror and you will see who He restores. The Christian has been charged with the responsibility to restore fallen saints. Will we be found faithful in this critical ministry?

Note the word "man." This means a person who is just like the rest of us; that is, he has desires, passions, and urges just like we have. He walks and lives in the flesh just like we do. Therefore, he faces the very same temptations we do, for *all temptation* is common to all men (1 Cor.10:13).

What is to be done when a Christian brother has succumbed to temptation, stumbled or fallen? What is to be the spirit and attitude of the church? How are we to approach the problem? Are we to...

- ignore him?
- criticize him?
- withdraw from him?
- shame him?
- censor him?
- dismiss him?
- isolate him?
- spread rumors about him?
- slander him

Note a fact: no sin is specified. The sin may be large or small, black or gray, despicable or acceptable (to man), serious or innocent, harmful or harmless. The point to note is this: a true Christian brother can be overtaken by sin. The word "overtaken" is interesting: it means to be taken beforehand, by surprise, or unexpectedly. A true Christian is *surprised* when he is overtaken by sin; he *never suspected* it. In fact, being overtaken by serious sin was seldom, if ever, a concern; for he belonged to Christ and lived in Christ.

However, when a brother is caught in sin and slips and falls, what should be done? Scripture is clear: Christian brothers are to restore him. The word "restore" is a word that is used for setting a broken arm or leg, for mending nets, or for cutting some growth out of a body.[1] Believers are to help the brother:

⇒ set him right
⇒ restore him
⇒ help cut the sin out
⇒ mend him
⇒ lead him back

However, there is a right way and a wrong way to help the fallen brother. This is the point that is being stressed and that is desperately needed by believers and the church. All believers are mere men of like passions with all other men, and there are always some being overtaken by sin. This, of course, means that we need to constantly stay alert and available to fallen brothers.

But again, how we approach a fallen brother is of utmost importance. It is a very delicate matter. The brother will be very sensitive and perhaps embarrassed and easily shamed. He could become so ashamed that he would be too embarrassed to return to the fellowship of believers. He could also feel that he would be unwelcomed, for what he has done is just not acceptable among believers. He has failed and failed publicly, and he has damaged the name of Christ and hurt the image of the church. He knows the attitude of the church and its believers about the matter.

Therefore, unless he is approached in the right spirit, he could be lost to the cause of Christ upon this earth. This, of course, means that the ministry of restoration is of paramount importance, for the life of a dear brother is at stake. What the church needs to realize is this: the ministry of restoration is the ministry of God. It is the ministry to which God has called us. We are to walk restoring men to the Kingdom of God and the fellowship of His church.

OUTLINE:

1. First, let the spiritual believers handle the matter (v.1).
2. Second, approach the brother in a spirit of meekness (v.1).
3. Third, consider yourself (v.1).
4. Fourth, bear one another's burden (v.2).
5. Fifth, confess your own nothingness (v.3).
6. Sixth, examine your own work (v.4).
7. Seventh, realize your own responsibility (v.5).

1. FIRST, LET THE SPIRITUAL BELIEVERS HANDLE THE MATTER (v.1).

Spiritual believers are those who walk in the Spirit. How can the church tell if a believer is spiritual, if he is truly walking in the Spirit? The former passage spells out how.

1. Does the believer bear the fruit of the Spirit? (Gal.5:22-23).
    - love
    - joy
    - peace
    - longsuffering
    - gentleness
    - goodness
    - faith
    - meekness
    - self-control
2. Does the believer live a crucified life with Christ, that is, a sacrificial, self-denying life? Has the believer crucified his flesh with the passions and lusts? (Gal.5:24).
3. Does the believer walk in the Spirit--live a life that is consistent with his position in Christ? (Gal.5:25).
4. Does the believer walk free from super-spirituality and envy, pride and jealousy, arrogance and selfishness? (Gal.5:26).

ILLUSTRATION:

Sometimes Christians can act just like sharks that sense blood in the water: they circle in for the kill. But this is not God's way! Here is an example of how restoration is to be done:

> *"One of the great preachers of the South was marvelously converted when he was a drunkard. His ministry was quite demanding and after a great deal of pressure and temptation he got drunk one night. He was so ashamed that the very next day he called in his board of deacons and turned in his resignation. He told them, 'I want to resign.' They were amazed. They asked why. He frankly told them, 'I got drunk last night. A preacher should not get drunk, and I want to resign.'*
>
> *"It was obvious that he was ashamed, and do you know what those wonderful deacons did? They put their arms around him and said, 'Let's all pray.' They would not accept his resignation. A man who was present in the congregation that next Sunday said, 'I never heard a greater sermon in my life than that man preached.'*
>
> *"Those deacons were real surgeons--they set a broken bone; they restored him. There are some people who would have put him out of the ministry, but these deacons put that preacher back on his feet, and God marvelously used him after that."*[2]

QUESTIONS:

1. Who do you personally know who fell into sin but was restored by other Christians? What kinds of things did these loving people do for this person?
2. What causes some people to be judgmental? How can trusting God help you to not be judgmental of others?
3. If you were to fall into sin, who could you count on to help restore you? Why? Who would not help restore you? Why?

2. SECOND, APPROACH THE BROTHER IN A SPIRIT OF MEEKNESS (v.1).

How desperately this charge is needed! Too often what is displayed is a spirit of...

- hardness
- indifference
- harshness
- rejection
- criticism
- censorship
- rumor
- slander
- reproof
- super-spirituality
- "holier-than-thou"
- ostracism

This approach, of course, is not ever concerned with restoring a brother. It is bent more on downing or destroying him. And the great tragedy is that it forces him to turn more and more to the world, to those who are more understanding of his weaknesses because they, too, are weak.

However, the spirit of rejection is not what Scripture is telling believers to show. Scripture is saying to approach the brother in meekness: to be gentle, tender, warm, loving, and caring. Discuss his sinning, yes, but with him not with others! Approach and love him, reach out to him, minister to him, help him, show care and concern and *above all else*, stay after him. Open your arms and welcome him back. Restore him into your fellowship. Let him know that he is forgiven, forgiven by all and accepted by all, warmly and tenderly.

> **"I therefore, the prisoner of the Lord, beseech you that ye walk worthy of the vocation [calling] wherewith ye are called, with all lowliness and meekness, with longsuffering, forbearing one another in love" (Eph.4:1-2).**

QUESTIONS:

1. How should you pray before you approach a fallen believer?
2. How do you cultivate a spirit of meekness?
3. How could your having a spirit of meekness affect the fallen Christian that you are trying to reach?

3. THIRD, CONSIDER YOURSELF (v.1).

Consider yourself, for you, too, can be tempted and overtaken by sin. This is a crucial point, for all believers are tempted with all kinds of sin (1 Cor.10:13). There is a real possibility that we may be overtaken by sin; therefore, we are to love and help our fallen brothers just like we would want to be loved and helped. The word "consider" means to look to oneself, to think about oneself and to give attention to oneself. It means to keep an attentive eye on oneself. If we really consider the matter, then we will reach out in love and meekness to help our fallen brothers. We have to help them, for we are all ever so subject to being overtaken by sin.

> **"There hath no temptation taken you but such as is common to man: but God is faithful, who will not suffer you to be tempted above that ye are able; but will with the temptation also make a way to escape, that ye may be able to bear it" (1 Cor.10:13).**

ILLUSTRATION:

Some of the most inaccurate words that glide across the lips of Christians are these: "I'll never fall. It could never happen to me."

> *"One of the first jokes of the age of automation describes a planeload of people soon after takeoff. A voice comes on the plane's intercom, 'Good afternoon, ladies and gentlemen. Welcome aboard. We are climbing to our planned cruising altitude of 39,000 feet. All of the plane's systems are working perfectly, and we expect to land at our destination on time. This is a fully automated plane. There is no pilot or copilot. Everything is guided and monitored by a computer. We want you to sit back, relax, and enjoy the flight. Nothing can go wrong...can go wrong...can go wrong....'"*[3]

Do not put your trust in man and his abilities, not even in your own. As you well know, we all fail...we all fail...we all fail--far, far too often. Place your trust in Jesus Christ, for He never fails.

QUESTIONS:

1. Have you ever said, "I'll never do this or that," but you did? Why did you think you were not capable of falling?
2. Pride has a way of producing blind spots in people. What kind of blind spots does pride produce in you?
3. What can you do to strengthen your ability to resist falling into sin?

4. FOURTH, BEAR ONE ANOTHER'S BURDEN (v.2).

The law of Christ is the law of ministry and love.

> **"Even as the Son of man came not to be ministered unto, but to minister, and to give his life a ransom for many" (Mt.20:28).**

Christ gave and sacrificed Himself to reach out to man. He bore the sins of man *for man.* We, of course, cannot bear the sins of men; but we can bear the burdens of each other, for we all suffer under the weight of sin--whether the sins are known or not. We can...

- be compassionate
- encourage
- pray
- forgive
- be warm and tender
- share the promises of God
- sympathize
- empathize

> **"Rejoice with them that do rejoice, and weep with them that weep" (Ro.12:15).**

QUESTIONS:

1. What was the heaviest burden that you had to bear that belonged to someone else? Why was it so heavy? What was the final outcome?
2. How do you feel when someone comes along side of you to bear one of your burdens?
3. Briefly describe the greatest burden that you are carrying. What has to happen before it crushes you? Can you carry it alone and remain spiritually healthy? Why or why not?

5. FIFTH, CONFESS YOUR OWN NOTHINGNESS (v.3).

This is the reason so many fallen brothers are locked out of the fellowship of believers and churches. They are looked upon as being...

- unfit
- less capable
- weaker
- less spiritual
- too tarnished
- insufficient

This attitude, of course, is contrary to the Spirit of Christ. Note the words, "When he is nothing." Christ came to save "nothings," that is, sinners. All men are sinners whether they know it or not. Even believers, after they are saved, are sinners. This is too often forgotten, yet believers are both *saved and kept* by the righteousness of Christ and not by their own righteousness. We must always remember this, for the only acceptable approach to God is through the righteousness of Jesus Christ.

The point is this: no person is better than any other person, not in righteousness and godliness. All men stand before God as sinners; in fact, they stand as totally depraved sinners. There is not a single man who is righteous, no, not one--not today, not tomorrow, not ever. If a man, believer or unbeliever, wants to stand in God's presence, he has to come by Jesus Christ and his righteousness alone. Therefore, there is absolutely no place among God's people for...

- super-spirituality
- spiritual snobbishness
- spiritual pride

There is absolutely no place for feeling superior or spiritually better than others. Only one person can make that claim: Jesus Christ. Within the church and its believers, there is to be only one attitude: that of confessing our nothingness before God--that of confessing our total dependency upon the grace of God--that of confessing the righteousness of Jesus Christ. Note that any other confession is a deception. If we think otherwise, we only deceive ourselves.

When a believer understands this truth, then he is ready to reach out and help restore the erring brother. He knows he is no better; he has to approach Christ just like the erring brother--as nothing, for he is nothing. Righteously and godly, he stands on the same footing as the fallen brother: neither one of them has any righteousness or godliness to offer God. Therefore, they both must approach God through His Son Jesus Christ. Knowing this truth is what will stir love, concern, and care within the hearts of believers for fallen brothers.

> **"And whosoever shall exalt himself shall be abased; and he that shall humble himself shall be exalted" (Mt.23:12).**
>
> **"Most men will proclaim every one his own goodness: but a faithful man who can find?" (Pr.20:6).**

ILLUSTRATION:

All ground at the foot of the cross is level. There is no spiritual hierarchy for men to climb in this life. A dynamic example of this truth was Saint Francis of Assisi, who was the founder of the Order of Friars (Franciscans). He lived out his life in an attempt to imitate Christ, to live just as Christ had lived upon earth. He set a dynamic example for all of us in one primary thing; he had a firm grasp on this eternal truth:

"When someone asked [him] why and how he could accomplish so much, he replied: 'This may be why. The Lord looked down from Heaven upon the earth and said, 'Where can I find the weakest, the littlest, the meanest man on the face of the earth?' Then He saw me and said, 'Now I've found him, and I will work through him. He won't be proud of it. He'll see that I am only using him because of his littleness and insignificance.''"[4]

Could God say the same things about you?

QUESTIONS:
1. What kinds of attitudes do you have to guard against?
2. Do you have a hard time controlling your pride when you are around people who are living carnal or fleshly lives? Why or why not?
3. Share an example of how you deceived yourself. What kinds of things would you do differently the next time?

6. SIXTH, EXAMINE YOUR OWN WORK (v.4).

The word "work" refers more to conduct and behavior than to employment. Of course, employment or work is involved, but the point of this verse deals with *all our behavior*. We are to be examining and judging our own lives, not the life of a fallen brother. Scripture is forceful on this point: *every man* is to keep busy examining *his own* work and life, and no man is exempt. There is so much evil flying around the world and the flesh is so weak that it is difficult for a person to remain unsoiled and clean. The flesh lusts...

- for acceptance
- for recognition
- for position
- for honor
- for compensation
- for approval
- to look
- to taste
- to feel
- to do
- to have
- to experience

Of course, every one of these desires is needful and beneficial until it crosses over into the forbidden or is taken too far. Tasting food is good; tasting too much food is bad. Wanting recognition is good; loving recognition is sin.

The point is that temptation just swirls around us--all of us. Therefore, we must be busy examining and judging ourselves and not others. In fact, so much temptation swirls around us that if we lower our guard to examine and judge others, we are immediately overcome by sin ourselves. Remember: criticizing and judging others is sin; therefore, by turning away from examining ourselves to judging others, we have sinned.

We must measure ourselves against the Word of God, not against others. Our attitude toward others is to be that of love and care, ministry and restoration, not criticism and judgment.

Note that the believer who constantly examines himself has reason to rejoice in himself and not only in others. It is when our hearts and lives are pure that joy fills us. Nothing fills us with joy as much as a pure conscience. True, we do joy when we see others walking as they should, but deep joy comes from knowing that we ourselves are pleasing God by the way we walk.

"Thou hypocrite, first cast out the beam out of thine own eye; and then shalt thou see clearly to cast out the mote out of thy brother's eye" (Mt.7:5)

QUESTIONS:
1. Who is to be the model for your life?
2. How can you keep from judging and criticizing others?
3. Do you ever examine yourself? What things need to be on your personal checklist?

4. Grade yourself on how you've done this past week. Have you passed or failed in these areas?
_____Had a daily worship or devotional time?
_____Attended church and Bible study?
_____Witnessed to someone about Christ?
_____Prayed for those who are backsliding?
_____Used your time wisely with your family/friends?
_____Spent your money wisely?
_____Encouraged or met the needs of others?

7. SEVENTH, REALIZE YOUR OWN RESPONSIBILITY (v.5).

The point of this verse is to warn the believer: he is personally responsible to the Lord for his own behavior and shall be judged for what he has done. Every believer has his own burdens, his own weight of faults and sins to bear. It is these that he is to be carrying, looking after, examining, and judging. He can never overcome them unless he gets his eyes off the failure of others and concentrates on the burden of his own failure.

> **"But I say unto you, That every idle word that men shall speak, they shall give account thereof in the day of judgment" (Mt.12:36).**
>
> **"For we must all appear before the judgment seat of Christ; that everyone may receive the things done in his body, according to that he hath done, whether it be good or bad" (2 Cor.5:10).**

QUESTIONS:
1. When are you least likely to own up to your responsibilities? Why?
2. What kind of failures in others capture your attention? Why?
3. Who do you tend to shift the blame on the most when things do not go your way?
_____God
_____Someone in your family
_____Your employer
_____Your circumstances
_____Yourself

SUMMARY:

You now have in your possession a great treasure--a treasure that has the power to grant another chance. God has called each one of us to be a "Wounded Healer." As a reminder, this is how restoration is to be done:

1. First, let the spiritual believers handle the matter.
2. Second, approach the brother in a spirit of meekness.
3. Third, consider yourself.
4. Fourth, bear one another's burden.
5. Fifth, confess your own nothingness.
6. Sixth, examine your own work.
7. Seventh, realize your own responsibility.

GALATIANS 6:1-5

PERSONAL JOURNAL NOTES

(Reflection & Response)

1. The most important thing that I learned from this lesson was:

2. The area that I need to work on the most is:

3. I can apply this lesson to my life by:

4. Closing Statement of Commitment:

---

[1] William Barclay. *The Letters to the Galatians and Ephesians*, p.58.
[2] J. Vernon McGee. *Thru The Bible, Vol.5*, p.193.
[3] Gordon MacDonald. *Rebuilding Your Broken World.* (Nashville, TN: Oliver Nelson Books, 1988), p.26.
[4] *From the Christian Herald.* Walter B. Knight. *3,000 Illustrations for Christian Service*, p.367.

GALATIANS 6:6-10

	E. A Walk Doing Good to One's Teacher: Sowing & Reaping, 6:6-10	to his flesh shall of the flesh reap corruption; but he that soweth to the Spirit shall of the Spirit reap life everlasting.	1) If one sows selfishly, he reaps corruption 2) If one sows spiritually, he reaps life
1. How to do good to a teacher: By sharing in the ministry of the teacher	6 Let him that is taught in the word communicate unto him that teacheth in all good things.	9 And let us not be weary in well doing: for in due season we shall reap, if we faint not.	b. Because a person will benefit from the good work—if he stands strong
2. Why do good to a teacher a. Because a person can be deceived about facing the judgment of God	7 Be not deceived; God is not mocked: for whatsoever a man soweth, that shall he also reap. 8 For he that soweth	10 As we have therefore opportunity, let us do good unto all men, especially unto them who are of the household of faith.	**3. When to serve with a teacher: As we have opportunity to** a. Do good to all men b. Do good to believers especially

Section V
THE BELIEVER'S LIFE AND WALK:
FREE AND SPIRITUAL
Galatians 5:13-6:18

Study 5: A WALK DOING GOOD TO ONE'S TEACHER: SOWING AND REAPING

Text: Galatians 6:6-10

Aim: To strengthen your commitment to your teacher.

Memory Verse:

"And let us not be weary in well doing: for in due season we shall reap, if we faint not" (Galatians 6:9).

INTRODUCTION:

Are you moved to take some sort of action after your teacher shares God's Word with you? Or do you just sit there and gaze with a blank stare at the wall? The student has a responsibility to respond to God's Word. Do you ever wonder why so many churches have to beg people to teach Sunday school? A large part of the struggle is a lack of enthusiasm from students.

One day, a frustrated teacher decided to pull out all the stops. He decided to take a risk and take a personal interest in each one of his students. The teacher concluded that "the cold facts" were not enough to attract the interest of his students. The only thing which would break down the walls of apathy was the power of relationships.

Months later, his class was the most exciting class in the entire Sunday school. When one of his students was asked what made the difference, the reply was: "Before, our teacher just read us the Bible stories. Now, we have so much more—he challenges us to act out the stories in the Bible and to join him in doing so. For the first time, we feel like we are *ministering together*."

Few people are as important to a society or to God as are teachers. The relationship between teacher and student is a subject that is never stressed enough within the church. The present passage deals with this subject, in particular with the student's responsibilities to the teacher. Keep in mind that every believer is a student who sits at the feet of God's teachers whether they be ministers or Bible teachers.

GALATIANS 6:6-10

OUTLINE:

1. How to do good to a teacher: by sharing in the ministry of the teacher (v.6).
2. Why do good to a teacher (v.7-9).
3. When to serve with a teacher: as we have opportunity (v.10).

1. HOW TO DO GOOD TO A TEACHER: BY SHARING IN THE MINISTRY OF THE TEACHER (v.6).

How does a believer do good to a teacher? Very simply, by communicating and sharing in the ministry of the teacher. This means much more than just giving financial support. Of course it means financial support; but as stated, it means much more. Note that Scripture is speaking directly to the *learner*, that is, to a believer in the church, to the person who is *taught in the Word of God*. The learner has a responsibility to the teacher just as the teacher has a responsibility to the learner. What is that responsibility? To share with the teacher in all good things and to participate in the ministry of the teacher. The learner shares in the ministry of the teacher by...

- *being present* when the teacher teaches.
- *being attentive and learning* what the teacher teaches.
- *sharing in discussions* of what the teacher teaches.
- *passing on* what the teacher teaches.
- *participating* with the teacher in his or her full ministry.
- *supporting* the teacher financially.
- *encouraging others* to come and learn from the teacher.

Note another point: the reference to the "Word" means the *Word of God*. A teacher should always be teaching the Word of God, and a learner should always be sure that he is sitting under a teacher who is teaching the Word of God.

> **"Let the elders [ministers] that rule well be counted worthy of double honour, especially they who labour in the word and doctrine. For the scripture saith, Thou shalt not muzzle the ox that treadeth out the corn. And, The labourer is worthy of his reward" (1 Tim.5:17-18).**

ILLUSTRATION:

One of the most rewarding experiences for a teacher is when his or her students capture the truth and apply it to other people.

> *Years ago, a Christian football coach invested a good portion of his life in his players and coaches. A stickler for details, his philosophy on offense and defense was branded into the minds of his assistant coaches. He spent just as much energy sharing his philosophy on what made up good character as he did on the actual game of football. An active member of the Fellowship of Christian Athletes, his faith in Christ became contagious. Through his witness, many of his coaches and players became believers.*
>
> *As the years went by, some of his players and assistant coaches went on to coach at other schools. Showing striking evidence that they had been mentored by this great coach, the philosophy for each of their teams mirrored what they had learned. The offense was the same. The defense was played the same. And in more important matters, godly character was stressed and expected. Like their former coach--their mentor, their teacher--Christ was seen in each of their lives. Through one man's influence, many young men came to know Jesus Christ personally. His students were sharing in his ministry--literally--both on and off the field of play.*

A good teacher reproduces what is in him. A good student shares what he has learned with others. Just as we are all teachers in some areas of life, we are all students in others areas. Are you sharing in the ministry of your teachers by passing on what you have learned to others?

QUESTIONS:
1. What practical things can you do to share in the ministry of your teacher?
2. Are you currently participating in your teacher's ministry? How valuable is the input of individuals in any class setting?
3. What would happen to your class if everyone participated in the teacher's ministry? What has to occur in order for this to happen? What would be your role in this? As the teacher? As the learner?

2. WHY DO GOOD TO A TEACHER (v.7-9).

Two very strong reasons are given.

1. A person can be deceived about facing the judgment of God. The word "deceived" means to be led astray. Some Galatians were being led astray in this matter. They were failing to share in the ministry of Paul, becoming critics instead of supporters. And note what attacking the teacher of God equals: it equals mocking God. The word "mocked" means to turn one's nose up at God. By rejecting God's minister, the teacher whom God had sent to them, the Galatians were rejecting God. They were not only mocking and turning their noses up at the teacher of God, but they were mocking God. However, Scripture declares in no uncertain terms: "God is not mocked: for whatsoever a man sows, that shall he also reap." If a man sows a life...

- that is not present when the teacher teaches
- that is not attentive and learning what the teacher teaches
- that does not pass on what the teacher teaches
- that does not participate with the teacher in his ministry
- that does not encourage others to learn from the teacher

...if a man sows this rejection, this turning up of the nose, he rejects and turns his nose up at God. And if he rejects God, he shall be rejected by God. Whatever a man sows toward his teacher, he reaps. He shall bear the judgment of his behavior toward God's teacher.

a. If a believer sows corruption to his flesh, he shall reap corruption (v.8). If he does not listen to the teacher's warnings about the lusts of the flesh, he shall reap the lusts of the flesh. He will be overtaken by the appeal, pull, cravings, passion, and lust...
   - to worship as he desires
   - to seek his destiny from astrology and sorcery instead of prayer
   - to live as he pleases
   - to seek earthly position, power, and honor
   - to strive against others as he pleases
   - to party as he likes
   - to have illicit sex
   - to hoard
   - to seek the things of this world

   The list could go on and on, but the point is well understood. The flesh perishes. It ages, dies, and decays. If a person sows to the flesh, he shall go the way of all flesh: die and face the judgment of God. God will not be mocked. His teachers must be heard and their lessons learned, for they teach His Word. If a man rejects God's messenger and chooses to sow to his flesh, he shall reap the flesh and its destiny: death and judgment. God is not mocked; there is no escape.

   > **"For to be carnally [fleshly] minded is death; but to be spiritually minded is life and peace. Because the carnal mind is enmity against God: for it is not subject to the law of God, neither indeed can be. So then they that are in the flesh cannot please God" (Ro.8:6-8).**

b. If a believer sows to the Spirit, he shall reap life everlasting. If he listens to the teacher's exhortations about the salvation that is in God's Son and the life God expects him to live, he shall reap the Spirit of God. The Spirit of God will actually enter his life and take up residence there. The Spirit will implant the divine nature of God within the heart of the believer, the divine nature that shall live now and forever. The believer will be enabled (given the strength and power) to live a life of...

- love
- joy
- peace
- long-suffering
- gentleness
- goodness
- faithfulness
- meekness
- self-control

And most importantly, as stated, he shall live forever with God in the new heavens and earth.

> **"And as Moses lifted up the serpent in the wilderness, even so must the son of man be lifted up: that whosoever believeth in him should not perish, but have eternal life" (Jn.3:14-15).**

2. A person shall reap if he does not faint in serving with his teacher. The believer or pupil must join with his teacher in the ministry if he wishes to reap the reward. He must not...

- withdraw
- fall back
- slack off
- allow weariness
- allow routineness
- give in to pressure
- allow interruptions
- cave in to persecution
- give in to temptation

The pupil must be constant, steadfast, and persevering—just as he is taught to be by his teacher. He must join right in with his teacher in serving the Lord Jesus Christ.

> **"Therefore, my beloved brethren, be ye steadfast, unmoveable, always abounding in the work of the Lord, forasmuch as ye know that your labour is not in vain in the Lord" (1 Cor.15:58).**

Note the motive for not fainting: the student shall reap in due season. The day of reaping is coming. God is going to reward the pupil (believer) who serves and works by the side of his teacher.

> **"And whosoever shall give to drink unto one of these little ones a cup of cold water only in the name of a disciple, verily I say unto you, he shall in no wise lose his reward" (Mt.10:42).**

QUESTIONS:

1. What kinds of things have you sown that will reap a blessing?
2. If you sow bad things, can you expect to reap life? Explain your answer.
3. What would cause some Christians to look for a blessing after they have knowingly sown to their flesh?
4. What kinds of things do you need to do in order to firm up your commitment to your teacher's ministry?

3. WHEN TO SERVE WITH A TEACHER: AS WE HAVE OPPORTUNITY (v.10).

When is a believer to serve with his teacher? Very simply, at every opportunity. He is to join right in and do good every chance he can. The idea is that he is to...

- stay alert to opportunity.
- keep his eyes open to make opportunities.
- rush to all opportunities.

GALATIANS 6:6-10

When a teacher goes to meet a need, the believer must not miss the opportunity to join his teacher and minister with him. No chance to minister should ever be missed. With each missed opportunity, a believer can miss the privilege of ministering and of being more greatly rewarded in the glorious day of redemption. Therefore, he must stay alert and not be weary if he wants a full reward.

Note to whom he is to minister: to all men (unbelievers), but especially to believers. A person is responsible for his own family first; then he adds on the burden of the world. God has placed us all within a family, and we are the ones who are first responsible for that family. Others may help us, but we are the ones who are primarily responsible. The same is true with the family of God. A Christian brother is the one who is responsible for the family of God. Therefore, we must always meet the needs of our Christian family before moving on out among unbelievers.

> **"But love ye your enemies, and do good, and lend, hoping for nothing again; and your reward shall be great, and ye shall be the children of the Highest: for he is kind unto the unthankful and to the evil" (Lk.6:35).**
>
> **"Therefore to him that knoweth to do good, and doeth it not, to him it is sin" (Jas.4:17).**

ILLUSTRATION:

How willing are you for His will? This is a question that every believer must answer whenever opportunities to minister are made available. God has provided plenty of work to do. The key is this: be ready to serve when He opens the door. Sometimes, that open door comes at a great personal sacrifice:

> *"'You are going out to die in a year or two. It is madness!' That is what a tutor in Oxford University, England, said to a brilliant student who was giving himself under the auspices of a missionary society for service in Africa.*
>
> *"It turned out that the young man did die after being on the field only a year, but he had answered his tutor in these wise and weighty words: 'I think it is with African missions as with the building of a great bridge. You know how many stones have to be buried in the earth, all unseen, to be a foundation. If Christ wants me to be one of the unseen stones, lying in an African grave, I am content, certain as I am that the final result will be a Christian Africa.'"*[1]

As the hymn reminds you, "Wherever He leads, I'll go." Is that true with you?

QUESTIONS:

1. How often do you skip regular times of Bible study with your teacher? What kinds of things cause you not to attend?
2. Do you have a role in your teacher's ministry? Are you fulfilling it?
3. Are you comfortable with your level of commitment to your teacher's ministry? What changes do you need to make?
4. When is the best time to serve with your teacher?
5. What is the priority of ministry? Who comes first? Why?

SUMMARY:

Contrary to popular belief, your teacher is not required by God to do all the work of the ministry. He or she is called to equip other believers for the work of the ministry. The responsibilities of the student are clearly outlined:

1. How to do good to a teacher: by sharing in the ministry of the teacher.
2. Why do good to a teacher.
3. When to serve with a teacher: as we have opportunity.

GALATIANS 6:6-10

PERSONAL JOURNAL NOTES
(Reflection & Response)

1. The most important thing that I learned from this lesson was:

2. The area that I need to work on the most is:

3. I can apply this lesson to my life by:

4. Closing Statement of Commitment:

---

[1] S. S. World. Walter B. Knight. *Knight's Master Book of 4,000 Illustrations*, p.619.

GALATIANS 6:11-18

	F. A Walk Boasting in the Cross of Christ, 6:11-18	I should glory, save in the cross of our Lord Jesus Christ, by whom the world is crucified unto me, and I unto the world.	**in the cross of Christ** a. The cross crucifies the world to men & men to the world
1. An important section Paul himself writes	11 Ye see how large a letter I have written unto you with mine own hand.	15 For in Christ Jesus neither circumcision availeth any thing, nor uncircumcision, but a new creature.	b. The cross creates a new man
2. False ministers make a good showing in the flesh—seeking popularity	12 As many as desire to make a fair show in the flesh, they constrain you to be circumcised; only lest they should suffer persecution for the cross of Christ.	16 And as many as walk according to this rule, peace be on them, and mercy, and upon the Israel of God.	c. The cross brings peace & mercy
a. To gain approval & to escape persecution		17 From henceforth let no man trouble me: for I bear in my body the marks of the Lord Jesus.	d. The cross gives purpose to the scars of life
b. To make a good showing by adding to their statistical numbers	13 For neither they themselves who are circumcised keep the law; but desire to have you circumcised, that they may glory in your flesh.	18 Brethren, the grace of our Lord Jesus Christ be with your spirit. Amen.	**4. Conclusion: A benediction of grace**
3. True ministers boast	14 But God forbid that		

Section V
THE BELIEVER'S LIFE AND WALK: FREE AND SPIRITUAL
Galatians 5:13-6:18

Study 6: **A WALK BOASTING IN THE CROSS OF CHRIST**

Text: **Galatians 6:11-18**

Aim: To focus our entire life upon the cross of Christ.

Memory Verse:

"But God forbid that I should glory, save in the cross of our Lord Jesus Christ, by whom the world is crucified unto me, and I unto the world" (Galatians 6:14).

INTRODUCTION:

Should a Christian believer ever boast? Is boasting ever justified? If you are a successful person, there is a great temptation to brag about all you have accomplished. And this is the point: many people take pride in boasting about all they have done. This attitude is particularly wrong when it is applied to salvation. Man had absolutely nothing to do with the saving work of Christ. Jesus Christ needed no help from man to solve the problem of sin. Consequently, the believer is exhorted to brag on Jesus Christ! Christ and Christ alone is worthy of our praise. We are to boast in the name of Christ and in His name alone.

This passage concludes Paul's letter to the Galatians. Paul's heart was pounding with concern over the Galatian believers and their churches. They had allowed false teachers to enter their ranks, and many of them had begun to listen and follow the false teachers. The churches were on the precipice of deserting God and destroying their witness for Christ and world missions. Usually Paul dictated his letters to a scribe, and when he was through dictating the letter, he closed the letter with a brief blessing and his signature. But note what he did as he closed this letter to the Galatians: he took the pen himself and closed the letter, closed it with a strong exhortation and with a defense of his ministry and of the gospel. He declared in no uncertain terms: believers—minister and layman alike—are to walk boasting in nothing but the cross of Christ.

OUTLINE:

1. An important section—Paul himself writes (v.11).
2. False ministers make a good showing in the flesh—seeking popularity (v.12-13).
3. True ministers boast in the cross of Christ (v.14-17).
4. Conclusion: a benediction of grace (v.18).

1. AN IMPORTANT SECTION—PAUL HIMSELF WRITES (v.11).

This is an important passage of Galatians, so important that Paul took the pen from his scribe and wrote it himself. The reference to writing a *large letter* means large print. Why did Paul write with large print? Several explanations are given.

1. Because Paul wanted to boldly emphasize the points of what he was saying. It should be noted that this is possible, but the scribe could have done this as well as Paul.
2. Because Paul could not write well, so he had to write in bold print in order for it to be read. This too is unlikely, for Paul was a well-educated man.
3. Because Paul had some kind of eye problem or blurred vision. Of all explanations, this seems most likely.

There is no question that Paul chose to personally write this section because he wanted to emphasize its message and to verify that he was the true author of the letter. Why he wrote in large print is unknown.

The lesson for us is this: the message of this passage is important enough for Paul to have taken the pen from the scribe and written it himself. Therefore, we need to give utmost attention to what is said.

QUESTIONS:

1. What is to be your response to this section? Why?
2. What kind of point was Paul making in this verse?

2. FALSE MINISTERS MAKE A GOOD SHOWING IN THE FLESH—SEEKING POPULARITY (v.12-13).

They want to be accepted and approved by the world. Remember: false teachers had infiltrated the churches of Galatia. They opposed both Paul and the gospel he preached. Their major stress was that a person had to undergo the basic ritual of religion, that of circumcision (baptism, church membership, etc.). They made circumcision necessary for salvation. If a person were circumcised, he was well on his way to being saved. Paul attacked this position, making a strong charge against false teachers. He charged them with being driven by worldly motives. Keep in mind that he was dealing with false teachers and ministers *within the church*. What he had to say is a strong lesson for teachers of every generation.

1. The false teachers sought to gain the approval of their peers and to escape persecution. They sought the favor of men over the favor of God. Many of the earliest ministers of the gospel were priests who saw Jesus Christ as the Savior of the world. However, they accepted Him only as an addition to the law. They said that Jesus Christ came primarily to show how God wants us to live; therefore, He only added to the law. The law was still important in approaching God: we were to approach God through both the law and Jesus Christ. Therefore, it was unpopular in the

ministry of that day to proclaim that Christ alone was the way to God. The ministers who proclaimed Christ alone were persecuted through ridicule, mockery, abuse, and rejection. A minister who preached salvation through the cross of Christ alone was thought to be destroying both the law and established religion. Therefore, the ministers of established religion persecuted the ministers of the cross. As a result, it took real courage to stand up and proclaim the truth. Most chose the easy way out, going along with the established ministry in order to avoid the persecution.

APPLICATION:

How many go along with the *established and popular religions of the world* instead of proclaiming the truth of Jesus Christ and His Word? How many fear the ridicule, rejection, and abuse of the cross? How often is a minister tempted to tone down the message of the cross to keep from offending some in the congregation? How many ministers have to fear reaction if they proclaim the simple message of salvation by faith in the cross of Christ *alone*? How many have to fear reaction from their peers and denominational leaders?

2. The false teachers sought to make a good showing by adding to their statistical numbers (v.13). Note exactly what Scripture says: they wanted to have people circumcised so that they could boast in their numbers. Their interest was not so much in teaching people to obey the Lord and the law as it was in building up their own security. They wanted recognition through the appearance of a growing ministry. They sought the approval and acceptance of people more than the welfare of the people. Of course, keeping the law and leading the people to obey God was important, just as every man's teaching is important to him. But their primary concern was the appearance of a growing ministry so that they could secure their own livelihood and position with the people.

APPLICATION:

People are impressed with increased numbers on statistical growth. Everyone knows this, both religious and lay leaders. As a result ministers are often drawn into the temptation to stress growth in baptism, church attendance, Bible study, programs, or activities. Increased numbers…

- build image
- boost egos
- convey success
- enlarge reputation
- secure position
- increase opportunity
- point to gifts and abilities
- stress charisma
- open doors
- help to increase income
- attract attention

QUESTIONS:

1. Can you give an example of a false ministry that was just for show? Why does God allow these kinds of things? How are you to respond to this type of ministry?
2. In what ways are you tempted to become popular with the world? How can you shift your focus to Christ?
3. Why do some people put a lot of emphasis on numbers? Is it always bad? Why or why not? What conclusion can you reach about a ministry whose focus is always on numbers, appearance, etc., instead of on Christ?

3. TRUE MINISTERS BOAST IN THE CROSS OF CHRIST (v.14-17).

The cross of Christ is the *only boast* of a true minister of God, for there is no other approach to God. God accepts a person only if he comes to Him by way of the cross. There is no other way to become acceptable to God. Therefore, the true minister has no other message, no other truth of which to boast. Paul gave four reasons why the cross is the minister's only boast.

1. The cross crucifies the world to men and men to the world. What does this mean?
   a. First, the cross crucifies the world to men. The world has all kinds of attractions that appeal to men, and men lust after the attractions. There are such attractions as...
      - position
      - power
      - acceptance
      - recognition
      - money
      - sex
      - pleasure
      - honor
      - food
      - possessions

      The list could go on and on to include every appealing attraction on earth, but what is the end of it all? Deterioration, decay, death, and a sense of judgment. Even man himself ages, dies, and decays. There is nothing on earth that lasts and lives eternally. If man wishes to live forever, someone with unlimited power has to restructure this world. Someone has to destroy the world and remake it, everything in it, including the flesh of man. The glorious news is that God has done this very thing. God has shown that He loves this world, and He has demonstrated His love in the most perfect way possible. How?

      God sent His Son into the world to *die for men* and to free them from the world. When Jesus Christ died upon the cross, He bore the penalty of our transgressions. He took the law's condemnation of death against us and bore the condemnation for us. Therefore, any person who believes that Jesus Christ died for him shall be saved from this world of death. God declares that he will count that person as having been crucified with Christ. The person never has to die. When the moment comes for the person to pass from this world into the next, God will transfer the person right into His presence to live eternally. It will all happen within the blinking of an eye. The person who believes in Christ will never die, never taste or experience death.

      This is what is meant by the world's being crucified to the believer. *The believer never has to go the way of the world*, that is, the way of sin, corruption, death, and judgment.

      ⇒ Jesus Christ died to deliver the believer from the world, all its bondages including the bondage of death.

      ⇒ The Spirit of Jesus Christ (the Holy Spirit) lives within the believer to give him the power to overcome the world in all its corruptible attractions. Through the Spirit of God, the believer has the power to conquer the lusts of the flesh.
   b. Second, the cross crucifies men (believers) to the world. What does this mean? When the believer dies to the world, he turns away from the attractions and pleasures of the world; therefore, the believer becomes unattractive to the world. Worldly men do not like what they see, for the believer is rejecting the life-style and pleasures of the world. Consequently, the worldly want nothing to do with the believer. They want him out of their way. They want him as non-existent, as a dead person to them. Therefore, when a person comes to the cross of Christ, the cross crucifies him to the world and its ways. He is no longer attractive to the world.

      "Knowing this, that our old man is crucified with him, that the body of sin might be destroyed, that henceforth we should not serve sin" (Ro.6:6).

      "I am crucified with Christ: nevertheless I live; yet not I, but Christ liveth in me: and the life which I now live in the flesh I live

by the faith of the Son of God, who loved me, and gave himself for me" (Gal.2:20).

2. The cross creates a new man. Nothing makes a person acceptable to God except God's very own Son, Jesus Christ. No religion, no law, no ritual—nothing can avail anything with God except Jesus Christ. Therefore, if any man wishes to live with God, he has to *believe in Jesus Christ and approach God in the name of Jesus Christ.*

Now a very practical question arises: How does using the name of Jesus Christ make a person live forever? Does a person become acceptable to God by just approaching God and saying, "God, I come to you in the name of Jesus Christ"? No! And there is one good reason. God knows who is really sincere and who is not. God cannot be deceived. *Words and false profession*—just using the words "in the name of Jesus Christ"—will not save anyone. A person has to be genuinely sincere.

The point is this: when a person is sincere in his belief, God gives the person a new spirit—a recreated spirit. God actually places His divine nature, the presence of His own Spirit, into the person's life. The person is "born again" spiritually. He becomes what Scripture calls a *new creature*, a *new man*.

"Therefore if any man be in Christ, he is a new creature: old things are passed away; behold, all things are become new" (2 Cor.5:17).

"Beloved, let us love one other: for love is of God; and every one that loveth is born of God, and knoweth God" (1 Jn.4:7).

3. The cross brings peace and mercy (v.16). Note who it is that experiences peace and mercy: those who walk by the *rule of the cross and of the new creature*. A person who walks after the cross, seeking to live as a new creature in Christ Jesus will be given...

- the peace of God.
- the mercy of God. He will experience both the forgiveness of sins and the acceptance of God. And most wonderfully, he will be given the *perfect assurance* of eternal life and of God's care.

Note that the church and believers are called "the Israel of God." This simply means that the church and believers are the true Israel of God, the ones in whom God fulfills His promises.

4. The cross gives purpose to the scars of life. Christ had suffered for Paul; therefore, Paul was willing to suffer for Christ. And suffer he did. He bore as much as any man has had to bear for Christ. The word for marks means the branding marks that masters put upon their slaves. The marks identified the slaves as belonging to them.

The point is clear: Paul had subjected his body so much and suffered so much persecution for Christ that his body bore the marks of such subjection and suffering. He could say that the marks upon his body were the branding marks of Christ—the marks that proved his slavery and service to Christ. Therefore, let no man deny his call and ministry for the Lord. He had strong evidence that he was a true minister of the Lord Jesus: the very marks upon his body. The cross of Jesus Christ drove Paul to serve Christ, even to the point of suffering beyond imagination.

APPLICATION:

The believer who suffers reproach, ridicule, mockery, and other persecutions because of his stand for Christ bears the marks of Christ in his body. Have you ever asked the *Why* question of God when...

- you are made fun of because of your love for Jesus?
- you lose a promotion at work because of your faith?
- you are slandered because you do not laugh at the dirty jokes you overhear?
- you turn the other cheek, only to be struck on the other?

The next time that you are tempted to ask the *Why* question of God, ask Him *How* instead. "Lord, *How* can I best glorify You in this circumstance?"

"Blessed are you when men revile you, and persecute you, and say all kinds of evil against you falsely, on account of Me. Rejoice, and be glad, for your reward in heaven in great, for so they persecuted the prophets who were before you" (Mt.5:11-12, NASB).

ILLUSTRATION:

If you need good directions to get somewhere, the last person you want to ask is someone who is just as lost as you. Like you, he needs a point of reference: how to get there from here.

"The geographical heart of London is Charing Cross. All distances are measured from it. This spot is referred to simply as 'the cross.' A lost child was one day picked up by a London 'bobby.' The child was unable to tell where he lived. Finally, in response to the repeated questions of the bobby, and amid his sobs and tears, the little fellow said, "If you will take me to the cross I think I can find my way from there."

"The cross is the point where men become reconciled to God. If we [are to] find our way to God and home we must first come to the cross."[1]

The only road sign that will do you any good is the one which points you to the cross. There, the lost can be found.

QUESTIONS:
1. What is the secret to the power of the cross?
2. What kind of life is lived by a Christian who avoids the cross?
3. How do you cultivate a habit of living through the cross?

4. CONCLUSION: A BENEDICTION OF GRACE (v.18).

Paul ends the letter to the Galatians abruptly. He will have no more attacks upon his ministry nor upon the gospel of Christ. The churches and their people need to repent and get rid of the false teachers. Until then:

"Brethren, the grace of our Lord Jesus Christ be with your spirit. Amen" (v.18).

ILLUSTRATION:

The choice is clear: either we choose a life that is bound to the law and its legalism, or we choose to bind our fate to the grace of God.

"Lillie Baltrip is a good bus driver. In fact, according to the Fort Worth Star-Telegram of June 17, 1988, the Houston school district nominated her for a safe-driving award. Her colleagues even trusted her to drive a busload of them to an awards ceremony for safe drivers. Unfortunately, on the way to the ceremony, Lillie turned a corner too sharply and flipped the bus over, sending herself and sixteen others to the hospital for minor emergency treatment.

"Did Lillie, accident free for the whole year, get her award anyway? No. Award committees rarely operate on the principle of grace. How fortunate we are that even when we don't maintain a spotless life-record, our final reward depends on God's grace, not on our performance!"[2]

GALATIANS 6:11-18

QUESTIONS:

1. How would you describe grace?
2. Are you convinced of God's unconditional love for you—even when you make a mistake? How can you be sure?
3. Grace is God's gift to you. What can you give Him in return?

SUMMARY:

Is the cross your point of reference? In order to get a better focus of the cross, you need to remember these major points:

1. An important section—Paul himself writes.
2. False ministers make a good showing in the flesh—seeking popularity.
3. True ministers boast in the cross of Christ.
4. Conclusion: a benediction of grace.

PERSONAL JOURNAL NOTES
(Reflection & Response)

1. The most important thing that I learned from this lesson was:

2. The area that I need to work on the most is:

3. I can apply this lesson to my life by:

4. Closing Statement of Commitment:

---

[1] Walter B. Knight. *Knight's Treasury of 2,000 Illustrations*, p.97-98.
[2] Craig B. Larson, Editor. *Illustrations for Preaching & Teaching*, p.101.

OUTLINE & SUBJECT INDEX

GALATIANS

OUTLINE & SUBJECT INDEX

OUTLINE & SUBJECT INDEX

GALATIANS

REMEMBER: When you look up a subject and turn to the Scripture reference, you have not only the Scripture, you have an outline and a discussion (commentary) of the Scripture and subject.

This is one of the GREAT VALUES of the Teacher's Outline & Study Bible. Once you have all the volumes, you will have not only what all other Bible indexes give you, that is, a list of all the subjects and their Scripture references, BUT you will also have...

- An outline of every Scripture and subject in the Bible.
- A discussion (commentary) on every Scripture and subject.
- Every subject supported by other Scriptures or cross references.

DISCOVER THE GREAT VALUE for yourself. Quickly glance below to the very first subject of the Index of Galatians. It is:

ABRAHAM
Covenant of. Gal.3:6-7; 3:15-18

Turn to the reference. Glance at the Scripture and outline of the Scripture, then read the commentary. You will immediately see the GREAT VALUE of the INDEX of the Teacher's Outline & Study Bible.

OUTLINE AND SUBJECT INDEX

OUTLINE & SUBJECT INDEX

OUTLINE & SUBJECT INDEX

OUTLINE & SUBJECT INDEX

OUTLINE & SUBJECT INDEX

OUTLINE & SUBJECT INDEX

OUTLINE & SUBJECT INDEX

OUTLINE & SUBJECT INDEX

OUTLINE & SUBJECT INDEX

OUTLINE & SUBJECT INDEX

SCRIPTURE INDEX

GALATIANS

SCRIPTURE INDEX

SCRIPTURE INDEX

(The Scripture Index follows the Order of the Books of the Bible)

SCRIPTURE INDEX

SCRIPTURE INDEX

SCRIPTURE INDEX

ILLUSTRATION INDEX

GALATIANS

ILLUSTRATION INDEX

ILLUSTRATION INDEX

ILLUSTRATION INDEX

ILLUSTRATION INDEX

ILLUSTRATION INDEX

PURPOSE STATEMENT

LEADERSHIP MINISTRIES WORLDWIDE

exists to equip ministers, teachers, and laymen in their understanding, preaching, and teaching of God's Word by publishing and distributing worldwide *The Preacher's Outline & Sermon Bible™* and related *Outline* Bible materials, to reach & disciple men, women, boys, and girls for Jesus Christ.

• MISSION STATEMENT •

1. To make the Bible so understandable - its truth so clear and plain - that men and women everywhere, whether teacher or student, preacher or hearer, can grasp its Message and receive Jesus Christ as Savior; and...
2. To place the Bible in the hands of all who will preach and teach God's Holy Word, verse by verse, precept by precept, regardless of the individual's ability to purchase it.

The ***Outline*** Bible materials have been given to LMW for printing and especially distribution worldwide at/below cost, by those who remain anonymous. One fact, however, is as true today as it was in the time of Christ:

• The Gospel is free, but the cost of taking it is not •

LMW depends on the generous gifts of Believers with a heart for Him and a love and burden for the lost. They help pay for the printing, translating, and placing ***Outline*** Bible materials in the hands and hearts of those worldwide who will present God's message with clarity, authority and understanding beyond their own.

LMW was incorporated in the state of Tennessee in July 1992 and received IRS 501(c) 3 non-profit status in March 1994. LMW is an international, nondenominational mission organization. All proceeds from USA sales, along with donations from donor partners, go 100% into underwriting our translation and distribution projects of ***Outline*** Bible materials to preachers, church & lay leaders, and Bible students around the world.

PO Box 21310 - Chattanooga, TN 37424 - (615) 855-2181 — FAX (615) 855-8616

LEADERSHIP
MINISTRIES
WORLDWIDE

Sharing

The

OUTLINED

BIBLE

With the World!